As Ancient Is This Hostelry

The Story of The Wayside Inn

Curtis F. Garfield and Alison R. Ridley

Illustrated by Robert R. Evans

PORCUPINE ENTERPRISES
106 Woodside Road
Sudbury, Massachusetts

The authors gratefully acknowledge the generous support of
the Wayside Inn and The Sudbury Foundation.

Printed by CSA Press/R.R. Donnelley & Sons
Hudson, MA 01749

ISBN 0-9621976-0-2

To Francis Koppeis
Innkeeper in the How tradition

Table of Contents

Acknowledgements... vii

Introduction xi

1630–1680

I. "If You Persecute Us In One City, We Must Fly To
   Another" I
II. "Wee Have Found A Place Which Lyeth Westward" .. 9

1664–1759

III. "200 Acres More or Less" 19
IV. "Best Accomdated And The Most Suitabel Man" 29
V. "A Hous Of Entertainment For Travellers..." 39

1746–1796

VI. A Red Horse And Revolution 55
VII. "The Dye was Cast and the Torch Lit" 63
VIII. "Establishing the Independence of America" 71

1797–1861

IX. "The Antiquarian of the Family" 81
X. "The Belle of Sudbury" 95
XI. "A Kind of Old Hobgoblin Hall" 103

INTERLUDE: ENGLISH ORIGINS 1576–1642

XII. "The Woodland of Warwickshyre" 117

1861–1900

XIII. "Alas, No Longer An Inn" 163
XIV. "Into The Hands of Strangers" 171

1900–1923

XV. "A Finer Hospitality than Any Known Of Yore"...... 183

1923–1955

XVI. "A Trustee For The Nation" 195
XVII. From The Three R's To Ford Cars 205
XVIII. A $1 Highway, A Chapel And A Mill 211

THE INN DIARIES: 1929–1950

XIX. "Hollyhocks Tall and Stately....Celery and Radishes
  Were Served...." 219
XX. "An Oasis of Peace" 235

1955–1958

XXI. The Inn's On Fire! 253
XXII. "Nothing That Is Good Ever Dies" 259
XXIII. A Phoenix Rises From The Ashes 265

1958–1988

XXIV. "Food And Lodging For Man, Woman And Beast" . 273

EPILOGUE

XXV. Signs of the Times—Horses of a Different Color .. 285

Endnotes 301

Appendices 315

Bibliography 331

Acknowledgements

Agreat many people have helped in the preparation of this book, both in the United States and in England. In the course of the last three and a half years we have asked numerous individuals to undertake seemingly impossible quests, often at short notice, and most of them have responded with admirable speed and vigor. We try below to acknowledge as many of them as possible.

Our special thanks to Francis Koppeis, Innkeeper of the Wayside Inn and to Barbara Deveneau, Assistant Innkeeper. They made available to us on a continuing basis the materials preserved at the Inn, many of which are unique. They put up with numerous inconvenient intrusions and showed remarkable courtesy and restraint in dealing with our ceaseless questions.

Antoinette Frederick, Assistant Vice President, Shawmut Bank of Boston, and author of several institutional histories, has been an indispensable part of this work from the beginning. She has advised and counseled us without flagging in interest or enthusiasm, and helped the book to grow from an idea to a final draft. She heartened us to continue, despite long periods of tribulation. Her wit and patience were as unwavering as her criticisms were just. Our gratitude is immense.

Richard H. Davison, Virginia R. Ellis, and Henry Lyman were kind enough to read the final draft and to bring to bear on it their separate and joint areas of knowledge. We are grateful for their time and their expertise which has saved us from a number of sins of omission and commission.

We appreciate the diverse skills of Merian J. Evans, who researched the Sudbury Town Records for relevant periods, examined Latin sixteenth- and seventeenth-century baptismal records in Warwick, England, and spent many rainy hours scraping moss off old gravestones to reveal previously illegible names. We are also indebted to James Evans who, in the last stages of research, assisted us in the Boston Public Library and in the New England Historical Association.

Roderick Bryant, who performed a number of unusual and hurried commissions in the counties of Warwickshire, Gloucestershire, Worcestershire and the surrounding countryside, deserves a special tribute, as does Philip Garfield, who undertook similar much-appreciated tasks over several years in Massachusetts.

Librarians and archivists on both sides of the Atlantic have been of utmost assistance. Carolyn Anderson, Julie Melly and Shelia Noah of the staff of the Goodnow Library in Sudbury, Massachusetts, all merit recognition for many long and patient hours spent on our behalf. We are grateful to Sally B. Linden, Readers Services Librarian of the Wellesley College Library, Dennis R. Laurie, Assistant to the Curator of the American Antiquarian Society, Gary Robertson of the New England Historic Genealogical Society in Boston, and Mary A. Terpo, Law Librarian of the Worcester Superior Court.

The continuing help of William Milhomme and Barbara L. Anderson at the Commonwealth of Massachusetts Archives at Columbia Point, Boston, Massachusetts, has been invaluable. Mr. William P. Johnston, First Assistant Clerk Magistrate at the Superior Court, East Cambridge, and his assistant, Mary Collari, have extricated us from several quagmires; Meg Dempsey of the Suffolk County Courthouse contributed her special knowledge and Joseph B. Baniukiewicz, Deputy Chief, Worcester Superior Court, was heroic in an hour of crisis.

We are particularly grateful for the efforts of M.W. Farr, Archivist in the County Records Office, Warwick, England. He has assisted us continuously both in person and in a lengthy correspondence. Whatever progress has been made in ascertaining John How's point of origin and the facts about the How coat of arms is in no small measure due to his unfailingly sound and good-humored suggestions.

In the last stages of the research on the history of Warwickshire before the English Civil War, important suggestions were made by Christopher Hill, for which we are especially grateful.

We also acknowledge the help of those who have previously investigated portions of the history of the Inn: Gladys Salta who, in the Ford era, did pioneering genealogical work about the How family; Priscilla Staples Rixmann, Curator of the

Wayside Inn Archives from 1935 until 1958, whose persistent research brought to light obscure and unusual points; and Frank H. Noyes, a descendant of Thankful How, who, in the course of his legal work in the 1950's, unearthed a number of important facts about old How family deeds and the ownership of the Wayside Inn property.

Members of the Howe family have assisted us in various ways. Mrs. Samuel Arthur (Ella Mae) Howe, of Hartford, South Dakota, whose late husband, Samuel Arthur Howe (1914–1988), was directly descended from Samuel How of Sudbury (1642–1713), and her daughter, Sandra Howe Dean, took the time and trouble to share with us their prior investigations of How family history and theories about the How coat of arms. Also, Richard H. Davison and Barbara Eaton Deveneau of Sudbury, Massachusetts, both of whom are directly descended from David How, the first innkeeper, helped us trace recent Howe genealogy.

We have conducted a large number of interviews on both sides of the sea. Several past and present Sudbury residents have contributed important information which added to our store of knowledge about the more recent past. We would like to thank, among others, Algy Alexander, Ira Amesbury, David Bentley, Forrest and Kay Bradshaw, Loring Coleman, Sheila Davison, Barbara Deveneau, Albert St. Germaine, James Greenawalt, Francis Koppeis, Priscilla Staples Rixmann, Louis Varrichione Sr. and Philip Way. Wayside Inn trustees Thomas Boylston Adams and Daniel Coolidge have provided information and anecdotes concerning the Francis Koppeis era.

Numerous individuals in Ladbroke, Brinklow and other villages in Warwickshire helped us in our quest. Canon George Ruben Fishley, Canon Ronald T. Murray, Canon Anthony Rowe and Mr. David Rutherford deserve special mention for assisting us with the history of Ladbroke. In Brinklow we are especially grateful to Miss Lucy E. Cryer, Mr. Harry Johnson, and Mr. David E. Williams, each of whom supplied a valuable missing piece of the puzzle from memories of the past and present knowledge of their village. We are also grateful to Brinklow residents Edna Walker Hallam, Betty Mawson, Dess Denyer Osden and Sarah Colledge Taylor.

Our warm thanks to Elizabeth and John Draisey, whose hospitality and encouragement in Warwick were of utmost help at a turning point in the book's fortunes. Our thanks also to Dick Heyelman of South Orleans, Massachusetts, who similarly succored the writers during the preparation of the final chapters.

Our thanks to Charles Cavanaugh and the staff of CSA Press for their painstaking efforts in the production of the book. We acknowledge particularly Jeanne LoCascio and Eileen Sullivan who shepherded the manuscript through its final stages with unusual timing and patience. Jeff Towner and Morgan Downs provided exceptionally skilled assistance with art work and maps, as did Brian Nelson with proofreading.

We are profoundly grateful to Virginia R. Ellis, Professor of English at Mt. Holyoke College, who bore with us during the final stages of the book's preparation and encouraged us with keen scholarship and discerning literary judgment.

Above all, we wish to acknowledge the help of two historians whose spirit and example have sustained us throughout this long endeavor—the late Forrest D. Bradshaw of Sudbury, Massachusetts and the late A.B. Rodger of Oxford, England.

Introduction

"The best home a man can have is a good inn..."
—Dr. Samuel Johnson

Old inns and taverns—in America as well as Europe—
can tell us much about the people who lived and
worked there. Just as churches, battlefields and mon-
uments speak to us of past ages, old inns are living books
which narrate their own story if we know how to read it.

The Wayside Inn in Sudbury, Massachusetts, has its own
special tale, as do the Rose and Crown and Red Lion in East
Anglia, the Mitre in Oxford or the Lygon Arms in Worcestershire. The Wayside Inn is not quite as old as its English
counterparts, but its story is just as varied and compelling. To
tell that story as honestly and completely as known facts will
permit is the object of this book.

One cannot tell the story of the Wayside Inn—or the Red
Horse Tavern, or "How's Place," as it was familiarly called—
without telling the story of the Sudbury How family. Their
lives and accomplishments over the centuries are closely
interwoven with their tavern and their town, and we have
made no attempt to separate the two. Many people with the
name Howe or How—and in England the spellings are interchangeable—have made pilgrimages to Sudbury in past and
present decades, and no doubt will continue to do so.

The founder of the line in Sudbury and Marlborough was
John How. He was one of five men with that surname who
settled in Massachusetts in the 1630s. There were also Abraham of Roxbury; Abraham of Watertown and Marlborough;
Edward of Lynn; and James of Roxbury and Ipswich. James and
Abraham of Roxbury were brothers, but none of the other
emigrant ancestors were related to one another.

Readers interested in tracing the How family tree should
consult Judge Daniel Wait Howe's comprehensive two-volume
Howe Genealogies. We are concerned here with John How,

who first settled in Sudbury and later helped to establish Marlborough.

While John How's life bears only indirectly upon the history of the Wayside Inn, and the first How innkeeping activity in Sudbury did not begin until 1692, when John's son Samuel received a license to operate an ordinary in the hamlet of Lanham, the previous half century is an important period not only in the history of Sudbury and the Massachusetts Bay Colony, but in the rising stature of the How family as well. Their wisdom at town meetings, their courage on the battleground, and their skillful hands and strong backs all served the community well.

John How's story is also the story of the early days of Sudbury and Marlborough. John helped establish not one, but two towns while starting a family innkeeping tradition that was to continue for six generations. What we have been able to discover about his English origins is discussed in detail in Chapter XII.

It is our belief that John How came from a village called Brinklow in Warwickshire sometime between 1621 and 1639. As far as we know, he did not sail on the *Confidence* with many of Sudbury's early settlers who came from villages in Wiltshire, Suffolk, Dorset, Hertfordshire and Hampshire.

Wherever he came from in England, he slowly became a leading citizen in both Sudbury and Marlborough, as did his sons and grandsons after him. His steady rise in stature is duly recorded in the Sudbury Town Book, which contains an unbroken record of the town's affairs since its incorporation in 1639.

During the next three centuries, John How's descendants would carry on this tradition and enhance it, both in war and in peace. His eldest son, John Jr., was killed by King Philip's braves in the Sudbury Fight in 1676; his great-grandson, Ezekiel, led Sudbury troops to fight at Concord just 99 years later on April 19, 1775. Samuel, Adam and Lyman How all served in other important and versatile ways.

The Hows made a colorful and lasting contribution to the history of their town, but their energy and resourcefulness stretched far beyond its boundaries. Their inn and the tradition of "ampler hospitality" they started in past centuries is ably carried on by the present innkeeper; it has grown from the roots of America and has become famous all over this country and the world.

"As ancient is this hostelry
As any in the land may be,
Built in the old Colonial day,
When men lived in a grander way,
With ampler hospitality."

Tales of a Wayside Inn
Henry W. Longfellow

I

"If You Persecute Us In One City, We Must Fly To Another"

Forty-four men and two women shivered and stamped their feet on the pine plank floor of the new Sudbury meeting house overlooking the Musketaquid River meadows that cold winter morning of January 22, 1655. The new house had gable ends to allow for the storage of powder and other town property; Thomas Plympton, Peter King and Hugh Griffyn had finished the interior work only the autumn before. There still remained the task of moving the pulpit and deacon's seat from the old meeting house next door.

John How knew the old house well. He had been on the committee to oversee its construction by John Rutter in 1643 and, in his capacity as town marshal, had rounded up enough able-bodied men to raise the 30- by 20-foot frame on May 16 of the same year.[1]

Sudbury had prospered since that first meeting house was raised 12 years before and John How with it. His original allotment of "two acres of river meadow plus an acre and a half for allowance"[2] had grown to 15½ acres, he had held several trusted town posts, and was raising a large family.

As first town marshal, appointed in December 1642 and paid "twenty shillings and twelve pence for every distrainte...."[3] How had signed several important and varied orders. Along with select men Pendleton, Haynes, Goodnow and Noyes, he concurred in the appointment of Hugh Griffyn to "take note of births, marriages and deaths" in March of 1643 and later, in the same spring, admonished residents about the control of "hogges." They were to "drive them out every morninge into the woods and when they come home at night to see them shutt up fast...or else if they be about the street to ringe and yoake...."[4] In June of the following summer, How was authorized to supervise Tymothy Hawkins in the building of the town's first cart bridge and empowered to "levy a rate"[5] to pay for it.

In November of the same year, How watched the passage of a law which was to affect the future of Sudbury drastically and bring about the controversial gathering 12 years later. This was the original "syzinge" law which would limit how many animals anyone could pasture on the town's common lands in direct proportion to the "quantity of meadow" an "inhabitant" owned at that early date.[6] First come, first served.

As Sudbury ceased to be a primitive plantation and grew into a thriving town with a second generation rapidly coming of age, ownership of more land became increasingly crucial. There wasn't enough of it to go around. Tensions started to mount in the spring of 1653 when the select men ordered John How, John Blandford and John Maynard to conduct a general survey of land all over the town.[7]

Sudbury's early settlers, petitioners Peter Noyes, Brian Pendelton and the Reverend Browne among them, had instituted an English open field system of government which gave each adult male economic and social ranking according to the amount of land he was allotted when the town was divided which, in turn, was determined on the basis of previously-held land elsewhere.[8] Thus, wealthy landowners such as Noyes and Browne, who were granted 16 acres of river meadow or more in the first division, had more power and prestige than the young men who were granted none.*

The growing dissent over the division of land had come to a head on January 9, 1654 when a town meeting was called to "take some course for dividing of the land that was last granted by the Court to the town."[9] The land in question was an extension "two miles westward next adjoyning to them for the further enlargement. . ." granted to the town by the General Court in March, 1649.[10] This became known as the New Grant and was located west of the Sudbury River bordering on what would later become Marlborough.

In an unusual aside in the town book, Griffyn noted that there was "much agitation."[11] Indeed there was, and with good reason. The townspeople were being asked to decide between two distinctly different and decisive ways of dividing the New Grant land: according to family and previous estate, as was the

---

*For the full story of the land allotments and the disagreement about sizing the commons, see Sumner Chilton Powell's admirable book, *Puritan Village*.

case in the past, or "To every man an equall portion in quantity."[12]

For whatever reasons, the young men of the town were conspicuous by their absence at that meeting and the old guard prevailed, but not before John Smith, Walter King and Obadiah Ward loudly voiced their dissent and stormed out of the meeting house to spread the word. The following day the young men were on hand in force as a majority called another "publicke town meeting for a full ending the difference about the way of dividinge the land last granted by the court...."[13]

This time there was no mistake. The old guard's bid to get a quick and inconspicuous vote and maintain the status quo had failed. Only three people voted for the original proposal, while 20 young men made it clear that they would stand for nothing less than "an equall portion in quantity."

The passage of this article was a blow to the older settlers, several of whom were select men, who wanted no more division of land within the town. Many of them, like Noyes, who had staked £76 to bring several people to the New World with him on the *Confidence*, left a prosperous living in England, and made order in the wilderness at considerable risk and discomfort to himself, were not about to sit back and let audacious newcomers call the shots if they had anything to say about it.

So they used a political tactic that is still popular in Massachusetts to this day. They delayed. No move was made to stake out plots. After all, the select men did control the land, and there was nothing in the article specifying WHEN "every man" would get his equal portion in quantity. The younger generation would just have to sit and wait. Little did they realize how high the price of their stalling would be.

It was more than a year before Noyes and other members of the old guard decided to take the offensive themselves in a last ditch attempt to preserve the open field system. At a private select men's meeting on January 15, 1655, Noyes raised the question of sizing the town's eight plots of common land. Was the town herd of cattle too large for the Sudbury commons to support? Noyes reminded his fellow select men that in 1643 the group had signed an order that all the common lands should eventually be "sized" or limited as to the number of livestock that could safely be placed upon them. In the light of the growth of the town and the scarcity of open land he felt that the commons should be "sized speedily." [14]

Four select men agreed with him and proceeded to draw up an article for approval at town meeting which would: "size all common lands and limit the number of animals to be placed thereon according to the number of acres of river meadow granted to the inhabitants in the first, second or third divisions of meadow or granted by some service done by them." For every two acres of river meadow owned, a townsman could graze one cow, heifer, steer or bull or six sheep on the town commons. Horses counted as a beast and a half. [15]

It was a loaded question and nobody knew it better than John How. If it passed, the young men would have no place to graze their cattle, since they owned little or no meadow land of their own. He was not much better off himself. His 11 acres of meadow would allow him to graze five head of cattle on the common lands, whereas Peter and Thomas Noyes, Walter Haynes and Edmund Goodnow would be able to graze three times as many. [16]

And now, just a week later, on this frosty January morning, it had come to a head. The voters settled into the newly-finished white oak pews and rose as Rev. Browne "by the desire of the town sought the Lord for his blessinge in the actings of the day." [17] Then Griffyn read the article out loud and the battle was joined.

Select man John Ruddock, whose sympathies lay with the younger men, immediately accused Noyes of trying to push the sizing order through the select mens' meeting in secret. Noyes defended himself at length, and the two men became engaged in a shouting match. Watching from his seat in a front pew, a man of principle thought, with rising anxiety, of the future of his town. John How decided to speak out.

Like Ruddock, How's sympathy was with the younger generation and they could have no better spokesman. Older by a score of years and involved in town government from the beginning, How had the respect of his peers and a long record of achievement. In 1640, when there was a threat that the Colony treasurer might distrain (seize) someone's goods or cattle to settle the town's unpaid tax bill, his was one of 17 signatures appearing in support of the following article:

"It is ordered by the town that if the Treasurer shall send up a distreynt for all or any part of the Country Rate that the goods or cattle Distreyned shall be replaced and *the town will bear all the charge that may arise* by standing suite with the Treasurer, the charges to be paid by a town rate (tax)."[18]

Fifteen years before, How had been in support of the town as a whole, not a particular individual. On this cold day in the unheated meeting house, his position had not changed. He asked if he could have the floor and speak for all those who had little meadow land.

How wasted little time getting to the point. "It is oppression," he said. "If you oppresse the poore, they will cry out and if you persecute us in one city, we must fly to another."[19]

His words rang out a solemn warning. He was reminding the large body of townsmen of the reason they had come to New England in the first place. Memories of events in Warwickshire in 1607—when there were revolts touched off by enclosure of common land—may have been in his mind, as well as the present need for fair play. He was not only accusing the elder statesmen of attempting to override a fair land policy, but "was threatening to lead a group out of the organization, which, as first marshal, he had done so much to establish."[20] How's was not to be an idle threat. Less than two years later he and Ruddock were among a group of Sudbury men to settle Marlborough. The elder statesmen's neglect of a fair land policy not only would cost Sudbury many of its bright young men, but some of its leading citizens as well.

When the time finally came for a vote, Griffyn wanted to be certain that there were no mistakes in the tally that would come back to haunt him later. "You that judge the act of the select men to be a righteous act, discover it by drawing yourselves to one end of the meeting house...and those who are of a contrary mind draw themselves to the other end of the meeting house..."[21] he instructed the voters.

The first vote was 27 to 27 with Edmund Rice, Robert Davies and Plympton abstaining. Griffyn went from one end of the building to the other, recording the voters name by name: Parmenter, the Noyeses, Haynes, Goodnow, Griffyn, Rev. Browne and others supported the select men. How, Rice, Bent, William Ward, Ruddock, Newton, Henry Loker and members of the younger generation were "of a contrary mind."[22]

There were claims of foul on both sides. The young men claimed that John Parmenter had no right to act as agent for Herbert Pelham and Thomas Walgrave, and the old guard countered that ten of the young men had no business voting at all since they owned no river meadow.

Although it solved nothing, the deadlock signalled that the winds of change were blowing. The younger generation would be denied its rights no longer.

The first signs came barely two months later. On March 5, 1655, old Hugh Griffyn sadly penned the following in the town book: "John Parmenter, William Ward, John Ruddock, John Maynard, Robert Darnill, Thomas King and John Toll are chosen select men from this day for one yeare."[23] Parmenter was the only member of the old guard to survive the purge. Noyes, Haynes, Goodnow and Griffyn, Town Clerk of 12 years standing, were suddenly on the outside looking in. John Moore, John How, and John Blandford were re-appointed as general surveyors for the whole town to see to fields and fences.

At the same time, How received another charge. "John How is appointed by the pastor and by the select men to see to the constraining of the youth from the profanation of the Lord's day in time of public exercise."[24]

While this is usually noted to show what a devout man How was, several other interesting explanations suggest themselves in view of the timing of the appointment. Browne, who was not at all pleased by the younger generation's rise to power, may have taken petty revenge on How for allying himself with them and not respecting his cloth in the land dispute; or Ruddock and Ward, who were sympathetic, but still not ready to make full public cause with the members of the young group, could have been indirectly warning How to be careful. Regardless of politics, both the pastor and the newly-elected select men recognized that How had a good deal of influence with the unruly youths and were merely trying to preserve the peace of the Sabbath in the best way they could.

Whatever their motive in putting him in the unenviable position of controlling roisterers on Sunday, the townsmen's trust remained with How. At the end of May in that same turbulent spring, he was appointed "to keep the court orders having been delivered by Hugh Griffyn to the town's hands."[25] Being entrusted with the town records, including all legal land titles, was a supreme vote of confidence in an hour of crisis.

Meanwhile, Rev. Browne, one of the town's largest landowners with 85 acres, was trying to keep the conservative cause alive and protect his own economic interests with the aid of the pulpit. He brought in clergy from neighboring towns to "endeavor to compose and settle the distractions at Sudbury."[26]

But their remonstrances fell on deaf ears. Then, as now, Sudbury citizens refused to tolerate outside interference in what they saw as a local matter and would not recognize the authority of the church in a civil issue. Church attendance fell drastically.[27]

Browne and his peers made the sad mistake of forgetting that these colonists had come to the New World to escape, once and for all, the jurisdiction of the church in government. Ruddock spoke for everyone when he told Browne in a public meeting: "Setting aside your office, I regard you no more than any other man."[28] In the same vein he objected to the censures of the other ministers by insisting: "We shall, or should be, judged by men of our own choosing."[29] Ruddock had not outlasted the long rule of Noyes and the conservatives to be duped by a group of pious churchmen, standing more by the old school tie of Cambridge, England than a strong belief in the will of God.*

While Ruddock and the churchmen argued, How quietly went about the task of breaking the deadlock and getting the New Grant land laid out and apportioned. On January 14, 1656 his efforts bore fruit as the town voted; "That there shall be some course for to get the land layd out which was last granted by the Court according to the order of the towne in a vote formerly made," and that there shall be "some course taken to keep a herde of cattle upon the land."[30] Ruddock, How and Henry Rice were appointed by the town to: "take some paynes for to see if they can get a surveyor to lay out the land last granted to the towne..."[31]

Meanwhile Ruddock and the other young select men made good use of their new-found power by striking the 1655 order for "syzinge" the commons from the town records[32] and moving decisively to start the allotment of the two-mile grant in equal lots. On one of those lots, which fell to Thomas King in the January 1657 drawing,[33] John How's son, Samuel, and grandson, David, would together build a house that would one day be world-famous as Longfellow's Wayside Inn.

---

*There was more than a touch of Archbishop Laud in the arrogant behavior of Rev. Browne, and he lost the respect of his flock accordingly. It must have crossed the minds of Sudbury citizens that it had been barely six years since King Charles I had lost his head on the scaffold, and his father's prophetic saying: "No bishop, no king," or its corollary, "no king, no bishop" (or no undue respect for the authority of any minister), had much the same force on both sides of the Atlantic.

John How's Petition to the Court of General Sessions, September 30, 1662.

II

"Wee Have Found A Place Which Lyeth Westward"

Old Edmund Rice put down his quill and moved the candlestick closer to the sheet of foolscap on the table. In his position as Deputy to the Massachusetts General Court he had worded similar petitions on several occasions, but this time he wanted to achieve something of exceptional skill and artistry. Ten years of hard-won experience went into the lines of ink that lay drying on the document before him.

Above his own signature and 12 others, he had penned the following:

> Whereas your petitioners have lived divers years in Sudbury and God hath been pleased to increase our children which are, now divers of them grown to man's estate, and we, many of us, are grown into years so that we should be glad to see them settled before the Lord takes us away from hence...as also God having given us some considerable cattle so that we are so straightened that we cannot so comfortably subsist as could be desired...and some of us having taken some pains to view the country...wee have found a place which lyeth westward about eight miles from Sudbury which we conceive might be comfortable for our subsistence...it is therefore the humble request of your Petitioners to this Honored Court that you would be pleased to grant unto eight miles square or so much lands as may containe to eight miles square for to make a Plantation.[1]

This masterful document was signed by William Ward, Thomas King, John Wood, Thomas Goodnow, John Ruddock, Henry Rice, John Bent Sr., John Maynard, Richard Newton, Peter Bent, Edward Rice and John How. The old settler's prophetic words about "flying to another city" had begun to take concrete shape.

On May 14, 1656 the General Court responded by granting a tract six miles square.[2] The 6,000-acre grant was first known by its Indian name, Whipsufferadge or Whipsuppenick, which

9

means "The Ledges" in the Nipmuc tongue. The new plantation later became known as Marlborough.

Meanwhile, Sudbury's New Grant land had finally been
surveyed and divided into squadrons and subdivisions. A town
meeting was called on January 4, 1657 to draw lots. John How
drew Lot 16 in the Second Squadron,[3] adjoining Henry Loker
and Edmund Rice. But by this time, How's eyes, like Rice's,
were already on new horizons.

For How had his own personal interests to protect in the
long-standing quarrel between old timers and newcomers.
During the previous 15 years when men were forming and
governing their township, raising crops and cattle, paying
rates, mending highways, protecting their boundaries from
Watertown's "drawing so near us," and arguing over the
division of land, John How, at the same time that he was a
leader in town affairs, was raising his own large family.

Sometime before 1640 he married, either in Massachusetts or
in Warwickshire, a woman whose first name was Mary. He
may have married her before leaving England since no marriage
record has been found in the colonies. In August, 1640, John's
oldest son, also a John, was born. In October 1642, his second
son Samuel followed. Between 1644, when daughter Sarah was
born, and 1656, three other sons, Isaac, Josiah, and Thomas, and
two more daughters, both named Mary, were born. One of the
girls died a year after birth. Two other sons, Daniel and
Alexander, also died in infancy. John's youngest son, Eleazar,
was born in Marlborough in 1662.[4]

With eight dependents to support, the words of Rice's
petition must have sounded forcibly in How's ears. For him,
"straightened circumstances" were a daily reality. More land
and livestock had become vital to his growing family. There
were many in like case all over town and the move westward
could not happen too soon.

No wonder John How and the other Marlborough proprietors
moved swiftly. In the fall after the Court's decision, their first
meeting was held and John How, William Ward, Thomas King,
John Ruddock and Edmund Rice were chosen "to put the affairs
of the new plantation in an orderly way."[5] How did not wait for
further formalities. Sometime in 1657 he built himself a cabin
"near the Indian planting grounds" and became Marlborough's
first white settler. This cabin, according to Rev. Joseph Allen,
was "a little to the east of the Indian planting field."[6] Charles

Hudson, Marlborough historian, elaborates that it was "situated some 100 rods from Spring Hill meeting house, a little to the east of the present road from Spring Hill to Feltonville...."[7]

In Marlborough, How was an acknowledged leader from the first. In 1661 he was elected to the first of four successive terms as a select man along with Rice, Ward, Ruddock, Thomas King and the two Johnson brothers, John and Solomon.

How became a leader in the new plantation not only because of his years of experience and his role in the Sudbury quarrel, but also because of his ability to make friends with his Indian neighbors. The Indians knew that they could trust John How to be fair in land dealings as in other things, and they came to have great respect for his judgment.

There is a time-worn legend that he settled a dispute between two fractious Indians over a pumpkin which was planted on the land of one and grew to great size on the land of his neighbor. How divided the pumpkin equally between the two contenders and acquired a reputation for great wisdom.[8] Relations with the Indians remained harmonious for a long time.

Indian goodwill was needed in the early 1660s when land was required for a meeting house. How and Ruddock reached an agreement with Anamaks, Chief of the Wamesits, to purchase a piece of land for: "the proper and only use of the inhabitants and proprietors of the said town of Marlborough. . . full and quiet possession of the aforementioned land forever."[9] This land was near the Indian planting field and the cabin of John How, who, soon afterwards, opened the doors of the Black Horse Tavern on October 1, 1661.

William Ward and his fellow select men made it official with a simple written request to the Court of General Sessions that: "John How is to be an ordinary keeper of Marlborrow if the Court approve of it." The little slip of paper is marked with faded ink: "Allowd."[10]

In 1662, How was one of a group which arranged for land and a house for the minister, Rev. William Brimstead. In the same year, the General Court thought enough of How's judgment to appoint him and Edmund Rice to mediate a claim by Thomas Danforth for further compensation for services rendered the Colony as a surveyor some years before.

The Court ruled that Danforth should have a "parcell of land" and asked John How and Edmund Rice to settle the exact amount and location.[11] The document was dated May 27, 1662 and was signed by Daniel Gookin, the father of Samuel How's future partner in real estate.

Despite adequate meadow for all, the new plantation was not entirely tranquil in its first eight years of existence. A dispute arose over a 1659 town ordinance that mandated that each man ''perfect his house lott'' and pay a tax of 20 shillings within less than a year or forfeit title to the lands. Petitions and counter petitions were sent to the General Court and two distinct parties emerged.[12]

One group, headed by Ward, Ruddock and many of the younger residents who were unable to raise the 20 shillings for their taxes, asked the court to send in a committee to settle the problems. The other side, led by Rice and How and most of the older men, maintained that the new township could solve its own difficulties. The Marlborough conservatives, who were the former Sudbury liberals, stated their case this way:

''We are willing with our persons and estates, to uphold the Authority of the Country, and do therefore desire the liberty of the law which gives towns the power to transact their own affairs.''[13] More than a century later, their descendants would take up arms against their mother country to preserve that liberty.

How was evidently trying during this period to mediate among the contending factions. Certainly his own ''person and estate'' were growing in substance. His family was increasing and prospering. Both John Jr. and Samuel were granted land in Marlborough, and John Jr. lived and married there. Samuel, in 1663 at age 21, married Martha Bent, whose father, John Bent, was one of How's old friends and colleagues in Sudbury. This was no doubt an advantageous marriage, since Bent Sr. was by that time well established in Sudbury. Samuel was deeded 44 acres in Lanham by his wife's family and he and his bride moved back to Sudbury.[14]

John's oldest daughter, Sarah, married William Ward's son, Samuel, in 1667, and raised a family of seven in Marlborough. His second daughter, Mary, married John Wetherbee and raised three children. Before his death, John How had at least 15 grandchildren.

The pressures of supporting a large family and running his ordinary at the same time must have been demanding, for on September 30, 1662, How petitioned the Court of General Sessions as follows:

Honrd. Sir:

My humble suit unto this Honrd. Court is that they would be pleased to grant me a freedom from Training and that my license for Ordinary keeping may be renewed unto me. My grounds which I request the said freedom are: 1. The consideration of a bodily infirmity I have had many years upon me which as I grow in age, increaseth in its tediousness in so much that is frequently interruptive to me in my calling. 2. I am also thick of hearing. 3. I do and am like to maintain three train souldiers in my family. Sr, I trust you will endeavor that I may obtain my desire in respects mentioned though I give you but a hint of things which if do, you will hereby more abundantly oblige me to subscribe myself as already I do.

> Yor Humble Servant,
> John How.[15]

This is written in a bold hand, unusually clear for documents of this period. Someone taught John How how to write clearly and distinctly when he was still a boy. Perhaps it was Pastor Bolton* of Brinklow, in Warwickshire, who writes with a clear hand himself, very much like How's.

Both How's requests were granted. His "ordinary"—the Black Horse Tavern—would be run by his descendants for several generations. His son John probably helped him start and run the business before being killed by King Philip's braves in April of 1676.

Having worked so long and hard to establish friendly relations with his Indian neighbors, the rise to power of King Philip and the threat of war must have been a great sadness for How. He was in his mid-seventies in 1675, but in October of that year he met with other town leaders to prepare for the defense of their settlement. Garrisons were set up in the houses of several citizens and the Colony sent a small and inadequate number of soldiers to help, 37 to man nine or ten garrison houses.

This peril leaps to life in this passage from the *Massachusetts Archives:* "In order to safeguard our town...These following proposals agreed upon in case of attack...The follow-

---

*A man by the name of John Bolton was the Pastor of Brinklow in Warwickshire, from 1584 until 1611. In the year 1600 he signed the christening certificates for John How and his own son, John Bolton, on the same day in November. He writes in a clear hand and would almost certainly have been the only source of schooling in an English village of that day and age. He probably taught both John and Mary How to write and read.

ing persons to remain at William Kerby's house...John How
(sr.) Thomas How....''[16] Kerby was allowed four of the limited
number of soldiers. John How's signature, again in a bold, clear
hand, is the first of 26 on the document.

Deaf and suffering from rheumatism, his oldest son killed in
the Sudbury Fight, his plantation decimated, and his Indian
neighbors who trusted him rounded up and marched off to
prison in Boston, How must have suffered mental anguish
wondering if all of his efforts had been futile. But a worse blow
was yet to come. After the war, his sons Thomas, Josiah and
Eleazar became involved in maneuvers to swallow up the
Indian plantation in their own.[17] The days of friendly adjudica-
tion about pumpkins were gone for good.

John How must have aged rapidly after this difficult year, for
sometime between 1676 and 1680 he gave up innkeeping, as his
wife's letter to the governor tells us (see below).*

On May 24, 1680, "expecting my departure out of this life
being under bodily distemper," How signed his last will and
testament. He died four days later, leaving an estate worth 511
pounds and an innkeeping legacy that would continue for six
generations.

Samuel, who had moved back to Sudbury, was given 25 acres
of upland and made executor along with his mother; Isaac was
given 25 acres of upland "on part of which his house now
stands and all that part of 'Patch Meadow' which lies next to
his upland."[18]

To Thomas, the fifth son, John gave "my now dwelling
house," a good deal of land adjoining "together with the horse
he troops on...my best oxen and my Cart and plow with all
Tackling pertaining thereto, he allowing his mother, my loving
wife suffit. maintenance both for food and raym't, attending to
her wants and fifty shillings a year during her widowhood."

---

*One of the only records we have of Mary How, which shows her to have
been a hard-working wife and loyal member of her frontier community, is a
letter she wrote to the Governor soon after her husband's death in 1680:
May it please your worshipe to understand that in my husband's days we
have capt the ordinary many years although we have for sume years since
dejested it yet we are so importuned by travelers to Renew our License that
wee cannot tell how to denie them—If it may please your worshipe thearfor
for to Renew the License formerlie granted to my husband which I humbly
crave it may be your worshipe's pleasure...unto mee.
Mary How, wife unto the Deceased John How
of Marlborough This 3 October 1681[19]

How must have loved his wife dearly, for in addition to the instruction to Thomas and the bequest "to my beloved wife ...thirty four acres of upland and meadow, ten acres of swamp and all his movable goods and estate not disposed of," he made an additional, unusual provision: "If she shall see mete to move from my house to dwell elsewhere, my said son Thomas shall defray the whole charge of her maintenance wherever she shall choose to reside."

Thomas was unmarried at the time of his father's death and the only son without a homestead of his own. His father's provisions for Thomas, and the close connection with his mother, were probably so detailed because future innkeeping activities in Marlborough, which Thomas eventually carried on, were already a matter of family consideration and conversation.

John How was careful to leave provisions for every one of his household. He asked his wife to look after one Joseph Graves, an indentured servant, who, at his departure after completing his obligation at the age of 19, was to be clothed and given "a cow or a hors, whichever he shall choose." To his youngest son Eleazar, who was only 18 at the time of his father's death, he left 28 acres of various land parcels and a "hors and colt and two steers." He left a ewe lamb to "John How my grandchild, son unto my son John How, deceased, I having done well by his father..."

From "two acres and an acre and a half for allowance" in 1639, John How had come a considerable distance in his 41 years in the New World. He would never know that he had founded a tradition in New England, nor that his family would start and run a world-famous hostelry for nearly two centuries. He could not realize that arguments would continue to this day about his ancestry in Warwickshire and the Red Horse of Saxon fame, nor that scholars and historians would puzzle over his origins.

But the old settler had lived as well as he could. Loyal to his own creed and steadfast to the last, he yielded up his soul to God, "who hath, in long suffering and goodness, lengthened out my days hitherto..."

SUDBURY 1640-1920

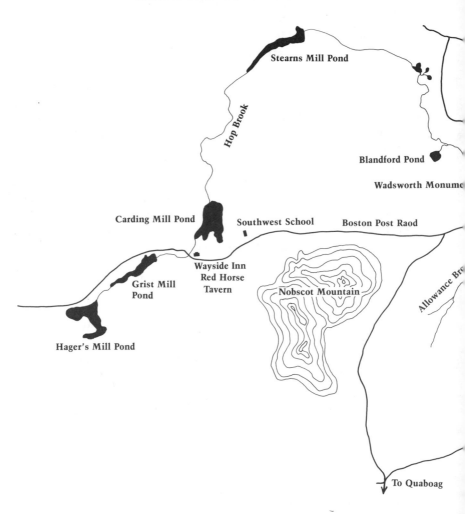

st Side
eeting
ouse

To Concord

Sudbury River

East Side

Goodman
Hill

Long Causey

Old Lancaster Road

West Side

Town Bridge

East Side Meeting House

Green Hill

Cakebread Mill

uth Sudbury

Parmenter
Tavern

Parmenter
Mill

Hop Brook

Ford

To Watertown

Pelham Island Road

Heard's Pond

Sudbury River

How's Cart Bridge

nham

Samuel
How

Samuel How's Appeal to the General Court for reimbursement for building the Cart Bridge, April 1674.

III

"200 Acres More or Less"

Samuel How could smell the smoke long before he reached the brow of the long, gentle hill that sloped down to the west bank of the Musketaquid River. The cart bridge that he had built two years before was still there, but only piles of smoldering ashes remained where his house and barns once stood. Philip of Pokanoket's braves had done a thorough job that misty morning of April 21, 1676.

Samuel's property in the hamlet of Lanham was an ideal location for doing business of any kind, and he had accepted the Court's suggestion to replace the old horse bridge with a cart bridge with that in mind.

The road that led to the bridge (today's Stone Bridge Road in Wayland and Potter Road in Framingham) was the best route from Sudbury to Quaboag (now Brookfield) and the frontier settlements to the west. It was far enough up the river to be passable even in times of high water and travelers preferred it to the "long causeway" (today's River Road in Wayland) that led to the Old Town Bridge further downstream, which was often under water and constantly in need of repair. Unfortunately, Philip knew this as well. The Wampanoag chieftain intended to send his braves across it to raid the settlements on the East Side of the river and eventually drive the English into the sea.

On April 21, Philip's main force of 1,000 braves had been occupied in a day-long battle with militia troops under the command of Captains Samuel Wadsworth and Samuel Brocklebank on the slopes of Green Hill, in what would become known as the Sudbury Fight, and only a few raiding parties made it across the river. The damage could have been worse.

For Samuel How it was bad enough. Later he would be one of 33 Sudbury residents to petition for aid from the Irish Charity Donation organized by Nathaniel Mather, the brother of Increase, for relief of colonists in Massachusetts and Connecticut. In "an accompt of the losses sustained by severall inhabitants of ye towne of Sudbury ye 21st April by ye Indian Enemy..." How listed his losses as £140. The only larger claims were those of Deacon John Haines for £180 and Sg. Josiah Haines for £190.[1] Fortunately he had received enough warning to get his family to a place of safety. He still had his land and his health and a reputation as a hard worker and astute businessman. He would rebuild.

Ever since he had left his father John's Black Horse Tavern in Marlborough to start a family of his own, Samuel had made a living as a carpenter and glazier. The inventory of his estate, following his sudden death in 1713, would include "carpentry tools, glazier's vise, glass and lead" valued at £21 and four shillings.[2]

The town had been one of his earliest and best customers. In 1664 the Town Meeting "voted and granted that the town of Sudbury will build a new pound sufficient and good as the old pound was when it was new...only ten foot longer and ten foot broader...Left. Goodenow, Sergent Grout and Thomas Noyes are appynted a committy to let out this pound to building unto Samuell How...and to pay and satisfye the said man with lands according to their best judgement and discretion."[3]

As time went on, Samuel How developed a reputation for striking when the iron was hot that did not always go down well with his fellow townsmen. On December 23, 1673, when the County Court sitting in Charlestown appointed "John Stone, Sen. of Sudbury, John Woods of Marlborough and Thomas Eames of Framingham together with John Livermore of Watertown... to lay out a road from Watertown over Sudbury River...for the use of the Country...leading from the house of said Livermore to a Horse Bridge (then being) near the house of Daniel Stone, Jun. and thence the nearest and best way to Quaboag,"[4] How sensed opportunity knocking.

By the following spring, How had enlarged this Horse Bridge into a full-sized cart bridge and forwarded the following petition to the Court:

> 'Wheras Samull How of Sudbury, having Built a Sufficient Cart Bridge over Sudbury Great River att ye place approved by the County Court of Charlestown...and having been incorridged by sume of ye Honored Magistrates, my humble request is that Some Compensation may be made from ye Country for said worke...it being goode for travilars...Your servant and Humble Subscriber
>
> Sam'll How."[5]

The magistrates may have "incorridged" this excellent carpenter, but the Court wasn't prepared to part with any money. However, the officials did the next best thing. In the very same month, they answered his petition as follows:

> "In answer to the petition of Samuel How, referring to some allowance to be made him for his expense about the bridge he has lately erected upon Sudbury river above the town, he is allowed to take toll of all travellers, for a horse and man 3d and for a cart 6d, until there be an orderly settling of the Country highway, and some provision made for repayment to him of his disbursements[6]

Samuel must have anticipated the outcome of his appeal, for in February of that same year, when the "comon medoes" were "lett out for this ensuing somer," he applied for and got permission from the town to use "the comon medow about Lanham Cart Bridge for six shillings."[7] He efficiently arranged in advance to combine his haying and toll collecting duties in the coming summer months. Possibly his oldest son John, who would have been ten at the time, may have helped him.

This must have touched a nerve amongst the older settlers living on the East Side of the river near to the old town bridge which was badly in need of replacement.* On October 12, 1674 a town meeting was called: "To consider of and determine the matters propounded by the select men then under consideration, especially considering all the highwaies that want repair within this town and particularly the deffects of such as have neglected theire duties herein, especially relating to the great causey."[8]

The great Causey or causeway led from the western end of the town bridge across the river meadows to the high ground near Sand Hill. Motorists can still travel over part of it from the Wayland Country Club across Route 27 and along River Road to Old County Road in Sudbury.

Thanks to ravages by the yearly floods and the local muskrat population, it was in need of constant repair. These repairs were divided amongst the townspeople, most of whom considered them a low priority.

---

*This is the same bridge for which Samuel's father John How, in 1643, was empowered to levy a rate in the month of March to pay Timothy Hawkins of Watertown for the work. John How was marshal at the time. (Town Records pp. 41–42)

The select men, evidently fearing that the new county road and Samuel How's toll bridge would take traffic away from the center of town, and smarting because he enlarged the bridge without the consent of the town, were determined to make examples of the shirkers. Earlier they had ordered the causeway surveyed and the names of those who had neglected their duty recorded; now they wanted some teeth in the regulations. All parties were to complete their work within ten days or be fined ten shillings. If necessary, the constables could levy the sum by seizing an offender's land.[9]

Fixing the causeway was just the first step. The town voted on December 21, 1674 that: "There shall bee a new Bridge built over the Great River as speedily as may be and to be Railed on both sides, the posts to rise four feet above the said bridge, the Bridge to be built at the same height as the old Bridge is of."[10]

The order went so far as to detail the persons who would provide timbers for the bridge and where they were to be delivered. Captain Goodenow, Peter Noyes, Sergeant Haines, John Goodenow and Thomas Read are mentioned. Samuel How's name is conspicuously absent. On March 1, 1675 fifteen pounds was added to the town rate "for and toward the building of the new bridge (in lieu of the old one) over the Great River."[11]

There is no Town record of this bridge ever being completed in 1674 or 1675, and in 1676, the town had other priorities following King Philip's attack on April 21. Some bad feeling between How and his fellow townsmen probably remained for some time, and How appears to have attempted to mend some political as well as wooden fences by a good deal of "public service" over the next decade.

In March 1678 there is a record of the sickness of Reverend Edmund Browne and the need for a "free contribution gathered by Deacon Haines toward carrying the charge of preaching that the pulpit might be supplied." Samuel How is listed with a group of eight men who volunteered to: "travell with horses and weekly go forth and return Preachers...every Lord's Day."[12] Rev. Browne died the following June so this additional burden must have been on-going until the new minister, James Sherman, was formally installed.[13]

In 1680, Samuel How undertook to build a new set of stocks and "set them before the Meeting House of this town [this was near the present old town cemetery on Old Sudbury Road in Wayland], and the said Samll. How hath promised to finish the same...before the next County Court to be held in April. For the same he is to be paid out of the Rate shortly to be made."[14]

By 1681, How was sufficiently well thought of to be one of six substantial landowners chosen as a "tythingman" for the coming year. He was assigned the precinct "beginning at John Smith's house and so to the new mill,* Nobscot and Lanham and so away Southward ending with David Stone's house."[15] The following year How and John Goodenow were charged with "taking invoyce of all rateable estate." They held their assessing posts for the next three years.

Little by little, How was regaining men's confidence and managing to look after his own interests into the bargain. His life was a pattern of perpetual movement both within Sudbury and in the wider world of Cambridge—the Court House and the pursuit of real estate purchases and sales. In 1684 he was chosen to serve on the "Jury of Tryalls at the said County Court,"[16] where he undoubtedly met his friend and future business partner Samuel Gookin.

But no matter how busy he was with his own lucrative projects, How seldom turned down a request to aid his fellow townsmen. When, in 1685, the town found it necessary to build a log house for an unfortunate member of the community, Jonathan Griffin, who seems to have been afflicted with some form of brain disease, How volunteered for this thankless, but important task.

> John Goodenow and Samuel How have engaged to dig a hole and build a house for J. Griffin often times distracted...to be shutt up in it for his and his keeper's security in his Lunatick or Frenzy Fitts...twenty shillings paid them by the constabel out of the town rate.[17]

As far as How was concerned, the good will of the town mattered more than the 20 shillings. Later that year he constructed a new town pound "forty foot square and of a Sufficient height for keeping in all sorts of creatures..." and agreed to maintain it for the next 20 years. "And his heirs and assignes after him...and for the same hee is to have five pounds out of the Town rate...." An ongoing family proposition.[18]

But despite the esteem in which How was held by his neighbors, in the winter of 1686-87 he lost a bid to build a new

---

*According to Frank Noyes this mill was built by Deacon Daniel Stone on the Sudbury River not far from the cart bridge. The four-arch stone bridge that replaced it is still known as Stone's Bridge today.

meeting house to Leftenant Daniel Pond of Dedham. How and Corporal John Brewer had each made a "proposition" for the construction of the new house and the subject was hotly debated for some months. People disagreed about whether to add to the old building or to start anew. After "long agitations and disputes,"[19] it was voted to have Pond build a house "in all respects for dimensions, strength, shape, necessaries and conveniences as Dedham meeting house is...but in all things else admitting...such variations as are particularly mentioned in the propositions of Corpl John Brewer and Samll How...."[20]

Pond's "proposition" must have been a good one for the town to award such a lucrative contract to an outsider while bypassing two local craftsmen. The phrase "all things else" suggests an uneasy compromise between the outsider, Pond, and locals Brewer and How. Nonetheless, the town thought enough of How to make sure his judgment was brought to bear on such an important project.

Less than a month later, in February of 1687, voters tried to smooth any ruffled feathers by appointing both How and Brewer to a committee to "...al along inspect the workemen and work of the new meeting house in building and to see the same be done in all ways according to agreement with the Town." This arrangement must have afforded satisfaction to How and some discomfiture to Pond. The latter's work in progress was to be closely watched by local experts.[21]

Although he may have had the last laugh with Pond, How did not hear the last of this meeting house for some time. He was rated among the highest in town for a special tax subsequently raised for "the fouer gables of the new meeting house ...seven shillings and sixpence...."[22]

This may not have hurt too much. For How's means were growing apace. Several times he is on record for advancing money to the town for good causes. In the spring of 1688, the Court of Sessions levied a fine on the town "for damage" in answer to a complaint from a Concord resident about one of the town bridges. How advanced a shilling which was used to repair a minor deficiency in the town bridge. In the same year he laid out sixpence for constables' staves.[23]

How was becoming a trusted elder citizen. When ammunition was issued in 1689 as new danger threatened from the French and Indian wars, he was one of a large group who took "the publick stock of ammunition into theare hands and ingaged to respond for the same in case it be not spent...in the resistance of the enemy...." How had 4½ pounds of powder, 33¼ pounds of shot and 13 flints, which is what was allotted to most of the older citizens.[24]

It must have been a satisfactory day for Samuel, at age 48, after long service, when on June 1, 1691, "At a general Town meeting being leagaly warned for the choise of town officers..."[25] he was elected one of the seven select men. It was the first of two terms. His place in town affairs was assured.

During these busy years, Samuel found time to prosper in his own trade and to raise a large family—13 children in all. By 1680, he already had seven children by his first wife, Martha Bent, who died that year, and he was to have six more sons by his second wife, Sarah Leavit Clapp, a widow whom he married in 1685.

Almost from the beginning of his bustling career, How had his irons in other fires, many of them involving real estate transactions. The best known of these was a deal made by himself and Samuel Gookin with the Natick Indians in 1682, which became known as the Gookin-How Purchase. The deed with the Indians, which bears the clear imprint of a lawyer for the other party, reads, in part: "a parcel of land lying and being in the bounds of Natick, containing by estimation 200 acres more or less, bounde with Sherborn line southerly, with John Bent and David Stone's land northerly, Henry Rice's lands and Cathechauitt pond (Lake Cochituate) easterly, to have and to hold the above premises be the same more ore less with all the privilages and appurtenances to the same appertaining...."[26]

Gookin's father was Major General Daniel Gookin, Colonial Commissioner to the Indians and a good friend of the Reverend John Eliot, the "Apostle to the Indians," but it didn't take the tribe very long to figure out that the father's good name didn't extend to the son. With no western boundary specified in the deed, Gookin and How took possession of an immense amount of land which they sold to homesteaders as opportunity offered.

Not surprisingly, the Naticks became dissatisfied and on June 22, 1695, Thomas Sawin, lawyer for the tribe, placed a claim with the General Court that How and Gookin had "fradulently obtained a large tract of land," and had made "encroachments" far beyond the land agreed to in the grant and asked for "satisfaction therefor...."[27]

Gookin and How weren't to be cornered that easily. Gookin presented the Court with a document which enumerated the monies he and his partner had paid to the Indians, and the support of "severall widow squaws," as well as Samuel How's expenses and time, a total of £81-11-6. On December 9, 1696, the Court confirmed 1,700 acres to Gookin and How. Even considering the 1,000 acres the Court returned to the Indians, it wasn't a bad increase over "200 acres more or less."

This was by no means How's first shrewd real estate deal. In 1676, two months after the Sudbury Fight, he purchased Lot #50 in the New Grant from young Peter King after the death of his father, Thomas.[28] It was a good time for an astute real estate dealer to make an offer for this remote lot with Indian raids still a real danger. How probably bought it on terms favorable to himself. Twenty-six years later he would deed the property to his fourth son David and help him build a homestead in the wild land.

Deed for the Gookin-How Purchase from the Natick Indians.

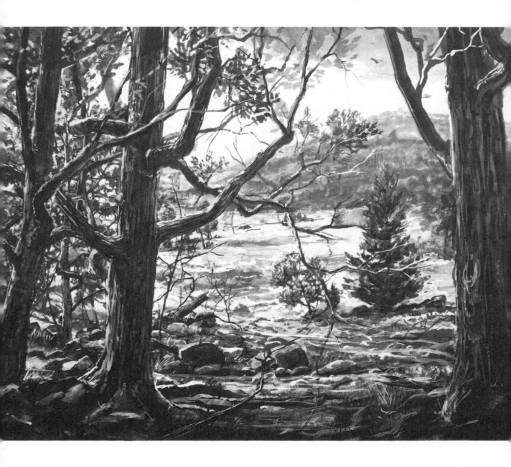

IV

"Best Accomdated And
The Most Suitabel Man"

In the years before Samuel How became a select man in 1691, more and more travelers were passing through the town and the Parmenter Tavern and Thomas Walker's ordinary couldn't accommodate them all. The Parmenter Tavern in East Sudbury, which began when John Parmenter Junior was allowed by the Court February 4, 1655, to "keep a house of publique entertainment...for selling beer, brandy, wine and strong waters"[1] was Sudbury's first and oldest tavern.* Thomas Walker opened his ordinary in 1672. He was the father of the Thomas Walker who, in 1687, married Samuel How's second daughter Martha.

The demand for strong waters was so great that some citizens had been selling liquor illegally and in nearby Marlborough, Samuel's younger brother Thomas, at the sign of the Black Horse, was chastised in 1682 for selling hard "sider" to an Indian. He had promised "not to sell it again."[2]

Drunkenness was rampant and resulted in an increasing fear of God's wrath. Taverns and ordinaries were carefully scrutinized. As a result, Thomas Walker found himself with unexpected visitors. According to a contemporary report, "Upon the uncomfortable representations and reports concerning the ordinary, the selectmen were ordered to make inquiry and if, upon examination, they found matters were as reported, to persuade Mr. Walker and his wife to take down their sign and sell no more drink."[3]

Walker "gravely" responded that "he guessed" the reports were not true and evidently the select men decided, for the time being, to let well enough alone since town meetings on January 10, 1685 and February 18, 1686 were "adjourned to the

*This tavern was probably run from John Parmenter Jr.'s house which, according to a map drawn in 1889 by J.S. Draper, was located near the end of the highway to Bridle Point on the east side of the Sudbury River (now Wayland).

house of Mr. Walker by reason of the extremity of the cold."[4]

But Colony officals were watching events in Sudbury and other towns. Sudbury was conspicuous in those days because it was one of the largest. In March, 1690, the General Court—spurred on by the general belief that the recurring Indian wars were a "particular manifestation of God's displeasure for the prevalence of vice and immorality"—published a proclamation for the reformation of manners wherein it was ordered that "the law of the country against vice and all sorts of debauchery and profane acts and all enticements and injustices be put into execution."[5]

Perhaps in direct response to this Court order, in 1692, the Sudbury select men took matters into their own hands and decided to bring order to the situation. They requested the Court that Samuel How, a newly-elected member of their board, be allowed to open an ordinary. Joseph Noyes spoke for the town:

To the Middlesex County Court:

In answer to the warrent received I have used what means I could to get the select men together, but by reason of one trobel and another it has been neglected.

It has been in the minds of most of us that ther should be none to retail drink amongst us by reason of the growing of the sin of drunknes amongst us. Oure fathers came into this wilderness to enjoy the gospel and his ordinances in its purity and the convertion of the hethen but instead of converting them, amongst other sins we have taught them to be druckerds which we may have cause to fear God has permitted them to be such a scourge as at this present.

Ther be those that desir licenses but such as cannot command themselves ar not fit for such an imploie or trust. Verbum spienti satis est quod suffisit. All things considered it is not mine one mind only but of some others that Col. Samuel How is best accomdated and the most suitabel man that presents himself willing to undertack to entertaine travillers wich as far as I understand is the only or at least the chef end of a howes of entertainment and not Town druckerds. Plain dealing I think is best-I pray pardon my boldness.

Your Servant
Joseph Noyes, Select man
Sudbury, July the 29, 1692[6]

Noyes' petition was approved by the Court that summer and, consequently, at the height of his prosperity and stature in the town, and in response to this official request, Samuel How opened his own ordinary. How is the only new licensed tavern keeper listed in Sudbury at that date as "persons that received theire licenses."[7]

It didn't take long for How's ordinary to become the headquarters for officials conducting town business on the West Side of the river. The Sudbury Town Records list some of the visits:

> August 8, 1694: The 5 assessors expended in necessary charges att Corpral Sammll Hows whilst they wear making the Kings Tax, on all 5 days: oL 12s 6d*
>
> October 5, 1694: The 4 assessors expended at Mr. Hows in Necessary charges: oL 4s 8d.
>
> December 4, 1694: Select Men expended at Corpll Hows in meatt and drink oL 4s od.
>
> December 25, 1694: Select Men expended in necessary charges att Corpll Samll Hows: oL 5s 6d.[8] (One wonders if this is in the line of duty or the seventeenth century equivalent of the office Christmas party).

In late 1695, the select men seemed to have developed the habit of conducting their monthly meeting over dinner at How's, as shown by the following accounts in the town book:

> July 2, 1695: Expended at Mr. How's 6 dinners oL 4s 04d.
>
> August 30, 1695: 6 dinners and a pint and halfe rum o1s 6d.
>
> September 6, 1695: 7 dinners select men a pint of rum 4s 08d.[9]

Since this is a record only of official matters which had to be set down by law, one can assume that the regular course of trade was equally brisk. How's was an ideal stopping point for travelers midway between the East and West sides as well as a gathering place for locals.

How still managed to find time between his ordinary keeping chores for a variety of small jobs for the town, such as "perambulator for the west side of the river with Watertown,"[10] in 1693, and fence viewer for his side of the river in 1694 and 1695.[11] He was also asked to perform a number of duties which drew on his business and carpentry skills. In 1693 he was sent "to Dedham to adjust the accompts and obtain a

---

*Pounds, shillings and pence were indicated by the symbols L-s-d. For example, oL-12s-6d would be 12 shillings and sixpence.

discharge from Lieut Pond conserning our new meeting house...." and, in the year following, to direct a group of men freed from all other highway work "to keep Lanham bridge and casway in good repair att all times."[12]

In 1696, How was put in charge of choosing among 20 young men those most qualified to "build a house for the Widdow Edge"[13] and, in 1695, "to take special care and cognoscence of the carpenters work all ways...to the hanging of a bell at the meeting house...."[14]

Meanwhile at the courts in Cambridge and Charlestown, How was sufficiently respected to be made an arbitrator for other men's court cases in 1697. Any man who was serving as an arbitrator during that period would have had to have steady nerves and a cool head. The year 1697 was a particularly bad one for people all over the Colony, since the epidemic which took place that winter resulted in "the terriblest coughs and colds and from which...passed many out of this into eternity...."[15]

It is remarkable that Samuel found the time and energy to encompass all these activities simultaneously, but he was a master at making sure that public service or "good works," whether at the Colony level or at home in Sudbury, were also expedient moves to advance his various businesses and his good name. The opening of his ordinary is a case in point. It was probably an advantageous sideline.

It is important to recognize that in this period when Samuel How received his license, the phrase "most suitabel man" meant exactly what it said. Those who ran town government were anxious to prevent the abuse of this license and Court records of the time are full of references to difficulties encountered with tavern keepers all over the Colony. A law was passed in November, 1692 which specified that "only those licensed by the Justices of the Court were allowed to keep a house of entertainment or sell strong liquor."[16] On December 10, 1695, a bill for more effective suppression of the sale of liquor without a license was introduced.[17] In March, 1697, it was required that "such persons as are of a Sober Conversation"[18] are allowed to have licenses. And only those. In 1693, an innholder, tavern keeper or retailer had to give the Clerk of Sessions a £10 bond* and two sureties at £5 apiece.[19]

*During this decade, Thomas How, proprietor of the Black Horse Tavern in Marlborough was required by the Colony to furnish a similar bond and agree to the following: "(The proprietor) shall not suffer or have any playing

All this suggests that opening and running an ordinary of any kind was not undertaken lightly and that those that did so had earned the confidence of their fellow townsmen. Samuel How was responding not just to the prospect of personal profits (he had plenty of more lucrative opportunities elsewhere) but to a summons which, as a loyal citizen of the town, he could not refuse.

But it is perfectly possible, in fact probable, that this first How ordinary in Sudbury simply served food and drink and did not put people up overnight. Nothing in the records suggests that it was a full-fledged inn. In fact, the contrary is suggested. A distinction was made at that time between an innholder and a retailer, the difference being that innholders lodged people overnight whereas retailers merely sold "strong waters" and sometimes food, "in doors" or, very frequently, "with out doors." It seems likely that How's activities were in the category of retailer, which would have interfered less with his other businesses. The references to assessors and other officials eating and drinking during the making of the King's tax during several years in the late 1690s, do not specify that the individuals stayed overnight.

Moreover, there are at least three specific references to How family retailing during the period that Samuel How was functioning as an ordinary keeper. In 1710, one of the years in which the renewal of his license is recorded,† the Court of

---

at cards, dice, tally, bowls, nine pins, billiards or other unlawful games in his said house or yard, or gardens, nor shall suffer to remain in his house any person or persons, not being his own family, on Saturday night after dark, or on the Sabbath days, or during the time of God's Public Worship...nor shall sell any wine to Indians, or negroes, nor suffer any children or servant, or other person to remain in his house, tippling or drinking after nine o'clock in the night...nor willingly or knowingly harbor in his house, barn, stable, or elsewhere any rogues, vagabonds, thieves, sturdy beggars, masterless men or women or other notorious offenders whatsoever...." (Charles Hudson, *History of Marlborough* pp. 382–383)

†How's license shows for the first time in the Court of Sessions records in 1692. It then shows as a renewal five other times—in the years, 1695, 1697, 1709, 1710 and 1711. There are gaps in between these years in which we can find no renewal. There are several possible explanations:
1. How's is not the only ordinary keeper's name which is missing for a year or two and then reappears. Possibly if the town and the Court were satisfied with a man's upright character, they did not, in this decade, insist on *annual* renewal.

Sessions preserves this message from the select men of Sudbury:

> June 11, 1710. Sudbury. We the select men of Sudbury to the Honord Court of ye General Sessions to be held at Charles-towne the 18th day of this instant...will allow Corp. Samuel How should be a retailer of strong drink without doors ...provided he obtaine approbation of this honoured Court...
>
> > John Brigham
> > David Haynes
> > John Rice[20]

The following year, 1711, when Samuel evidently enlisted the help of one of his sons, Elisha, the select men say to the Court of General Sessions:

> June 24, 1711
> We...give our consent that Elisha How of Sudbury be a Retailer of strong drink out of doers...
>
> > John Rice
> > Ephraim Curtis
> > Joshua Haynes
> > John Noyes....[21]

By 1712, the year before his death, Samuel must have given the business entirely over to Elisha, who by then would have been in his early twenties. Elisha is recorded that year as "Elisha How, Ret" or Retailer, along with Susanna Blandford, who is listed as "Innholder". She pays a license fee of two pounds, five shillings whereas he pays two pounds. The distinction between retailer and innholder is clear.[22]

These three references, which all specify retailing, or the sale of strong drink out of doors, point to the fact that Samuel How and one of his younger sons were running an ordinary, pure and simple. It was left to Elisha's brother, David, to run an inn as such.

---

2. Gladys Salta, who did extensive Court research for Henry Ford in the 1920s, theorizes that Samuel Gookin, whose name frequently shows at the Court, was arranging How's renewals to save Samuel long horseback trips.

3. There may have been some years when Samuel was too preoccupied with other business to run the ordinary. It was not uncommon for tavern keepers to cease for short periods. Samuel How's mother, Mary How, tells us that she and her husband, John, for "sume yeres desisted" from running their Marlborough tavern in John's old age. Her son may simply have followed the same practice for a brief time.

Where was Samuel's ordinary located? We are relatively certain that Samuel ran this first How tavern in Sudbury from his house in Lanham on the property originally deeded to him by the Bent family, or at least from a nearby location in Lanham, close to the cart bridge he built in 1674.

Although, as a shrewd real estate operator, Samuel undoubtedly owned land on both sides of the Great River, he is usually mentioned in town records as a West Side resident (as in his large claim for damages from the Irish Charity Donation in 1676). We believe that both his house and his ordinary were on the West Side.*

Wherever the ordinary was operated, it was not on the present site of the Wayside Inn. The deed Samuel gave to David in 1702 specified "a parcell of land and meadows...being a New Grant Lott in the New part of said Sudbury..."[23] There were no buildings on this lot until after 1702. One building, the homestead built by Samuel and David in 1703, shows on a 1707 map.[24]

Records apart, common sense suggests that Samuel's ordinary was in Lanham. His house, burned by the Indians in 1676, had been rebuilt at considerable expense and it is most unlikely that he would have had the time or inclination to build and operate a tavern on the outskirts of town where customers would have been few and far between. He was operating his ordinary as a convenience for travelers, at the request of his town, and would have concentrated his efforts in one place as far as possible. He would simply not have had the time nor the inclination to ride several miles a day to a new location in the wild land.

In addition, Samuel's second wife and family would have demanded his attention. Six young sons arrived in the 1690s— Daniel†, Nehemiah, Moses, Elisha, Ebenezer and Micajah. The youngest, Micajah, was born in 1700[25] when his father was nearly 60 years old. By that time, the two oldest sons, John and

---

*In the mid-1950s, attorney Frank H. Noyes extensively researched deeds made to and from members of the How family in the 17th and 18th centuries. He left his unpublished research notes to the New England Historic Genealogical Society (MSS 47). For those interested in a more detailed discussion of the location of Samuel How's property and ordinary in Lanham, and in How family history, they are well worth examining.

†The first Daniel, How's third son, born in 1672, had died in 1680 at the age of eight. The second Daniel, born in 1690 as part of this second family, later came to prominence as an Indian fighter.

Samuel, who had been active in Sudbury affairs for many years as constables and in other offices, had both moved to Framingham to start their own businesses. The fourth son, David, had married Hepzibah Death in 1700 and was looking for a place of his own.

Samuel had just the place in mind. On June 4, 1702, he deeded the New Grant lot he had purchased back in 1676 from Peter King to David:

> ...out of the natural love and affection that I do bear to my beloved son David How...I have also the consent and good will of my beloved wife Sarah How...Have given, granted, aliened, enforced and confirmed, and by these presents fully, freely, clearly and absolutely give, grant a lien, enforce and confirm unto my said son David How, his heirs, executors, Adms and assigns a certain parcell of land and meadows containing by estimation one hundred and thirty acres, be it more or less, being a New Grant Lott in the New part of said Sudbury...[26]
>
> Samuel How

The spring and summer of 1703 was a busy one for both Samuel and David. His new daughter-in-law was pregnant and there was much to be done if she and her husband were to have a place of their own by the time the baby arrived in December.

How's years as a carpenter and glazier had taught him how to make the best use of time and outwit the vagueries of New England's climate. In fair weather he was busy outside with hammer, saw and chisel, while snowy and rainy days were spent indoors cutting glass and framing windows. The windows in David How's two-room homestead, which are of a style common in the late seventeenth century, were probably prefabricated at a much earlier time or salvaged from another house.* Glass and lead were expensive and hard to come by in the early 1700s and Samuel wouldn't have wasted them.

When Samuel's granddaughter, Thankful, was born in 1703, Samuel was 61. When Israel, his second grandson by David arrived in 1712, he had turned 70, but showed no signs of

---

*Frank Noyes, who investigated the origins of the Wayside Inn during the 1950s, put forward this very plausible theory. He also suggested that after the 1955 fire, Roy W. Baker, who was in charge of the restoration, was influenced consciously or unconsciously by these windows, and concluded that the first house was put up before the end of the 17th century. Noyes proved conclusively by deeds, maps, and logic that this was not the case. (Letter to Miss Priscilla Staples, September 29, 1958.)

slowing down. In 1704, the town paid How nine shillings for building three casks to store the Town's stock of ammunition,[27] and in 1711 he purchased a quarter interest in Deacon Daniel Stone's corn and saw mill along with the water rights.[28] This proved to be a shrewd investment. His interest was valued at £30 after his death and his administrator sold it back to its original owner for £32.

Samuel continued, as far as we know, to live in Lanham with his second wife until his death in 1713 at the age of 71. He must have died suddenly and unexpectedly, because, able man of affairs though he was, he left no will.

Old friends Thomas Brinton and Abraham Wood inventoried Samuel How's estate at £793, including homestead and meadow land at £230, ten additional acres at £23, and one fourth part of a corn and saw mill at £30. It was to be 16 years before John How and his younger brother, Nehemiah, finally settled their father's affairs.[29]

Although John, the eldest son, who was nearly 40 at the time of his father's death, was named administrator, it was Nehemiah, 20 years his junior, who did the most to bring order to the estate. The committee that appraised its worth gave it as their opinion in February, 1714, that "it will be a damage to this estate to divid to every child a peace of land out of...this estate...."[30]

Nehemiah solved the problem by buying the entire estate and settling with the other 12 heirs and their spouses, a transaction that would have made his father proud.[31]

We know little of Samuel How except as a public figure from public records, but in his actions—prudent management of money and land, participation in town and Colony affairs, gifts to his children, particularly David—Samuel How paved the way for the coming centuries of achievement by his descendants. Samuel How was a trail blazer in the wild land.

V

"A Hous Of Entertainment For Travelers"

Threw Lot #16 in the second squadron. Thomas
building in the clearing beside Hop Brook on Lot #50 of
the New Grant that spring and summer of 1703 was not
an imposing one, but to David that did not matter. He would be
29 years old on the second of November and soon after that
would be a father. It was time that he and Hepzibah Death How
had a place of their own.

Samuel had deeded him the lot the summer before. The land
was a part of a two-mile extension to the town's western
boundary granted by the General Court in 1649 and divided into
four squadrons, each of which contained a number of 130-acre
lots.

The select men didn't get around to surveying or allocating
the land until 1657. In that year it was distributed to the
townsmen literally "by lott". That January, John How, David's
grandfather, drew Lot #16 in the second squadron. Thomas
King, another freeman of the town, drew Lot #50 in the fourth
squadron.[1] It was the latter lot that Samuel How had purchased
from Peter King shortly after Thomas King's death in 1676.

David How was born just two years before this transaction
took place. Samuel's fourth son grew up in Lanham, absorbing
what schooling was available. Samuel had a demonstrated
interest in education, so his sons may have fared better than
some. There had been books in the household since John How's
time and David learned to read and write, which many could
not.* In 1679, when David was five years old, an early town

---

*Before schools existed, it was the responsibility of parents and other
adults to instruct children and bondservants. About the same time that the
Sudbury select men toured the homesteads to inquire into the state of
learning, town officials replied to an inquiry from the court of Middlesex
County: "Although there are not stated scholes in the town for that the
inhabitants are so scattered in their dwellings that it cannot well be, yet
such is the case by having school dames in each side of the river that
teacheth small children to spell and read which is so managed by their
parents and governours at home presented..." (*Stearns Collection*, pp. 51-52)

record tells us that the select men decided to:

> ...visit the families of the town and speedily Inspect the same...especially to examine children and servants about their improvement as to Reading and catechism....[2]

Later on the visitors reported that they found that "children and young persons are in a forward and growing way...as to reading and catechizing...."[3]

When Samuel became a select man in 1691, he was party to a decision to once again send officials throughout the town to "examine children and servants about their reading and catechism" and shortly after this, six school masters and school dames were appointed in different areas of town. "...the wif of our brother Daniel Stone...att Lanham" was specified among others and "John Long was chosen a writing master to teach children to write and cast amounts."[4]

Certainly by the time he married Hepzibah Death of Framingham on Christmas Day, 1700, David How could "write and caste amounts..." Just five years later he signed his name in a bold, clear hand to a petition to Governor Dudley while others simply made their mark. In the meantime he became a property owner and head of household in his own right, when on June 4, 1702, Samuel deeded him Lot #50 which had been lying undeveloped since the elder How purchased it 26 years before.

The deed, which specifies a transaction of land and land only, makes it clear that there were no buildings on the lot at that time. The first written record of a building on Lot #50 is a map drawn in the year 1707[5] which shows a small homestead on the lot.*

Father and son had started to clear the land the year previous. There were plenty of big American chestnut trees† nearby on Nobscot Mountain for beams and framing and stands of white pine for boards and planking. Deacon Daniel Stone's saw mill was near Samuel How's farm in the hamlet of Lanham, but that was a ten-mile round trip from David's homestead. More

---

*See also Sumner Chilton Powell's *Puritan Village*, Map facing p. 109. This clearly shows the layout of the New Grant Lots and squadrons and the location of the lots drawn by John How and Thomas King.

†Russell Kirby, former Fife Master of the Sudbury Ancient Fife and Drum Company, used pieces of old beams salvaged from the 1955 fire to make a set of ceremonial colonial wooden fifes for the Inn. The wood proved to be American chestnut.

than likely the boards, planks and framing were cut at Hager's mill, which was just a mile west on Hop Brook (now the site of the Wayside Country Store in Marlborough). Daniel Woodward's mill, four miles to the north on the same stream, was not built until 1740, although there is some evidence that a mill existed on that site somewhat earlier.

The house was a simple, two-room building with an entrance hall on the west end, which sheltered a steep circular staircase winding around the chimney to a common bedroom on the second floor. The building was 26 feet long by 20 wide and of post and beam construction. The windows were small and shuttered in case of Indian attack, and Samuel How had glazed them carefully, probably in the warmth of his own home during the cold winter months.

The first floor common room, which is the old bar room in today's Wayside Inn, served as a combination kitchen, dining room and parlor. It was heated by a great fieldstone fireplace on the west wall. Samuel and David carefully notched the girt (supporting) beam and lined the space with clay before setting the hearthstone for the upstairs fireplace. Bits of clay can still be found there today.

Things were in order in time for David to get in wood and make other preparations for the winter. His first child, Thankful, was born that December with four more to follow in the next nine years—Hepzibah on October 1, 1706, Eliphalet on June 3, 1710, Israel on May 6, 1712 and Ruth on February 23, 1715. Later, two more sons were born, David in 1717 and Ezekiel in 1720.[6]

David's early years on the West Side were busy ones, but they did not include innkeeping, despite traditions to the contrary. There were fields to be cleared, walls to be laid up, and barns and shelters for livestock to be built. With a growing family and a two-room house, David How was in no position to put up travelers.

But a couple of events were in the wind to change all that. In 1707, David How was one of 31 people to sign a petition to Governor Dudley and the General Court to allow Sudbury to divide into two separate precincts, each with its own meeting house. The petition pointed out that West Side residents had to travel a great distance in bad weather to reach the East Side meeting house and were often:

> forced to seek our spirituall good with the peril of our
> Lives...God...hath cast our lott to fall on that side of the
> River by Reason of the flud of watare which for a very great
> part of the yeare does very much incommode us and often by
> extremity of water terrible and violent winds and a great part
> of the winter by ice...so that we are shut up and cannot come
> forth...whereby many of our children and little ones, ancient
> and weak persons, can very Rarly attend the public
> worship....

The petition was dated January 15, 1707.[7]

This petition did not exaggerate the hardships. Far more than just politics between the East and West sides was involved. The distance from the first meeting house in East Sudbury (now Wayland) to David How's homestead was more than ten miles or a round trip of 20 miles on foot or horseback in good weather or bad. It is not surprising that David How and other West Side residents moved strongly for a safer and less uncomfortable way to take their families to church and to conduct town business. Try a brisk hike from the Wayside Inn to the old graveyard in Wayland on a snowy morning in February. And take two or three children along.

Only a few years before this petition, the town meeting usually held in February for the election of town officers had been put forward to November because West Side residents "attended it with too much difficulty...on account of the water of the great river being risen too high on the causeway that they cannot pass on horses and so much frozen that they cannot come over in canoos...."[8]

An additional danger was attack from wolves. A bounty of ten shillings per wolf was in effect at this date,[9] and later the town voted an extra ten shillings a head.[10] Hungry wolves prowled in lonely places on winter days.

East Side residents protested the 1707 petition, countering it with one of their own in which they cited the expense of a new minister and offered to help build a new causeway over the river as an alternative. They pointed out that a meeting house on the West Side would simply result in: "many of their dwellings being as remote from the meeting house as they are now."[11] This counter petition was signed by 54 people, 24 of them from the West Side.*

---

*The uneasiness between East and West Side residents, which had been an issue of greater or lesser moment in town politics for a long time, escalated

Seven years later, the West Siders took a more drastic step and petitioned for a separate township.[12] The General Court compromised and ordered on October 27, 1714, that "there be allowed a distinct precinct and a meeting house built for the public worship of God on the west side of ye river."[13] The import of this news was not lost on David How. He applied for and received his first license to run a house of entertainment just two years later.

Creating a somber backdrop to these activities was the ever-present threat of the French and Indian wars. Sudbury felt the impact of the conflict more closely than some communities nearer the sea, since many relatives and friends had settled in the outlying districts of Brookfield and Rutland in what is now central Massachusetts.

For a period of nearly 40 years, 1700 until 1739, the white settlers and various Indian tribes throughout New England were caught in a squeeze play between England and France. While these two European powers struggled for supremacy on the North American continent, both old and new inhabitants of the colonies were forced to take sides. Various stages of the conflict were called King William's War and Queen Anne's War and so on. To David How and the residents of Sudbury the British and French monarchies meant little. Ever-present danger from attack, possible imprisonment and death were what counted. Memories of relatives killed and missing in King Philip's War in 1676 were still vivid in men's minds.

There are records of Hows serving in various parts of the Colony in 1724 and 1725, and it is probable that they participated in skirmishes in the Queen Anne's War before that time. In 1706, when it was rumored that a large force of Indians was approaching New England, Chelmsford, Groton and Sudbury were alerted. The following year, the Indians were reported near Groton and Marlborough and in May of 1704, Sudbury was mentioned in a resolve of the province in which: "soldiers shall, each of them at his own charge, be provided with a pair

---

during this argument, and the question of two meeting houses dragged on for years. It finally ended in 1721 when Rev. Israel Loring accepted the invitation of West Side residents to become their new minister. In March of 1724; twenty five West Siders "entered into and renewed a holy church covenant." (Hudson p. 291) David How's name does not appear on the document, perhaps because the Inn was only eight years old at the time, David considered it injudicious to involve himself in a dispute involving potential customers from both sides of the river.

of good serviceable snow shoes, mogginsons at or before the tenth of Nov. this present year which they shall keep in good repair and fit for the service."[14]

There was a brief peace in 1713 with the Treaty of Utrecht, but hostilities soon resumed when the Indians of Maine allied with other tribes to prevent further settlement by white men. Rutland, where David's son Israel later settled and was killed, was already a center for new settlement by sturdy Sudbury townsmen such as Captain Samuel Wright, who had served as town treasurer. In 1724, Wright wrote the General Court of a recent skirmish with the Indians.

> These are to inform your honors that what I feared is come upon us for want [of men] to guard us at our work, this day about 12 o'clock five men and a boy [were] making hay in the middle of town.
>
> A number of Indians surrounded them and shot first at the boy which alarmed the men, who ran for their guns, but the Indians shot upon them and kept them from their guns and shot down three of the men and wounded another in the arm who got home, the fifth got home without any damage.
>
> The men that are killed are James Clark [Sr.], Joseph Wood, Uriah Ward, the boy missing is James Clark."[15]

Wright's letter shows how swiftly and unexpectedly Indians could strike in outlying places. It was no wonder that Sudbury, along with other Massachusetts towns, was often called upon to send men and arms to the imperiled frontier towns.

Awareness of constant danger at their very doorsteps built a strong tradition of Indian service in the How family. They knew the peril from firsthand experience through several generations. David's uncle John, son of the first John How, died in the Sudbury Fight in 1676. His cousin Sarah, who married Peter Joslin and moved to Lancaster, was massacred by the Indians in 1692. Another cousin, Elizabeth,* was carried away on the same occasion.[16]

David was 18 years old when the Lancaster raid took place. His younger brother Daniel, who moved to Brookfield in 1715, served under Captain Samuel Willard in the ranks of the Indian rangers. David's second son, Israel, was killed by Indians in

---

*Elizabeth How had a beautiful singing voice which the Indians prized. They carried her away to Canada where she remained for some years, and was later ransomed and rescued by her uncle, Colonel Thomas How of Marlborough. (D.W. Howe, *Howe Genealogies*, p.7)

Rutland. There is a poignant entry in the settlement of David's estate, many years later, in which Israel's widow, Elizabeth Barrett How, signed for Israel's children and their portion of their grandfather's estate.[17]

There is strong tradition that David How himself was an Indian ranger* along with his brother Daniel, but we have been unable to unearth any definite evidence to support this. The only suggestion that David How may have been an Indian fighter is for a much later period and quite unspecific. In the year 1739, during renewed hostilities, a David How is mentioned in a list of "Gentlemen of Horse" under Captain Josiah Brown of Sudbury.[18] This is probably David's son, David How, Jr. who would have been 22 years old at this date. It is possible, but unlikely, that David senior was skirmishing with the Indians at the age of 65.

Other members of the family, and most especially David's younger brother, Daniel, were certainly involved in the continual fighting. Daniel, who was born in 1690, 16 years after his brother, was granted land in Brookfield in 1715 and later moved to Rutland where he lived from 1722 to 1725. He is listed as an assessor there.[19] This Daniel appears in Captain Willard's Journal for a 1725 Indian campaign in which Willard recounts mustering in Lancaster and marching on to Rutland, "foul weather," and sending out to look for Indian signs. Willard's entry for November 28, 1725, reads: "Mr. William Brintnall being sick and Daniel How lame, I sent them home...."[20] It was no wonder that they were sick and lame. The average day's march was about 24 miles.

This campaign, of which Willard's Journal is one of the few records, may have been the result of an appeal by the settlers of

---

*The tradition of David How's Indian service seems to have resulted mostly from the fact that Hudson (p.299), in his *History of Sudbury*, mentions David How as appearing in Captain Willard's Journal which Hudson apparently examined in the State Archives. Hudson must have misread the name 'Daniel' as 'David'. Since William Brintnall, also from Sudbury, is mentioned on the same page, it is an understandable error. David's younger brother, Daniel, lived in Rutland and was a leading citizen there. Hudson's error was later compounded by the Rev. Martin Lovering who states flatly in his *Genealogies of the Howe Family*: "David How was an Indian ranger," (page 72) with no source mentioned. This reference was, even more unfortunately, picked up by Dr. John van Schaick, Jr., who remarks in his introductory chapter to *Characters in the Tales of a Wayside Inn*, 'Five Generations of Howes:' "There is a deal of suggestiveness in the sentence from Lovering: 'David How was an Indian Ranger.'" (p. 16)

Rutland to Governor Dudley in February of 1725 in which they ask for help because:

> The summer previous they laboured under great difficulty and hardship by reason of war with the Indian enemy and not being able to raise their crop and other provisions were obliged to travel near twenty miles for the same and purchase it at a very deare rate which made it very difficult to subsist themselves and their families more especially the soldiers posted there....[21]

By the mid-1700's, the Indian troubles had subsided enough for settlement of the outlying lands to the west to resume. This, in turn, brought more traffic over the rough dirt path that ran past David How's homestead. Drivers and drovers were moving livestock from the fertile valley of Lake Quinsigamond and the hills of Quaboag to Boston and needed a place to rest their animals and spend the night.

Consequently, in the late summer of 1716, the Sudbury select men forwarded a rectangular scrap of paper to the Court of General Sessions sitting in Concord. It read:

> To his Majesties Justices of the Honour'd Court of the Sessions at Concord, August 28, 1716: We the select men of Sudbury are willing and give our Consent that David How of Sudbury should keep a hous of entertainment for travelers if the honored justices think meet.
>
> Peter Haynes
James Haines
Joshua Haynes
Ephraim Curtis
Select Men[22]

Plans for that first How Tavern in Sudbury may have been sparked by the 1714 petition for a separate township. Samuel How may even have helped his son enlarge the building to make way for wayfarers before he died. Two more rooms were added to the west end of the building and the chimney was doubled in size to accommodate two new fireplaces on the east end of the new addition. David chose to have a higher ceiling in his new downstairs parlor and to this day there is a six inch difference between the upstairs floor levels in the new and old sections of the house.

David took naturally to innkeeping. He had had plenty of time to learn the trade during his father's ordinary keeping days in Lanham, which started when David was 18. It is also possible that, as a very young child, he watched his grandfather, John, at work in the Black Horse Tavern in Marlborough. His memories of the Black Horse would have been dim, since the Indian wars interrupted family life and David was only six when John How died. But the innkeeping tradition was probably instilled by both relatives in practice and in reminiscence by winter fires.

There is a popular tradition of long standing, ably encouraged by the Inn's present signboard, that David or his father operated a tavern on the present site in an informal way well before 1716. This is, at best, questionable. Upright, law-abiding citizens that they both were, it is most unlikely. Samuel had his own license to run an ordinary "out of doors" and did so with the help of his son, Elisha, much closer to the center of town, probably from his own house in the hamlet of Lanham.

Licenses were carefully protected in this decade. The Court had become more particular and there is a clear and specific record of innholders and retailers in Sudbury, both before and after 1716. Other than Samuel How, Stephan Blandford was the only listed ordinary keeper in Sudbury in the late 1690's.[23] After his death, his widow took over and Susanna Blandford and Samuel How held sway together for several years. Jonathan Willard joined the list in 1702 and Enoch Cleveland in 1708. By the year 1711, Samuel seems to have been assisted by one of his sons, Elisha, who is on record as a Retailer for that year.[24]

By 1712, only Susanna Blandford and Elisha How are listed— this is the year before Samuel's death—and in 1713, only Susanna Blandford. She was joined in 1714 by Joshua Parker and the same two are listed in 1715.[25] In 1716, for the first time, David How joined them and in 1717, Samuel Wright replaced Joshua Parker.[26]

There is a record of David's innkeeping license every year from 1716 onwards. In 1722, Sudbury had no less than five licensed keepers of houses of entertainment: Mr. David How, Mrs. Susanna Blandford, Widow Rachel Knight, Hannah Gleason and Mr. Phineas Rice. By 1726, only Hannah Gleason and David How continued from this group. By that date a Mr. David Baldwin was also licensed and Mr. Jonathan Rice replaced Phineas. These four continued while Knight and Blandford dropped out. Jeremiah Wesson and John Ebeloth appeared for the first time in 1733.[27] Innkeeping must have been a fairly competitive business although it was clearly divided between the East and West sides.

David How's last annual listing appears in 1747. Ezekiel How is listed for the first time in 1748.

In this orderly procession of innholders, licensed annually, there is no room for anyone to run an inn or an ordinary on the present site prior to the listed date. Innkeeping in the early eighteenth century was a well-regulated, highly-competitive business with no room for interlopers. Even when things were above board there was occasional squabbling. Only a few years before David How opened his doors to the public, Susanna Blandford complained to the Court about the number of inn holders licensed in the town; she asked for and received an abatement of her annual fees. No one could have operated sub-rosa for long.

Moreover, in addition to the recorded license, there is another piece of telling evidence to support the fact that the inn opened in 1716, or at least that the first signboard didn't go up any sooner. Henry David Thoreau kept a daily journal from 1837 to 1861, leaving us with a clear record of the times. In an entry dated May 22, 1853, when he was on his way to Nobscot Hill, he writes:

> This is the third windy day following two days of rain, a washing day...such as we always have at this season, me-thinks. The grass has sprung up as by magic since the rains. The birds are heard through pleasant dashing wind that enlivens everyt...Left our horse at the How Tavern. The oldest date on the sign is 'D.H. 1716.' An old woman*, who had been a servant in the family and said she was ninety-one, said that this was the first house built on the spot. Went on to Nobscot.[28]

This is Thoreau writing a casual account of a pleasant spring day, complete with weather and other details. He was a good observer, noted for accuracy. There is absolutely no reason to doubt him.

Licenses and signboards apart, it can possibly be argued that David How was operating informally at least a few months or a few weeks before he received his official license. There are two references to an ordinary in Sudbury in Judge Samuel

---

*This old woman is undoubtedly 'Aunt Margey' who is mentioned in newspaper accounts of Lyman Howe's day.

Sewall's diary, the first of which is suggestive. It reads: "1716. Monday, August 27. Set out with Davenport for Springfield...Treated* at N. Sparhawks. Dine at Wilsons. Mr. Justice Lynde came to me at Watertown Mill. Got to How's about ½ hour by Sun."[29]

Were the good Justice and his friends meeting at How's tavern illegally? Perhaps, but since the Court met only twice a year, allowances were often made for this sort of timing. It's also perfectly possible, since times and distances are an estimate at best, that Sewall was at David How's cousin's place in Marlborough.

Sewall's second entry reads: "1718. Thursday, July 25. Have a fast in Westborough this day in order to settle a minister. We bait† at Sudbury; dine at Larned's in Watertown."[30] This notation may have nothing at all to do with David How's tavern, even though David was certainly legal by then. The Judge and his companions may have lunched at one of the other ordinaries in Sudbury. Phineas Rice, Samuel Wright and the widows Blandford and Knight were all licensed in 1718.

By the time David How received his license he was 42 years old and his family and farm were flourishing. He had the time and talent to devote to innkeeping, and his tavern swiftly became successful and known as a comfortable place to eat, drink and rest horses on the main line to the west. By the time that Benjamin Lynde recorded in his diary in October of 1734 that he "dined at How's, Sudbury" David was the only How tavern keeper in town and he was prospering.

David was also branching out in other directions. He dammed Hop Brook and built a mill a short distance northwest of the site of the present Grist Mill. Colony and town records both make this clear.

The mill was originally equipped only for sawing logs, with millstones added later to grind corn, wheat and rye for wayfarers' meals.‡ Probably this mill was built to serve David's own

---

*The term "Treat" meant "To entertain, especially with food and drink." *Oxford English Dictionary* Vol. II, p. 308

†The term "Bait" meant "originally to feed and water the horses, but later to rest and refresh passengers—a brief stay or sojurn." *Oxford English Dictionary* Volume I, p. 628

‡This dual use of mills is suggested by the fact that when Samuel How's interest in a mill was sold after his death to Deacon Daniel Stone, it was described as "One fourth part of a saw and grist mill on Sudbury river..." in a deed dated February 14, 1714. The fact that a saw mill usually preceded a

needs—to provide lumber for improvements to his home and outbuildings. It later became a profitable side business which enabled David to sell lumber to the town.

There are several disbursements in Town Records[31] which show that David provided lumber for town use. Two typical entries are:

> April 3, 1732. Allowed to Mr. David How for four hundred feet of plank when delivered to surveyers...2-4-0.
> April 9, 1733. To Mr. David How for two hundred feet of plank. 1-0-0

Since the rate appears to have been roughly ten shillings per hundred feet of plank, and there was plenty of cheap standing timber available nearby, the mill undoubtedly paid for itself quickly. It was certainly operating by the spring of 1732 and may have been operating sooner. It is described in detail in a deed dated February 4, 1744, in which David and Hepzibah conveyed a tract of their property to their third son, David junior. One of the identifying boundaries to the transfer of ''...thirty six acres of upland and meadows...with the buildings thereon ...the land he now lives in...'' is ''...the easterly end of my New Grist Mill.''

How senior reserved for himself and his other heirs:

> ...the one moiety or half part of my New Grist Mill standing and being in the above premises with one moiety or half part of the sd Mill Dam and Mill Pond with the privileges of one half part of the stream belonging to sd Mill with one half part of the Utensels that...belong to sd Mill...with the free liberty of coming to and from and round sd Grist Mill from time to time...[32]

David How deeded his third son a portion of his lands and buildings outright, but reserved for himself and other members of the family—at least for the time being—the use of the Mill and its appurtenances.

In the years that followed, three family members are on record for frequent sales of lumber to the town:

> October 19, 1747. To Ezekiel How for providing planks for bridges. 0-7-6

---

grist mill is further borne out by David's own phrase: ''my *New* grist mill'' which implies that another sort of mill was operating on the site in prior years.

October 3, 1748. To David How for plank....0-7-6
October 2, 1749. To David How junr. for 100 feet of plank.
0-10-0[33]

Six years after the first deed, David How, Sr., sold the remaining half of the mill and its rights to David How, Jr. absolutely.

> For and in consideration of the Sum of thirteen pounds Six Shillings and Eight Pence lawful money...truly paid by David How Junr of Sudbury, miller...give, grant, sell and Confirm unto him...the one half of a Grist Mill in Sudbury with the half of the Mill Dam and Privileges of the Stream and flowing forever which I now have in possession...the other half of ye said Mill and Dam and Stream was my Said Son David's before by a deed of gift from me...and with whatsoever belongs to the said Mill to Have and To Hold...forever....[34]*

As time went on, David junior seems to have concentrated on milling while his brother Ezekiel devoted himself to running the tavern. But the two brothers cooperated closely in all business matters. David, at various times, gave a hand at the tavern, as did other relatives when needed, and later Ezekiel used the mill for his substantial improvements to the tavern between 1750 and 1760.

In 1730 and 1731, David How's innkeeping routine was interrupted by another duty. He was called as a witness in a court case against one Robert Allen of Shrewsbury, who had been "making and spreading a false news on ye 26th of November last in Sudbury and in other places that in Boston he saw sundry people sick of the smallpox."[35]

David and Hepzibah doubtless overheard this rumor during a visit Allen made to the tavern. Smallpox was dreaded and a "false news" of this kind was brought to court as a serious offense. How and his wife, who was also a witness, had to travel twice to court in Cambridge and were reimbursed three pounds and two shillings for their travel. It seems likely that innkeepers frequently overheard important pieces of informa-

---

*David's wish that mill should remain in the family "forever" was carried out for several generations. One of David junior's sons. Joseph Howe, born in 1760, operated a mill on the site in 1794. This Joseph had a son named Buckley, whose son, Joseph Calvin Howe, born in 1817, later ran a tack and nail factory at the same place. (D.W. Howe, *Howe Genealogies* p.38, p. 286) Joseph Calvin lived until 1905. Soon after that another landlord reopened a Grist Mill in 1929 on the present site.

tion in the line of duty which later required their presence and their sworn testimony in a court of law. The court records make it clear that Mrs. How did not attend court 20 miles from home, necessitating two long, round-trip journeys, simply for the pleasure of accompanying her husband. Hepzibah was a witness and the Honoured Justices insisted on her presence.

Like his father and grandfather before him, David How took his service to his town and colony seriously. He was called to Cambridge to serve on the Grand Jury in 1736 [36] and at about the same time embarked on a 20-year period as a leader in town educational affairs.

In June of 1727, he was one half of a two-man school committee, the other being Samuel Abbott, to appoint a school master. An agreement is recorded between these two and one Zachariah Hicks to keep school for 45 pounds, with a proviso that if Hicks's living costs exceeded 5s and 6d per week, he would be compensated by the town. [37]

In 1733, How was once more responsible for "providing a school master" and received six shillings for the service. He chose his brother's old comrade in arms, William Brintnall, a member of an old Sudbury family, who had begun keeping school as early as 1727. [38]

David How became a select man in 1741 and continued his already-demonstrated interest in education. In October 1741 he signed an agreement with John Mellen for the grammar school for the coming year. Mellen agreed to: "teach children to read, write and cypher, for the space of a year upon condition of ye sum of £87-7-0." [39]

Ironically, at about the same time he was elected a select man, David How became a leader in a controversial movement to carve out a new township once again. A petition to the General Court was made jointly by "David How and other inhabitants of Framingham, Sudbury, Marlborough and Stow." David How, by reason of his age and position in the community, was apparently the natural leader in this venture.

The petition, which is dated March 14, 1739, asked that certain citizens of the four towns be allowed to start a separate township because, as they explain in a carefully-worded plea to His Excellency and the Honoured Court, reminiscent of former such requests, they have been:

> A long time greatly incommoded by the great distance from the place of public worship...some of our families being three, four or six miles distant therefrom...roads very diffi-

cult, especially at some seasons of the year...allowe us therefor to...make a separate township...the center of the town to be at a pine tree...nigh the great Country road...sixty rods from Mr. Ebenezer Hager's sawmill....[40]

This document is signed by more than 20 people. Some of them, How, Parmenter and Brintnall, are the same family names that appeared on the 1707 petition. David How's name heads the list, in large, prominent handwriting.

It is not hard to see why. The "pine tree" mentioned as the "center of town" would have been less than a mile from the site of How's flourishing tavern. This must have been the powerful motivation which caused the old man to bestir himself and play a militant role in one more fight. In 1740, he was 65 years old.

But the new township was not to be. A counter-petition was presented and the request of the West Side inhabitants was denied by the Court. The officials gave as their reason: "The very great charge the town hath lately been at in building two new meeting houses, two school houses and settling two new ministers..." The counter-petition added pointedly: "The meeting house on the West Side of the river was placed where the Petitioners desired it and...they signed to the place where it standeth with their own hands..."[41]

This last flourish of leadership for his fellow West Siders may have worn David How out. Soon after this he turned over the operation of the tavern to Ezekiel and lived out the remainder of his long life in relative obscurity.

David How lived to a "great age." He was 85 when he died in 1759, 13 years after turning over the management of the tavern to his youngest son. The old man would have been pleased that at the time of his death, his family and the location of his homestead, farm and inn were well enough known to be cited in official documents and deeds. In the Court records there is the following note about a highway being considered by the Commonwealth in 1758:

> September 12. Concord. The Committee appointed do report that the ways petitioned for are of public necessity and conveniency and that there be a way laid out by order of this Court from Sudbury Line where the Great Country Road is already laid, near David How's, through a corner of Framingham and so thro' the town of Marlborough leading to Worcester....[42]

The How Tavern was already a landmark.

David How's First License, August 28, 1716.

VI

A Red Horse And Revolution

The toddy and flip were flowing before the blazing hearth that December afternoon in 1745, and young Ezekiel How and his new bride Bathsheba Stone could sense excitement in the air. Christmas had always been a special day for the How family. It was on that day in 1700 that Ezekiel's father, David, had married Hepzibah Death, and now, on his 45th wedding anniversary, surrounded by several generations of his large family, the old man was about to make a special announcement.

David How was 70 years old and the 130-acre lot of wild land his father, Samuel, had given him had prospered. His homestead had expanded to a busy tavern, and his sons had families of their own. It was time to give them more responsibility.

And so, at this family Christmas gathering, he made it official. With brother-in-law Justice of the Peace John Death officiating, David and Hepzibah swore to the documents that had been prepared the previous February, which divided his property between sons Ezekiel and David.

David junior and his wife, Abigail, received a tract of land and a half interest in his father's saw and grist mill. The deed to Ezekiel made it clear that David How had decided that Ezekiel should carry on the tavern. It reads in part:

> To my beloved son Ezekiel all the rest of my estate both real and personal...to his assigns and heirs forever. One half of all my lands and meadows with one half of the buildings thereon including the land I bought from Joshua Parker and the land that was laid out to me in the middle 30 rods Highway so-called. The whole is to be in quantity and quality considered and is all Scituate lying and being in Sudbury aforesaid and on the westerly side of said Sudbury river and is bounded Southerly on land of Captain David Bateman, Easterly on the aforesaid middle 30 Rods Highway, Northwesterly on land of Solomon Parmenter, westerly on land I have recently given by deed of gift to my son David How Jr. and is further bounded the northwest corner of said premises being

a stake and stones and from thence southerly running a straight line to a small black oak tree marked and so on the same poynt to a small white oak tree marked and so on from thence the same poynt until it comes to ye said Baldwin's land having the highway or road leading from Sudbury to Marlborough running through some part of the Northerly part of said premises.[1]

Today that property would extend from the eastern slopes of Nobscot Mountain west to just beyond the Inn. It would include the fields and meadows to the north of the present Inn buildings, as well as the ridges and woodlots to the south extending into what is now Framingham. David's message was clear. While he loved all of his children dearly, he wanted his youngest son, who had only recently passed his 25th birthday, to carry on the work that he had begun. Little did he know then that Ezekiel How would do much, much more.

David and Hepzibah had previously signed this deed in the presence of John Hayne and Ann Collester on February 5, 1745. It was to be four years before the document was offically recorded by the Middlesex County Registrar of Deeds on January 5, 1749. For at least three of them, the tavern license remained in David's name.

Meanwhile, Ezekiel was busy raising a family. He married Bathsheba Stone in 1744 and by 1750 she had born him three daughters: Ruth (1745), Ann or "Anna" (1747), and Hepzibah (1749). Bathsheba and "Molly" followed in 1752 and 1754 respectively before his first son, Ezekiel junior, arrived in 1756. Daughters Olive (1758) and Eliphalet (1761) preceded Adam How's birth in 1763.[2]

As his family grew, Ezekiel began to see the need for larger quarters. The tavern's four rooms, at least two of which were occupied by travellers for much of the time, were just not enough. Something had to be done to give his family some privacy.

There was plenty of raw building material nearby. The slopes of Nobscot Mountain were covered with American chestnut trees, some of which had been cut and hand-hewn for the great girts and summer beams placed by David and his father Samuel in the original house.

The problem of sawing large quantities of boards and planking was easily solved. He used the mill that his father had built and his brother David was now running. In the late 1740s the mill was apparently a joint venture because both Ezekiel and David are on record for selling various quantities of lumber to the town.

Between 1750 and 1760 there are no recorded lumber dealings between Ezekiel How and the town.[3] It is possible that the mill was kept busy sawing planks and boards for Ezekiel's four-room addition to the back of the house, which also included replacing the old pitched roof of the original structure with the now-familiar gambrel roof that provided attic space to accommodate overflow guests and servants.

The addition consisted of a small sitting room to the rear of the original parlor and a private kitchen and dining area behind the bar room. On the second story, a long room with a fireplace on the west side of the house was used for dancing. A bedroom (now the Lafayette room) was across the hall.

More barns and sheds went up across the road from the house to accommodate the increasing traffic between the western settlements and Boston. As business increased, Ezekiel is supposed to have added his own initials and "1746" to the back of the horizontal wooden sign that his father had put up. On the reverse side, rumor has it, he caused to be painted a prancing red horse, or a horse who walked in a manner spirited enough to suit the growing reputation of the Red Horse Tavern.*

The first rumblings of conflict with England were still years away, but the Hows were military men and Ezekiel was no

---

*Tradition says this horse was red and that Ezekiel was the first landlord to call his place the Red Horse Tavern to distinguish it from his cousins' Black Horse Tavern in Marlborough. However, the first two specific references we have found to the signboard—the diary of Isaiah Thomas, the printer, in 1808 and a memory of a visit by the well-known author Lydia Maria Child in 1828—both mention a black horse.

If there were only one reference to a black horse, one might assume someone had made a mistake. But two references to a black horse, twenty years apart, suggest that there was, in fact, a black animal on the sign at those dates. Mrs. Child saw the signboard in a late afternoon, but the month was June, so it would still have been daylight; Mr. Thomas saw the sign in a winter forenoon, and was by his profession, accustomed to accuracy and details. He is not likely to have mistaken Sudbury for Marlborough, since he frequently travelled the road, nor to have imagined that he saw a black horse where there should have been a red animal. We must conclude either that Ezekiel's horse had weathered black with time—this could have happened since the paint would have been ochre and produced a roan or sorrel color, not bright scarlet—or that for some reason the image on the old signboard had been changed to a horse of a different color.

exception. In 1757 he compiled the muster roll of Sudbury's Second Foot Company as clerk under the command of Josiah Richardson (109 men).[4]

The following September he set a precedent that has been followed ever since by "vitalling" a company of 97 of General Jeffrey Amherst's troops who were returning from the Canaday (Louisberg) Expedition and on their way to join the Western army.[5] Journalists of the day tell of the great army marching west from Boston followed by Amherst's collection of wild beasts.[6]

By 1764, Ezekiel had risen to the rank of captain. He is listed by that rank in the Sudbury town records as one of the overseers of the poor.[7] As the war drew nearer, he became more and more involved in town affairs. He was appointed to committees to see to the building of bridges, enlarging the West Side meeting house, building a powder house and later petitioning the Court of General Sessions of the Peace for the removal of Mary Knight to the town of Marlborough. Mary Knight was a "poor indigent" who was a burden to the town, which was obliged to spend large sums of money for her support.[8]

The Mary Knight affair trundled on unsettled throughout the War of Independence and there are numerous mentions in town records of Captain and later Colonel How being reimbursed for trips to the Court in Cambridge.[9]

News of the Boston Tea Party on December 16, 1773, didn't take long to reach Sudbury. Not long before Christmas, Constable Jonas Holden nailed to the doors of the East and West Side meeting houses a notice of a meeting "Of all Freeholders and other inhabitants of and belonging to Sudbury qualified to vote in town affairs to meet in the West meeting house on Monday the third day of January next."[10]

The first article on that warrant was short and to the point. "To see if the town will take into consideration the papers sent to them by the town of Boston relating to the tea sent to this province by the East India Company, subject to a duty, or do or act on said affair, as the town shall think proper when met."[11] Among the members of the committee appointed to "Take into consideration the above papers and report their opinion theron (sic) at the adjournment,"[12] was Ezekiel How.

It was obvious that the committee's opinion of the tea tax was pretty well established. Just a week later, when the adjourned town meeting resumed, it submitted a five-point resolution condemning British and Tory tyranny, saying, in part:

> The British Ministry, assisted by the inveterate enemies to American Liberty, on this as well as on the other side of the Atlantick; combining together to Rob us of our dear Bought freedom; have Brought us to this sad Dilemma, either to Resolve like Men in the defence of our Just Rights and Liberties or sink under the weight of their Arbitrary and unconstitutional measures into a state of abject Slavery. Therefore as Freeborn Americans, Intitled to all the immunities, Liberties and Privilidges of Freeborn English Men; we look upon our selves under the Strongest Obligations to use our utmost Exertions in defense of our just Rights in every constitutional Method within our power even though the cost of the defence should equal that of the purchase.[13]

The town meeting ordered that the resolves be recorded in the town book and a copy be forwarded to the Committee of Correspondence at Boston. At the same time, How, along with Thomas Plympton, John Maynard, Sarson Belcher and Phineas Glezen were chosen as a Committee of Correspondence for Sudbury.

As winter began to give way to spring and word of the Boston Port Bill spread through the countryside, strangers began arriving at How's Tavern for quiet conferences with the Landlord. Among them was William Molineaux Jr., an important member of the Boston Committee of Safety, a group charged with making contingency plans in case the British troops now occupying Boston should make a foray into the countryside. On June 24, 1774, he scratched the following ditty on a parlor window pane with a diamond:

> What do you think?
> Here is good drink.
> Perhaps you may not know it.
> If not in haste, do stop and taste.
> You merry folks will show it.
> —William Molineaux Jr. June 24, 1774

Molineaux obviously had more on his mind than a hearty meal and a mug of flip.* By the following September, town

---

*Flip is the ancestor of today's hot buttered rum. There were many recipes, but one of the most popular included hard cider, brown or maple

records show How's title as both "Col." and "Capt." and at a series of town meetings starting on September 20 and continuing through October 3, he was reimbursed some 62 pounds for "20 guns and bagnets, 600 pounds lead, 300 French flints and a chest for arms and carting them,"[14] as well as for six half barrels of powder. The arms were obviously ordered in a hurry not long after Molineaux's visit. The pot of revolution was beginning to bubble.

But the town was also occupied by other crises. At the same series of meetings, How was appointed to a committee to appeal to the General Court against dividing the town at the Musketaquid River and ordered to Cambridge to pursue further the Mary Knight problem.

His frequent trips to Cambridge served him well. He was able to meet other patriot leaders and keep abreast of the talk in Boston. He knew only too well that if the British carried out their threat to march into the countryside and destroy colonial military stores, the men of Sudbury, one of the largest frontier towns, would be counted on heavily.

How and Colonel James Barrett of Concord did everything they could to prepare. Through the winter of 1774–75, minute and militia companies carried out drills on the barn floors of their officers, but many of them were reduced to using pitchforks and hoe handles instead of muskets. On March 27, 1775, How submitted the following pessimistic report:

> The return of the Severall Companys of Militia and Minute in sd town viz: Capt. Moses Stone's company, 92 men of them 18 no guns. At least one third part ye forelocks unfit for Sarvis. Others wais un a quipt.
> Capt. Aaron Haynes company—60 men weel provided with arms the most of them provided with Bayonets or hatchets aboute one quarter part with Cartridge boxes.
> Captain Joseph Smith's Company consisting of...75 able Bodied men forty well a quipt twenty promis to find and

---

sugar, a stick of cinnamon, and a generous portion of thick, dark rum. This was heated by thrusting a glowing loggerhead poker into the mug. For his best India Flip, Ezekiel charged 15 pence. The common New England variety cost 12. Some of Ezekiel's other prices included:
A good dinner 20 pence
Common do 12 pence
Best Supper and Breakfast 15 pence each
Common do 12 pence each
Lodging 4 pence each

a quip themselves Emedetly fifteen no guns and other wais un a quipt.

The Troop Cat. Isaac Locer...21 besides are on the minit Role well a quipt.

Returned by Ezekiel How Leftn. Conl.[15]

Despite the pessimism, the drills went on. Captain John Nixon's company mustered on March 13, 20 and 27 and April 3, 10 and 17. While the manual of arms may have been rusty, the resolve certainly was not. Two days after that final muster, the words that Ezekiel How helped draft in Sudbury's Tea Tax resolution took on added meaning.

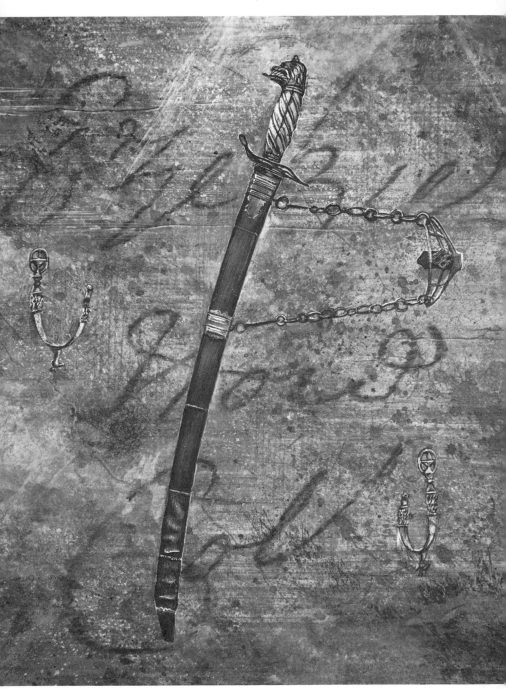

VII

"The Dye was Cast and the Torch Lit"

Sound carries a long way on quiet April nights and there was nothing between the West Side meeting house and Captain John Nixon's farm high on the slopes of Nobscot Hill but a lot of thin air. So when the peal of the church bell and the staccato bark of musket shots drifted across the valley at four o'clock on the morning of April 19, 1775, Nixon already knew what the breathless rider galloping along the 30 Rod Road* was going to tell him. The time for action had come.

Old John Weighton, who was to fight in the first of his eight battles in the Revolution, remembered later that the morning was "remarkable fine".[1] He marched with Nixon's West Side Minute Company to the Sudbury Common training field, where Captain Moses Stone's South Militia Company and Lieutenant Colonel Ezekiel How were waiting.

How had taken the time to dress equal to such an important occasion. His dress cocked hat was trimmed with lace, and he wore a short sword commonly called a "hanger", the end of its ivory handle carved in the shape of a snarling lion's head. He was riding his best horse.

The stop at the training field was a brief one. How had already received reports from Thomas Plympton, a member of the Provincial Congress who had sent his son to arouse the sexton and ring the West Side meeting house bell. Only the day before, How had met with Col. James Barrett of the Middlesex Militia to consider the removal of military stores from Concord to Sudbury. Now it was too late. The British were on their way.

How's oldest son Ezekiel Jr., at age 19, was a private in Moses Stone's company. More than half a century later, shortly before he died at the age of 90, he told Framingham historian William Barry that he and his neighbor Benjamin Berry ran the 12 miles

---

*When the New Grant Lots were laid out, thirty-rod-wide pathways running both east and west and north and south were left between squadrons for the convenience of landowners. The 30-Rod road leading past John Nixon's farm ran north and south just below the eastern slopes of Nobscot Mountain.

to Concord in two hours.[2] He would go on to fight at White Plains and come home a wounded hero.

That would have put the Sudbury men, now strengthened by the addition of Captain Aaron Haynes' West Side Militia who joined them during a brief stop for refreshments at Samuel Dakin's farm, near the South Bridge in Concord around eight o'clock. The chances are it was a little later, as the British arrived in Concord at about that time, and there was already a Redcoat detachment under Captain Mundy Pole sealing off the South Bridge.

Barrett had sent his son Stephen to intercept How and his three companies at Duggan's corner with orders to proceed cross country to Barrett's Farm. Several cannon and some other military stores were concealed there and he needed all the help he could get.

How, being mounted, took off for Barrett's, leaving orders for Nixon, Stone and Haynes to follow suit as quickly as possible, but Deacon Josiah Haynes, a member of the alarm company who had insisted on riding to the fray despite his great age (he was 80), had other ideas.

"If you don't drive them British from the bridge I shall call you a coward," he told Nixon, who was the senior officer present. "I'd rather be called a coward by you than called to account by my superiors for disobedience of orders,"[3] replied the Captain, who in five days, would be commissioned a colonel and serve under General Artemis Ward.

Undaunted, Haynes decided to take matters into his own hands. According to Lieutenant Jonathan Rice,* Nixon's second in command, he wheeled his horse, galloped to the bridge and confronted the British sentries. Only the intervention of Captain Pole, who was determined to prevent violence if at all possible, prevented him from being shot on the spot.[4]

It is about three miles from the North Bridge to Barrett's by road and slightly less than that from the South Bridge. By the time the three companies had rejoined How at a vantage point some distance from the farmhouse, a detachment of three British companies under Captain Lawrence Parsons was searching the house and burning cannon carriages in the front

---

*Stearns does not refer to Jonathan Rice by name as the source of this and following accounts, but Concord Historian Rev. Ezra Ripley in his *History of the Fight at Concord* published in 1827, attributes the same story, including the reference to the Deacon Haynes incident, to Rice.

dooryard. Barrett had alertly ordered the cannon barrels carried to the field in back of the house, where they were plowed under. The British did not discover them, nor did they find several barrels of military supplies concealed under feathers in the attic.

How knew that there was nothing he could do to help his commander, but was determined to discover all he could about the strength of the enemy and their intentions. Hiding his sword under his long overcoat and stripping the lace from his hat, he rode down the road toward the soldiers.[5]*

"I'm going down along on some business," he said when they stopped him and asked where he was going. "I shouldn't like to be hindered." Supposing him to be a countryman headed for town on private business, the detachment let How pass, but he had gone less than a mile down the road before the firing at the North Bridge began. Tacking about, he galloped back toward Barrett's only to be stopped once more. "I find there's trouble ahead," he said. "And I believe on the whole I

---

*Accounts differ as to whether this incident took place at the South Bridge or at Barrett's. Rice, who was interviewed by Thomas Stearns in his old age, says the latter. Abigail Eaton of Shrewsbury, stepdaughter to Lieutenant Ezekiel How, who inherited Colonel How's sword and other military accoutrements when Lyman Howe's estate was settled, wrote in a description of the sword that the incident took place at Concord Bridge.

"On the morning of the 19th of April, 1775 while riding to alarm and collect men and find where the trouble was, he came very suddenly upon the British Soldiers at Concord Bridge. He was alone, but self-possessed. He requested the office(r) to let him pass the bridge. The soldiers opened to the right and left and he passed, but soon found out what was the state of things and, turning his horse, rode calmly back and asked to repass. Observing he saw there was trouble ahead, the British officer replied 'Tis your own stupidity that has brought it upon you', at the same time letting him return. He probably supposed Colonel How a countryman on some peaceable errand. He was clad in his uniform with his hanger by his side all concealed by his overcoat."

Rice is a better source than Miss Eaton because he is an eyewitness, while she heard the story second hand from her stepfather. Also, the distance involved makes it hard to accept the idea that How was at the North Bridge. Not only would it have taken the Sudbury troops too long to get there, but they would have had to pass Parsons' detachment somewhere between the Bridge and Barrett's Farm.

The South Bridge theory fits. Duggan's Corner was only a short distance from this bridge and it wasn't much more than a mile from that point to the milldam where British soldiers were rolling barrels of flour into the millpond. How wouldn't have needed to go very far to see what he needed to see, before returning and instructing Nixon and Stone to proceed to Barrett's.

may as well get back to my family."[6]

The soldiers, who had heard the shots as well, had more important things to worry about than arguing with a civilian. Soon after How disappeared down the road to rejoin his companies, Parsons ordered his detachment to retreat. The Sudbury companies followed at a discreet distance.

Rice's deposition in the Stearns Papers says little more about Col. How's movements on April 19, but it is apparent that the three Sudbury companies and their commander reached the North Bridge and rendezvoused with Colonel Barrett and the Concord, Lincoln and Acton troops just minutes after Parsons and his companies recrossed the bridge and hastily retreated into town.

Barry writes of Ezekiel How Jr.'s introduction to the realities of combat. "The first object that struck him upon his arrival was a British regular weltering in blood (probably one of the soldiers wounded during the skirmish at the bridge who was later struck on the head with a hatchet by a teen-aged patriot on his way to join the companies). It being his first experience with the horrors of war, he was so shocked that he almost fainted."[7]

"But," How added, "they pushed me along and a few hours afterward I could see men dying around me with as much indifference as if they were sheep."[8]

And there were plenty of men dying. By the time Lieut. Col. Francis Smith had started his retreat from Concord, the Sudbury companies had poured across the North Bridge with the Concord, Lincoln and Acton men and cut across the meadows to the spot where the Bedford road joined the road from Concord to Lexington. It was known then and still is today as Meriam's Corner.

The British, who had marched forth from Boston less than 12 hours before as the hunters, suddenly found themselves the hunted. Just before reaching the intersection of the Bedford and Lexington roads, they were forced to pull in their flank guards in order to cross a narrow bridge over a brook, allowing the companies of militia and minute to close within easy musket range.

Whether the British or the Americans fired first is the subject of a debate that has raged on for 200 years, but the result was the same. Volleys of musket balls ripped into the regulars crowded on the bridge from behind houses, walls and hedges.

As old Amos Barrett of the Concord militia recalled years later: "A grait many lay dead and the road was bloddy."[9]

As the retreat continued toward Lexington, Nathanial Cudworth's and Joseph Smith's East Side Minute and Militia companies set up an ambush with devastating effect at Hardy's Hill, after taking the most direct route to Concord on the east side of the river. There they were joined by Captain Isaac Loker's troop of horse.

Ensign Henry DeBerniere of the British 10th Regiment of Foot, who less than two months before had trudged past the Red Horse Tavern with Captain William Brown on a spying mission for General Gage, was in the thick of the action.

"All the hills on either side of us were covered with rebels," he said in his report. "There could not be less than 5,000; so they kept the road always lined and a very hot fire on us without intermission; we at first kept our order and returned their fire as hot as we received it, but when we arrived within a mile of Lexington, our ammunition began to fail and the light companies were so fatigued with flanking they were scarce able to act and a great number of wounded scarce able to get forward made a great confusion..."[10]

The rest of the story is well-known. By the time the British had made it back under the safety of the fleet's guns in Charlestown, 73 regulars had died, 174 were wounded and 26 were missing. American casualties amounted to 49 killed, 39 wounded and five missing.

Two of the dead were from How's command. Ashael Reed, a private in Nixon's company, was shot at Tanner's Brook, and old Deacon Haynes was killed at Fiske Hill not long after he picked off a British sergeant and took his Brown Bess musket. He tried to get the soldier's belt and cartridge box as well, but had to give up his quest when the squad re-loaded and fired a volley in his direction.

Elsewhere, Weighton was getting a quick lesson in the art of guerrilla warfare. "I was running across a lot where there was a bend in (the) road in order to get a fair shot at the enemy in company with a Scotsman who was in Braddock's defeat 19 years before. After we had discharged our guns, I observed to the Scot, who appeared very composed, I wish I felt as calm as he appeared to be. (he said) It's a trend to be larnt.

"Before I served through one campaign, I found the Scot's remark to be a just one."[11]

Ezekiel How Jr. and most of Moses Stone's company served four days as the Provincial troops surrounded Boston. When exactly his father returned to the familiar confines of his tavern we do not know but it does not matter. As old John Weighton was to say years later: "The Dye was Cast and the Torch Lit by which we have becom an independent nation and may the present generation and those unborn preserve unimpared the Liberteys sivel and religeous as long as time endures..."[12]

Life would go on at the gambrel-roofed tavern on the road to Marlborough and in the rest of Middlesex County, but things would never be the same.

CONCORD, MASSACHUSETTS April 19, 1775

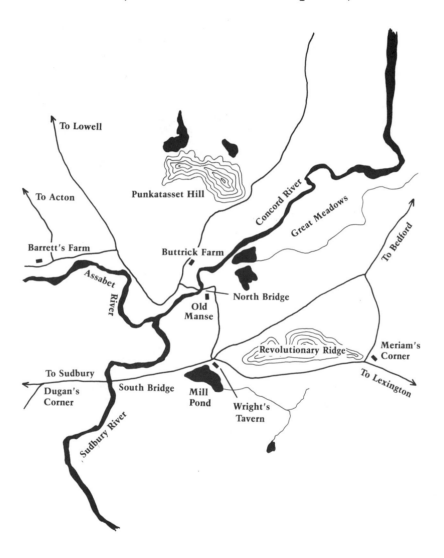

Military Dispatch to Col. Ezekiel How from Brigadier General Oliver Prescott.

VIII

"Establishing the Independence of America"

The 29th of July, 1778 broke hot and humid. Across the dirt track that served as the Boston Post Road, sweating teams were drawing loads of freshly cured hay into Colonel Ezekiel How's barns, hoping to win the race with the afternoon thunderstorms that are a common occurrence in Massachusetts in late summer.

Colonel How, the commanding officer of the Fourth Middlesex Militia had other problems besides the weather. Leaning on the trestle table in the common room of his tavern, he studied a document that had arrived by express that morning.

JULY 28, 1778

Sir,—Wheras General Sullivan, by the express order of General Washington, is directed to make a sudden attack upon the enemy at Rhode Island in conjunction with the French fleet there; and in consequence of a resolution of Congress by virtue of the same order has called upon this state to aid him with three thousand of the militia to cooperate in the entire reduction of the British Army under so bright a prospect of conquest and putting a final period to a bloody war and establishing the independence of America. And in consequence of an order of Council this moment received by express, you are hereby commanded to detach from the regiment under your command one captain, two subalterns and 60 non-commissioned officers and privates to form a company and march them to Tiverton in the state of Rhode Island by Thursday night next, if possible, to be under the command of General Sullivan six weeks from the time of their arrival, if not sooner discharged and all officers and soldiers will consider themselves under every obligation to be speedy in completing and marching this detachment and may depend upon adequate reward for their services at the next sitting of the General Court. This is the most important hour; you will therefor execute these orders with punctuality and despatch and make return to me of your doings by express or otherwise without delay. You will order the whole of the militia under your command to hold themselves in readiness to march at a moment's warning.

I am your very humble servant
Oliver Prescott,
Brigadier General[1]

How and his Sudbury Companies of Militia and Minute had been in on the start of the war with Britain just over three years before. Now it looked as if some of them would be in on the end of it as well. General John Sullivan had been informed by General George Washington that the French Fleet, 834 guns strong and carrying 4,000 troops under the command of Admiral Charles Henri Theodat, Comte d'Estaing, was sailing from Sandy Hook to Newport, Rhode Island.

Sullivan's plan was to reinforce himself with at least 5,000 militiamen from Massachusetts, Connecticut and Rhode Island and, with the support of the French, attack and capture the 3,000-man British garrison which had been occupying Newport since December of 1776. With the Continental Army now more than 16,000 strong and the British, under Major General Henry Clinton, reduced to fighting a holding action, it was the opinion of Washington and his staff that such a blow would force the British to surrender and bring the war to an end.

But How had his own difficulties. It was haying season and the harvest would begin soon. Most of the men in his Fourth Middlesex Regiment were farmers who could not afford to be away from their crops for three weeks, let alone six. Less than a month before, he had been reprimanded by Prescott and the Council for failing to provide troops to help guard the Prisoners of Convention—General John Burgoyne's defeated British army—at Cambridge. Stung by the reprimand, the Colonel had fired off a testy order to Captain Jonathan Rice, who, as a lieutenant, had marched to Concord two years before with Moses Stone's Militia Company.

"July 17, 1778
In consequence of express orders from the General and a reprimand from the Council for my defishency of the gard to guard the Prisoners of Convention and the publick stoors: you are ordered to raise the Co. a signed you and order them to repair to Cambridge to the commanding officer of the

guards. Their to receive orders. Of this you will not fail and make return to me of their being marched by Monday next at furthest.

This from your humble servant
Ezekiel How Col.[2]

The Prisoners of Convention had been a thorn in the Council's side ever since Burgoyne's surrender on October 17, 1777, ten days after the second battle of Freeman's Farm. On November 7, they straggled past How's tavern in a long, thin line on the way to Weston where they spent the night, half staying in the church, which sent a bill to the Council for cleaning up after them, and the rest camping out near the old town cemetery.

The vanquished army's final destination was Cambridge where it was to remain under guard until it was sent south to internment in Virginia, but How and Rice hadn't heard the last of it yet. On March 18, 1778 How ordered Rice to send one corporal and three privates to Cambridge to relieve the guard and serve for three months. How's reluctance to commit any more of his men to guard duty during haying and harvesting was quite understandable.

Consequently, Prescott's request for "punctuality" fell on deaf ears in Sudbury, and it took some prodding before How, on August 22, 1778, finally issued orders to Captain Jonathan Rice to: "Make return of the names of the six month men by Monday next and march the men by Tuesday to meet at Mr. Sanger's in Framingham at 2 o'clock p.m. Herof fail not as I must report those that don't comply herewith."[3] It was to be his last recorded military order.

As it turned out, the Sudbury men would spend little time in Tiverton. Sullivan and Green had moved on Newport on August 9, but lost the support of the French army and fleet over a question of protocol. A severe northeast storm scattered both the French and British fleets off Block Island Sound and the French didn't return to Newport until August 20. D'Estaing, still unhappy that Sullivan—whom he outranked—had chosen to move without informing him, sailed off to Boston to refit his ships the following day, taking his troops with him.

With his militia returning to their crops by the hundreds and British reenforcements due any day, Sullivan reconsidered his situation and withdrew back to Tiverton. By September 1, he had dismissed his remaining militia and dug in for the winter.

Thanks to bad luck and bad weather, his bid to bring a quick end to the war had failed.

How knew the trials of the citizen soldier well. Even before the Concord fight, he had been hard put to balance his public and private lives. His tavern and sawmill were doing a booming business, but much of the responsibility for running them had to be delegated to others while he dealt with the problems of town and country.

April 19, 1775 had been a crossroads for John Nixon and How. One would go on to raise a regiment and, a year later, receive a commission as a general in the Continental Army from Congress, while the other returned to his tavern to serve as a leader in his community. Although he was commissioned Colonel of the Fourth Middlesex Militia on May 10, 1776, Ezekiel How would never raise his sword in battle again. A builder, mover and shaker he was. A warrior, he was not.

While Nixon was leading a Sudbury company in defense of Bunker Hill on June 17, 1775, neither How nor any member of his family were involved. The following February How was offered a commission as Lieutenant Colonel of the Fourth Middlesex. He turned it down and on May 10 was commissioned as a full colonel. The post was largely an administrative one.

Ezekiel How junior, a private in Moses Stone's Company, served a month of garrison duty in Cambridge following the Concord Fight before returning to his father's tavern. More than a year later he enlisted in Captain Cranston's company of Marlborough and marched to White Plains, New York in time to participate in the battle there on October 28, 1776.

"It was soon after haying," he recalled in a deposition taken August 30, 1832 when he applied for a military pension at age 76. "Col. Brooks and Lt. Col. Micah Stone of Framingham commanded the regiment. They both took off their white wigs before the battle and tied handkerchiefs about their heads. General Washington was there." [4]

Less than a year later, the trickle of written orders from General Prescott and the Council to How's Fourth Middlesex began to turn into a torrent. As the Revolution heated up in the summer of 1777, Washington called for militia units to augment his Continental Army regulars. On July 23, in How's absence, Adjutant Daniel Loring issued orders to Captain Jonathan Rice to march half his company to Providence, R.I.

"With the greatest dispatch." Less than three weeks later, How was ordered by Prescott to draft a company of his best militiamen, see that they were properly trained and equipped, and dispatch them to Saratoga.

"The state of our military affairs is very alarming," wrote Prescott. "It requires the most speedy and vigorous examinations to put a stop to the brutal ravages of our enemies. The (pub)lick eye is on the militia whose virtue is now loudly called upon and whose vigerous exertion in the common cause cannot faile.

"Agreeable to these resolutions you are ordered without delay to muster and march the detachment from your regiment to the Northern Army near Saratoga with all possible dispatch consistent with the good of the service and I expect that your known attachment to the cause of your bleeding country will lead you to a close inspection of the detachment from your regiment so as to see that they are well equipt in every respect and furnished with all the necessaries agreeable to said resolve.

"And you are to form the men drafted from your regiment into one company. Hereof, fail not, making return to the Council on or before the 18th day of the next instant of the number of men drafted....

"You are also, with your field officers, to meet at Captain Jones innholder in Concord on Thursday next ten o'clock before noon appointed field officers for the detachment from my brigade."[5]

Captain Jonathan Rice was chosen to lead the Sudbury detachment. One of his corporals was Ezekiel How junior, whose second trip to New York was to be much more auspicious than his first. He was so severely wounded in the second battle of Freeman's Farm (How called it "Stillwater") that he bought a silver pocket watch from a defeated British officer for 30 silver dollars which he directed to be sent home to his sweetheart if he did not survive. "The officer, out of money, sold it under price,"[6] he was to write later after returning home triumphantly and making the presentation himself.

Two years later, on January 26, 1779, Ezekiel's father, Colonel How, petitioned the Council to be allowed to resign his commission for reasons of ill health. His request was approved on February 4.[7]

With his military responsibilities decreasing, How resumed his activity in town affairs. He was one of a committee of six to estimate the services of each of Sudbury's soldiers during the "present war" * and also sat on a committee charged with agreeing on a line to divide the town. On August 9, 1779, he was appointed a delegate to meet in convention on September 1 in Cambridge for the sole purpose of framing a new state constitution.[8]

As the years went on, How continued to draw the sticky assignments from the town. On December 6, 1779, he was named to a committee to petition the General Court to "set aside the bill for dividing the town," citing several disadvantages to West Side (Sudbury) residents:

> Such a division deprives them of all the gravel and obliges them to maintain the one half of the Great Causeway on the Easterly part of said town, notwithstanding the necessary repairs of the Highways on the Westerly part of said town are near duble to that on the East.

This division would also rob residents of the use of the Pound and Training Field and would make no provision for the support of the poor, which would be a "heavy burden to the West Side of the town...."[9]

The bickering went on until the town was formally divided on April 23, 1781, but in the meantime there were other problems more pressing than the cost of repairing roads.

*Deciding how to apportion pay for military service during the previous several years was a tricky business and the opinion of an experienced soldier like How was invaluable. There were numerous categories and distinctions. Some examples follow:

That the Minute Men be allowed each	3-10-0
That the six weeks men to Roxbury be allowed each	4-0-0
That the two months men to Cambridge be allowed each	6-0-0
That the year's men to York and the Northward	7-5-0
That the five months men to Ticonderoga be allowed each	50-0-0
That the thirty days men to Saratoga be allowed each	20-0-0

That no person shall be intitled to Receive pay for any of the above services unless he shall first be taxed towards the payment thereof. Also that each person shall receive pay only for the time he was in actual service.

Ezekiel How
Phineas Glezen
Jona. Rice
Asahel Wheeler
Issac Loker
Thos Walker
Committee

(Town Records, June, 1778)

Congress fell into the habit of printing more money whenever it was needed to pay the army or buy supplies. Consequently 20 Continental paper shillings were required to purchase what one silver shilling would buy and General Washington was wont to comment that: "A waggon load of money will but barely buy a waggon load of provisions." Sudbury's quota of beef for the use of the army in 1780 set the town back £24,300, and Colonel How was one of a committee responsible for its purchase.[10]

.Worse than that, a colonel's pay in Continental money wouldn't even buy enough oats to feed his horse. Small wonder that Ezekiel How resigned his commission to concentrate on private business.

And business was good. After Lord Cornwallis surrendered at Yorktown October 19, 1781, an increasing number of overnight guests were brought to How's door by the mail coaches plying the Boston Post Road to New York and Philadelphia.

Whether or not Washington himself was one of these guests is a question that has been debated over the years. There is a tradition that he stopped to refresh himself in late June or early July, 1775 on his way to Cambridge to take command of the Continental Army, and a tablet in front of today's Wayside Inn attests to that fact.

It is also possible that President Washington stopped at the How Tavern on October 23, 1789 on his way from Marlborough to Weston on a tour of the New England states to acquaint himself with "the temper and disposition of the inhabitants towards the new government..."[11]

According to the *Massachusetts Spy*, Washington travelled from "Spencer, to Leicester to Worcester, then to Marlborough and on to Weston for the night."[12]

There is no definite evidence that Colonel How and the General had ever met before, much less were comrades in arms as some accounts would have us believe. If Washington stopped on October 23 it was probably just to refresh himself and feed and water his horses.

Since Isaiah Thomas, editor and publisher of the *Massachusetts Spy*, often passed How's tavern on his own business travels, it is likely that he would have mentioned in his October 29th edition that Washington had stopped at a tavern with which he himself was familiar.[13]

There were plenty of other travelers besides presidents and printers, and sheltering and feeding them all in the eight rooms of his tavern was often a problem. Ezekiel decided to enlarge. The new addition is described later in the Colonel's will which he signed shortly before his death in October of 1796: "A new kitchen at the west end of the dwelling house with the lower room adjoining thereto, also the long chamber over the aforesaid room, with the north west bed chamber in the old part of said dwelling house."[14]

The "new kitchen" is today's tap room with its two fireplaces and the "long chamber" above is the 1800 ballroom. The addition was probably started in the spring of 1785, for in that year, Ezekiel was billed for 528 feet of white pine, 426 feet of pitch pine, 308 feet of white pine and 25 feet of "sash stuff" for which he paid Daniel Loring two pounds, 24 shillings and nine pence.[15]

Evidently, How sawed the timbers and summer beams for the new addition at his brother's mill and purchased the rest of the material from Loring. The white pine was probably used for roof and sheathing with the pitch pine—much cheaper and tougher—reserved for the floors.

With the new wing complete, How converted what is now Hobgoblin Hall, which he had been using for a ballroom, into a large bedroom. The old family kitchen to the rear of the bar room became a private dining room.

Ezekiel's will lists some other interesting items, among them the first public mention of the How coat of arms which was appraised in an inventory of his estate at $4. How it got to the Inn and where it came from is a matter of speculation which will be discussed later.

The will also contains, in a codicil, a provision for "My old negro servant, Portsmouth...He shall be well and comfortably supplied with all things necessary and suitable for a person of his age and quality...." How had purchased this dwarf slave in Portsmouth, New Hampshire, hence the name.

Ponto, as he was nicknamed, had a bunk in the attic equipped with a ladder that remained there long after his death.* He was a shy man, often hiding in an alcove near the

*Artist Arthur A. Shurtleff made a series of sketches of the interior of the inn as it looked before Edward R. Lemon's extensive renovations. One drawing shows the shelf-like bunk with ladder in the attic and is captioned "Dwarf's Bed". These drawings are displayed in the Ford sitting room at the Inn.

fireplace when strangers were about. There is a legend that in his old age, How is supposed to have offered him his freedom, but he declined, saying: "Well Massa, you've had the meat. I guess you can pick the bones." Ponto went on to outlive his master and Adam How saw to it that he had a Christian burial.

Even though he was in his seventies, Colonel Ezekiel How continued to serve the town that his ancestors helped settle. He was a member of the committee[16] to build a new West Side meeting house* as his great grandfather John had been before him and in 1791, served on a committee for the drafting of a plan for a new school.[17]

On the morning of October 15, 1796, as the first frosts of autumn turned the leaves of the big elm that supported his Red Horse sign to shades of yellow and gold, Ezekiel How died at the age of 77. Twenty-one years had passed since that early morning ride to Concord that had helped give birth to a tottering new nation. A nation that was now firmly on its feet.

---

*The building of this West Side meeting house was delayed until 1795, the year before Ezekiel How's death. It was dedicated in November, 1796 and is now the First Parish Church in Sudbury Center.

IX

"The Antiquarian of the Family"

Lydia Maria Francis was young, in love and not yet very famous that summer of 1828. Her first two novels had enjoyed moderate success, but it would be five years before she and husband-to-be David Lee Child would publish the bombshell abolitionist document "An Appeal in Favor of That Class of Americans called Africans". On this particular sunny June day, a ride into the country was in order.

"Many years ago when it was June in the seasons and the June of my youth, I went to ride with the young lover who is now my old lover," she recalled years later. "We rode on like a prince and princess through fairyland until we came to an old inn...known to all surrounding regions as Adam How's Tavern."

Adam How's tavern was in its heyday as the new nation approached its 50th birthday in the mid-1820's. Each dawn, with the exception of the Sabbath, was greeted by the creaking of the ponderous market wagons, their hooped canvas tops sheltering a bounteous array of goods destined for Boston from as far away as Western Massachusetts and New York. Later in the day they would return empty to fill the large gravel park in front of the tavern, their drivers refreshing themselves in the tap room while stable boys fed and watered their horses and oxen in the barns across the road.

Mail coaches on the Post Road from Boston to New York stopped to rest and water horses and to allow passengers to stretch their legs and refresh themselves. The early coach left Boston at 3 a.m., arriving at Adam How's in time for a hearty breakfast for its passengers. The landlord, clad in a long blue woolen frock, was on hand to greet them at the door, eager for the latest news.

The success of How's enterprise was no accident. Adam, the youngest son of Ezekiel How, had been carefully groomed for his duties as landlord by his father and gradually took over the day-to-day responsibilities of running the tavern a few years before the old colonel's death.

Gentlemen from Boston made it a regular practice to hitch up a coach and two and drive to Sudbury for an overnight stay, and it wasn't uncommon for a deputy on his way to the General Court or a minister on church business to ride dustily to the front door. These last were often ushered into the landlord's private quarters for food and drink a cut above that served to the ordinary guest.

Adam How was 65 years old when he greeted Mrs. Child and her husband-to-be that June afternoon, but he showed no signs of slowing down. He had successfully raised three sons and a daughter and his tavern and farm were prospering.

"How well I remember that quaint old room where we dined," Mrs. Child recalled years later. "The posts that supported the ceiling stood jutting out and the massive beams that held the form of the house together were visible overhead-...Through the open window in the rear of the house came the fragrance of lilac bushes and the pleasant prattling of a copious brook that ran sparkling across the green meadow.

"Before the front window strutted a peacock with his tail spread to the sunshine like a great oriental fan studded with gems...on the opposite wall hung a framed picture of the family coat of arms, brought from England by the ancestor whose axe first let sunlight into these woods...

"The dinner was plain and old fashioned like all else around us, but everything was delicious...we were served by Jerusha, sole daughter of Adam How, aided by a faithful house friend near 70 years old who has served in the family all her days and was still as indispensable to the house as the house was to her...

"Miss How's father and brothers treated us more like welcome friends than like travelers stopping at a tavern. It reminded me of Dr. Johnson's remark that the best home a man can have is a good inn!"[1]

Just a few feet away in the old bar room a more rustic scene was unfolding. Here sat the teamsters, horse jockeys, and cattle drivers, the dust of the road still clinging to their clothing. They were joined by travelling agents, itinerant showmen, peddlers, and even the occasional mysterious stranger. The blaze from the broad hearth glowed and glanced upon the faces of this motley crew as discussions arose, stories were told, and jokes were cracked while mugs of foaming flip went round before, one by one, they retired to the common bedroom directly above.

There had been some changes since that day in 1796 when Adam sadly followed his father's coffin to its final resting place in the old burying ground near the West Side Meeting House. He had moved a small barn from another location on the property, attached it to the northeast corner of the house, and fitted it with second story bedrooms and a large fireplace. We know the lower room today as The Old Kitchen. Later he added English touches and conversation pieces such as the peacocks strutting on the front lawn described by Mrs. Child in 1828.

Despite the fact that his boyhood occurred in the decade just preceding the Revolution, and his teen-age years were spent in the midst of the war and his father's military duties, Adam had acquired a good education. He developed a thirst for knowledge and an interest in books that he later passed on to his own children. There are testimonials in the Inn today to both Adam Jr. and Lyman. Adam Jr.'s reads: "This is to certify that Mr. Adam How merits the approbation of his instructress for his application to his studies by which he will store his mind with useful knowledge." It is signed by Lucy Maynard.

The exploits of his father and older brother, Ezekiel Jr. and the excitement of the Revolution may have whetted Adam's appetite for history and made him curious about his own ancestors. One authority maintains that: "The third proprietor of the Red Horse Tavern was the antiquarian of the family. The ancient coat of arms, hanging during his boyhood in the parlor of the Inn, gave his thoughts a heraldic turn and he was proud of the lineage he derived from an English ancestry..."[2]

The same writer credits Adam How with circulating the How genealogy "founded on a tradition which traced the family from John How of Sudbury, son of John How of Watertown, to a Warwickshire ancestor..."[3]

Whether the coat of arms was actually hanging on the parlor wall during Adam's boyhood is still open to question. We find the first public record of the heraldic crest, valued at $4, in Ezekiel How's will, which was executed shortly before his death in October of 1796.[4]

Three decades later, Reverend Allen, who lived in nearby Northborough, was the first author to mention the How family's Warwickshire roots in a chapter written in the *Worcester Magazine and Historical Journal* in the year 1826. In this chapter, which deals primarily with the history of North-borough, Allen states:

"According to a tradition handed down in the family, the first English person that came to reside in Marlborough was John How, son of a How of Watertown, supposed to be John How Esquire who came from Warwickshire in England, and who, as appears from a record in the possession of Mr. Adam How of Sudbury, also a descendant of John, was himself the son of John Hull of Hodinhull and connected with the family of Lord Charles How, Earl of Lancaster in the reign of Charles I."[5]

Rev. Allen's language as he describes the ancestry is almost identical to that on the coat of arms. This suggests that he had visited the How Tavern in person, seen the coat of arms in a place of honor, and talked with Adam about the family pedigree. It is just the sort of talk that would have interested and stimulated Adam. Allen uses the word 'record', which, at that time, meant rather specifically a historical record of some kind, written or artistic, or, in this case, both. There are references in the same period to 'Jerusha How's Record' which is a family tree put together by Adam's daughter about the same time. The coat of arms and how it may have come into being is discussed in detail in Chapter XII, but we have reason to believe that Adam helped originate it and that it was created shortly before Ezekiel's death by a well-known heraldic painter, John Coles of Boston. Our reasoning runs as follows:

First, it is highly unlikely that any heraldic symbol crossed the sea with John How in 1637 or 1638. A man leaving England in those hard times, even if he had been willing to take the oath of supremacy, would be most unlikely to cumber himself with extra baggage. Space on shipboard was at a premium and people took the bare necessities of life.

Second, from what we know of How's life in Massachusetts, it does not seem that he was the sort of man to have Royalist leanings or a desire to associate himself with royalty or nobility.

Third, several reputable genealogists have given it as their opinion that the coat of arms was "created" sometime in the eighteenth century.

Fourth, in the inventories of the estates and the wills of John, Samuel and David How there is no mention of a coat of arms. This is out of character. All items of any value, great or small, were mentioned, particularly in the case of Samuel, who died intestate and had 13 greedy heirs picking over his property with a fine-toothed comb. If a coat of arms had, in fact, been in existence, it would surely have been dragged into the light of day, inspected for monetary value, and listed.

Last, and most important, the coat of arms *is* mentioned in Ezekiel's will.[6] Mentioned and appraised at $4.00. It was left to Adam along with "Firearms, Clock, Silver Tankard" and the bulk of his property and the tavern.* How did it get there?

We think what probably happened is this. In the first published *Boston Street Directory* for the year 1796,† there appears an entry for a "John Coles, Heraldry Painter, Back Street." The same entry appears in 1798, 1800, 1803, 1809 and 1813.[7] Since no street directories were published prior to 1796, Coles could have had a flourishing business in Boston some years before that date.

In 1927, William Prescott Greenlaw, then librarian of the New England Genealogical Society, in response to an inquiry from the landlord of the Wayside Inn, expressed the opinion that: "the coat of arms which was said to have been brought from England by John How in 1630 and adorned the walls of the Wayside Inn or tavern in Sudbury...was undoubtedly painted by one John Coles of Boston...John Coles Sr., as early as 1776, undertook to supply all inquirers with a family arms at a moderate cost. He is said to have been a carriage painter, but in

---

*Ezekiel How's will is open to more than one interpretation. Depending on one's reading of the will, the coat of arms remained in the tavern, Adam's property. Or it went to the nearby house of Ezekiel's grandaughter Hepzibah Brown. We incline strongly to the first of these alternatives. The reason for confusion is the paragraph in which Ezekiel discusses what he is leaving to his wife. Here there occurs the phrase: "...also the one half of my indoor moveables and Household Furniture (except Firearms, Clock, Silver Tankard, Coat of Arms and that part of household furniture which is now the property of my well-beloved grandaughter, Hepzibah How Brown) to be hers forever...."

Some have taken this to mean that Ezekiel left the coat of arms to Hepzibah. We think this is a mis-reading of what Ezekiel intended and of what happened. Quite apart from grammar and the fact that if five items were left to Hepzibah, the sentence should read "are" and not "is," it would not have been in character for Ezekiel to leave *out of the inn* such important items as the clock, tankard, firearms and coat of arms. He left these to Adam along with the bulk of the property. The phrase in question details *the exceptions to what he leaves his wife*: the furniture he has already given Hepzibah and four heirlooms he wishes to stay in the family inn where they very properly belong.

†Directories were published in June and covered the previous six months.

the *Boston Directory*, 1800–1813 he appears as a heraldry painter. The spurious armorial paintings are easily recognized by the form of the shield, the mantlings and the palm branches. These are widely scattered throughout New England and of course are entirely worthless....

"As far as can now be ascertained, he made no researches in genealogy for the purpose of tracing the family descent...but he seems to have assigned arms to his customer without regard to the question of whether or not the person who employed him was lawfully entitled to them...which cannot be defended under the rules of heraldry...for these so called 'researches' he charged a guinea fee...."[8]

It is not difficult to imagine Coles making a foray into the countryside in search of new business and making How's tavern his base of operations. What better place to have a sample of his work on prominent display? An evening's discussion with aging Ezekiel and Adam, over a mug or two of flip, could easily have persuaded the two that the How family was entitled to a Warwickshire crest, based on the Spencer arms from Wormleighton. Coles would be only too happy to create this for a mere guinea.

Ezekiel's will sheds some light on just when this was done. How did those who appraised his estate in the fall of 1796 determine the value of the coat of arms? They probably based their figure on what Ezekiel actually paid for it. A guinea was equal to 21 shillings or a pound and one shilling. After the Revolution, the dollar—an adaptation of the German silver coin "thaler"—did not come into use until 1792 after the Coinage Act was passed. There is no recorded rate of exchange for dollars and pounds in the year 1796, but the first one, in 1800, shows the pound to be worth roughly $4.40. Four years prior to this date, a guinea would have been very close to a $4 value.[9]

Despite his interest in his ancestry and his family tree, Adam didn't get started on a family of his own until a year before his father's death, when he married Jerusha Balcom in 1795. Jerusha, the eldest of his six children, was born in 1797, followed by Rebecca in 1799, Lyman in 1801, Winthrop in 1804, Adam Jr. in 1805, and Abiel Winthrop in 1807. All but Rebecca and Winthrop survived to adulthood.[10]

Why did Adam not marry until he was 33, while his father and grandfather had both started their families at a much earlier age? We can only guess. He became very active in town affairs from 1790 into the late 1820s, but in the decade before that he is not mentioned in the Sudbury Town Book at all—most unusual for a younger member of the How family.[11] He may have been away at college, or have crossed the ocean to trace his roots in England.

But from 1790 onwards, Adam made up for lost time in Sudbury. He served the town in capacities ranging from perambulating town boundaries and erecting bounds to repairing roads and bridges. On several occasions he is on record for the sale of oak plank and stringers to the town for bridge repair. Particularly suggestive is the entry in the Town Book for October 1802.

> To Mr. Adam How for two stringpieces twenty eight feet long for a bridge. $5.60.
> For String Pieces for the Bridge west of my House $1.40.
> For seven day Myself to Plow, five days and Cart, three days at Highway work $6.92—$13.92.[12]

How was doing the work on the bridge nearest his house, work which he knew how to do better than anyone else and continuing a tradition started by his great-grandfather more than 125 years before.

Adam How began serving as a select man in 1801 and continued in this capacity through 1808. In 1804 he was named to the Southwest District School Committee and later that year had his powers broadened to include: "inspecting the several School houses in said Town and reporting to the Town on necessary repairs which ought to be made and the probable expense of making said repairs...."[13]

As the years went on, his responsibilities grew and so did the respect of his fellow townsmen. In 1806 he purchased one of six new pews in the West Side meeting house for $83. Only Abner Walker paid more.[14] It was a far cry from the times nearly two centuries before when Adam's great-grandfather John How had to sit back and watch other wealthier settlers divide the choicest portions of meadowland amongst themselves.

Adeline Lunt, wife of George Lunt, a Boston editor, journalist, and lawyer, and sister to Thomas Parsons, the "Poet" of Longfellow's *Tales*, paints an intimate picture of life at the tavern in an article for *Harpers New Monthly Magazine* of September, 1880. She visited the Inn on several occasions with her brother in the 1830s.

"It was a place busy with custom and proud in being so," she wrote. "Mr. How was a proud and painstaking farmer and his broad acres stretched through meadow and woodland for miles away. His good wife with ample force of male and female accessories, conducted the menage and two sons, Lyman and Adam and one daughter, Jerusha, made up the family picture. They were indeed a pleasing representative of old fashioned New England respectability and prosperity in its best sense combined with domestic happiness and virtue."[15]

During this busy and prosperous time, recorded by numerous journalists, it is probable that Adam How's alleged most famous guest, the Marquis de Lafayette, never stayed at the How Tavern at all despite legends to the contrary.*

General Lafayette visited Eastern Massachusetts at least nine times between 1778 and 1824, when he made his final triumphal tour to help the nation celebrate its 50th birthday. But, if accounts are correct, spending the night at How's tavern was a real possibility on only two occasions.

The first of these was in the fall of 1784 when, on his third visit to America, he travelled from Albany to Boston via Hartford, Connecticut, passing through Worcester on October 13. According to the *Boston Gazette*, on October 14 Lafayette "slept at some point betwixt Worcester and Watertown"[16] before receiving a formal welcome in Watertown and being escorted with much pomp and circumstance to Boston the next day. How's would have been a logical halfway point between Worcester and Watertown, but there is no record that he spent the night there.

During the 18 months he was in the United States between July, 1824 and mid-winter of 1826, as "The Nation's Guest," the Marquis made two lengthy visits to Boston.[17] The first was from the 23rd to the 31st of August, 1824, when he attended Harvard commencement and was feted at receptions, banquets, balls, and official functions. Wherever he went he was expected and publicized, and great crowds turned out to

---

*The two most complete sources are J. Bennett Nolan's *Lafayette Day By Day* published in Baltimore by Johns Hopkins Press, 1934, which includes a detailed account of Lafayette's known movements in all his visits to America, and *France and New England*, by Allan Forbes and Paul F. Cadman. This was published in 1925 by the State Street Trust Company of Boston in commemoration of the 150th anniversary of the battle of Bunker Hill. Volume I devotes a chapter to Lafayette's eight visits to Boston and his journeys throughout New England.

welcome him, even when he tried to keep his movements quiet, as in his surprise visit to Ex-President John Adams in Quincy on August 29.

Unlike his earlier visit, it would have been virtually impossible for him to elude the public and the press long enough for a trip to Sudbury in this ten-day period without someone recording the event for posterity.

Lafayette left Boston for Portsmouth, New Hampshire on August 31, stopping at Lexington and Concord on the way. A procession escorted him through Lynn to Marblehead, a town he was anxious to visit because of the exploits of its soldiers during the Revolution. He returned to Boston on September 2, but stayed only a few hours before leaving via West Cambridge, Lexington and Concord for the Wilder estate in Bolton, where he spent the night. He reached Hartford on September 4, and then went on to tour most of the existing states of the new nation he had helped bring into being.[18]

Lafayette started to make his way back toward Boston in early June of 1825. He was scheduled to lay the cornerstone for the Bunker Hill Monument on June 17. On June 12, he wrote Boston Mayor Josiah Quincy from Albany:

> Albany, June 12
> Thus far I am come to redeem my sacred and most cordial pledge. We shall reach Boston on the 15th. I will tell you between us that I have been informed the legislature intend to receive my personal respects, in which case it becomes proper for me to be arrived two days before the Bunker Hill ceremony. As to what I am to do, I cannot do better than to refer myself to your friendly advice and shall offer you and your family my most affectionate, grateful respect.[19]

According to the diary of Miss Eliza Susan Quincy, the Mayor's daughter, "My father was immediately obliged, although it was the midnight, to go out in order to give it [the letter] to the printers and have it published in the papers the next morning..."

Miss Quincy's diary makes it clear that Lafayette intended to arrive in Boston on June 15, 1825. He wrote his letter on Sunday, June 12 and Mayor Quincy received it very late on Tuesday, June 14, rushing out to get it in the morning papers of the 15th in time for the General's arrival.

In J. Bennett Nolan's book *Lafayette Day by Day*, there is this detailed account of the General's movements after dispatching his letter to Mayor Quincy on June 12:

> Monday, June 13th. Leaves Albany for Boston at 8 a.m. by way of Pittsfield. Escort to the ferry. Reception at Pittsfield. Arrives at Worthington, Mass. at 9 p.m. Spends the night at the tavern of Noah Pierce. (See *Lafayette in Worthington* by Katherine McDowell Rice.)
> Tuesday June 14th. Leaves Worthington, proceeds through Chesterfield and Northampton. Dinner at the old Warner House. Reception. The Worthington account places Lafayette at the Union House in Belchertown the night of the 14th. The Worcester account asserts that he drove all night to arrive in Worcester at two o'clock on Wednesday morning.
> Wednesday June 15. Arrives at two a.m. on the stage from Brookfield. Sleeps and breakfasts at the Exchange Hotel. Leaves in the morning for Boston. Arrives at Boston at noon. Descends at mansion of James Lloyd, esq. (Senator Walls' *Reminiscences of Worcester*)[20]

We give this account exactly as it is written because, in the course of this particular journey, it would have been possible, from a geographical point of view, for Lafayette to stop at How's Tavern which was on the direct stage route from Albany to Worcester and Boston. *The Farmer's Almanac* for 1825 shows the "old" stagecoach route passing through Sudbury on the way from Albany to Boston.

Moreover, Lafayette did have every facility for doing something on the spur of the moment and with great speed. When Miss Quincy marvelled at the swiftness and scope of his recent journey, he said: "Oh, there is nothing surprising in that. When people have carriages, horses, boats, all of the first order, prepared for them and awaiting them at every step as we have had, they do not deserve any credit for travelling fast..."[21]

But if Lafayette *did*, in fact, make a stop of any length in Sudbury, one must assume that Nolan's account of his overnight stay at Belchertown on June 14 is not accurate and that Lafayette either drove straight from Worthington to Worcester, using many relays of horses, and made an early start on the morning of the 15th, or that he didn't stop at Worcester at all and drove directly to Sudbury, which would mean that Senator

Walls is reminiscing incorrectly about his breakfast at the Exchange Hotel!*

The only point which allows one to consider such an exhausting itinerary is the fact that the Worthington and Worcester accounts do not agree about Lafayette's movements in the crucial 24 hours between noon on June 14 and noon on June 15. It is barely conceivable that with no sleep and a great deal of effort and discomfort, Lafayette could have stopped in Sudbury sometime during that time span. Why the aging war hero would have wanted to undergo such an endurance test is another question.

There were other occasions when, in theory, it would have been possible, although not likely, that Lafayette could have visited How's Tavern. The possibilities include the winter of 1778 when he travelled to Boston after his illness at Fishkill, New York and three short spring days in 1780 after his arrival in Boston from France. In the first instance, Lafayette had just recovered from a life-threatening fever in December of that year, and the winter was "the severest cold of many years."[22] In the latter case, he was in a hurry to reach Washington's headquarters in Morristown, New Jersey,[23] and Sudbury wouldn't have been a logical first night's stop.

The trouble with this convenient assembly of facts is that if the celebrated Frenchman had in fact spent a night at the Red Horse Tavern or even stopped for a meal and to feed and water his horses during one of his many journeys, every newshound within miles would have heard of it and trumpeted the glad tidings, but we have not been able to discover even a single item in the archives of local papers. Moreover, one would think that residents of Sudbury would turn out in great numbers and that someone would have kept a record or a diary of the happening. Mrs. Child, who visited the tavern two years later, would have mentioned it, and Adeline Lunt would certainly have written about it.

But they are all distressingly silent.[24] And even worse, nothing exists in the Wayside Inn Archives, which preserve material on all other major events. Unless Lafayette came in disguise, late at night, on foot and unaccompanied, it is unlikely that he was able to stop un-noticed at How's Tavern.

*There is a discrepancy between Nolan's account and Miss Quincy's diary for June 15. Nolan says Lafayette arrived at Lloyd's at noon and Miss Quincy pinpoints the time as 3 p.m. which is more logical considering the distances involved.

The peace and prosperity in the half-century following the Revolution, which Lafayette was on hand to celebrate, brought even more traffic past the tavern. One of the best descriptions of Adam and his family at this time is preserved in an exchange of letters in the *Boston Journal* in August, 1868, between "Zed" and "Medicus," the pen names of two old newspaper correspondents who visited the Inn when they were boys in the 1830s. Zed writes:

> Thirty years ago it was a treat to the boys to pass an hour beneath the trees at the inn and watch the callers at the trough quench the thirst of their horses and maybe the longing of their own appetites. Then too, in the summer, gentlemen with their families used to drive with coach and two from Boston to Sudbury to pass the night at the Red Horse Tavern as we called it; and such a paraphernalia as they presented was no unattractive sight to eyes like ours in those days.
>
> 'Uncle Adam', as he was familiarly known, was the landlord then and briskly did he move about in his long blue frock of wool, regardless of the style of his guests, while his good spouse in plain calico gown presided with honest zeal over the details of the house though both were grown gray from many labors and many years. The How boys were all at home then, Young Adam, Winthrop the working son and the Esquire (Lyman), the last of the family to pass away...[25]

The years of long hours and hard labor began to take their toll, and early in 1840, Adam How set down his last will and testament.

Stating that he was "weak in body but of sound and disposing mind and memory," he left his estate, real and personal, to be divided equally between his two oldest sons. He made provisions for his "well-beloved wife, Jerusha, in sickness and in health...to live in my dwelling and receive two thousand pounds within one year from my decease..."[26]

How made Lyman and Adam Jr. joint executors and requested that they pay sums of money both to their sister Jerusha and to their younger brother Winthrop, who was weak and sickly. Winthrop died five years after his father at the age of 38.

When the old man died later that year it was apparent that the end to an era had come. According to one account: "there was a great concourse of people at his funeral gathered from many towns and the neighbors shook their heads knowingly and solemnly said that Adam 'had left no boy that could make his place good....' '' [27] The speculation that Adam's sons could not cope with their legacy of centuries had already begun.

Sadly, that speculation would prove to be correct. Thomas Parsons summed up the situation in a few short lines penned 21 years later.

> Adam's love and Adam's trouble
> Are a scarce remembered tale;
> No more wine cups brightly bubble,
> No more healths, nor cakes, nor ale.
>
> ————
>
> Never to his father's hostel
> Comes a kinsman or a guest
> Midnight calls for no more candles
> House and landlord both have rest.[28]

As he lay dying in the homestead built by his great-grandfather so that his grandfather could raise a young family on the outskirts of the wilderness, and so that, in later years, he and his father could build it up and enlarge it into a flourishing inn and well-known meeting place, what thoughts went through Adam How's mind? A coat of arms? The unrelenting toil of farm and plow? The winds of Warwickshire? New England or Old England? What voices came to him from the shadows—the future or the past? An age had passed with Adam How. And no future age would be the same.

X

"The Belle of Sudbury"

On winter nights when there are few guests at the Inn and the wind is howling about the eaves, it has been said that one can hear an old piano playing the strains of the 'Copenhagen Waltz.' Guests assigned the big bedroom over the Old Kitchen often sense a haunting, faintly-perfumed presence and a light, swift step on the narrow, twisting stairway. The sad, rather wistful figure of Jerusha How is supposed to haunt certain rooms in the house where she spent most of the 44 years of her life.

The eldest daughter of Adam How and sister to Lyman, the last of his family to keep the tavern, Jerusha was born in 1797 and died unmarried in 1842.[1] She was educated at a far-away boarding school, probably in Philadelphia. She painted, read, dressed particularly well, played the piano from girlhood and sang, especially romantic songs like 'Bonnie Doon' and 'Highland Mary.' She was kind to visiting children and helped them pick wild flowers in the spring.

In her younger years she was known as "The Belle of Sudbury," but she refused all her suitors and did not approve of her brothers marrying. According to George Hunt, who was Postmaster at South Sudbury for many years early in the twentieth century, she was engaged to an Englishman who sailed home to arrange the match and never returned.

"I can never forget that wholesome repast without being reminded of Milton's Allegro and the neat-handed Phyllis," recalled Lydia Maria Child of a supper with Adam How and his family in June of 1828, when she rode to the old tavern from Boston with her husband-to-be David Lee Child. "In our case, the neat-handed Phyllis was Jerusha, the sole daughter of Adam How. Miss How seemed like one who had never been young and gay. Her manner had somewhat of Puritanical primness and she looked as if she took life very seriously.

"But her father said: 'Jerusha is as good as gold,' and her sober face was an index of a thoroughly honest and guileless character. Her father and brothers treated us more like welcome friends than like travelers stopping at an inn."[2]

"Miss Jerusha was, for that period, far above the average Country girl," wrote Adeline Lunt in an article entitled "The Red Horse Tavern", published in the September 1880 issue of *Harpers Magazine*. "... she possessed great common sense combined with refined tastes, musical accomplishments and rare domestic qualities.

"She had been educated at a fashionable boarding school in a distant city and in many families of the merchants of the day was a most welcome guest. She was delicate in person and not of robust condition which kept her much at home under the care of watchful parents.

"In the neighborhood of the surrounding country she was looked up to with much respect and regarded as an authority and model in matters of superior taste. Her home was truly a happy one. With devoted parents, two brothers who worshipped her as if she were indeed a creature almost too bright and good for human nature's daily food, she was, indeed, a very queen of the mansion."[3]

Jerusha spent most of her years in the three small rooms over the Old Kitchen. Following the fire of 1955 they were made into one large guest room, which is still known as the Jerusha room today. She was a woman of some refinement and was encouraged to be so by her parents and brothers.

"Well do I recall the piles of music books which lay upon her piano in the old parlor, handsomely-bound with her name outside in gilt letters," Mrs. Lunt went on. "And what a marvel in those days was this same instrument! The only one in town at the time and what visitors flocked to see it! 'Wa'al, I've seen Jerushy's pianny, and heerd her play on't too,' was the collective ejaculation of every gossiping woman in the town as the uneventful weeks went on."[4]

Nearly half a century after Jerusha's death Mrs. Van D. Chenoweth paints an equally bright picture in an article in the *New England Magazine* for May, 1894.

"Miss Jerusha Howe, the eldest sister of the Landlord [Lyman Howe] and four years his senior, was ever cherished by the doughty squire with peculiar tenderness and her death, which occurred some twenty years before his own, remained a lasting sorrow. Fascinating stories are told of the fragile Miss Jerusha's beauty and her gentle manner.

"The old spinet* of the inn parlor, the first musical instrument of its kind to appear in the town of Sudbury, was purchased for Miss Jerusha who used to play upon it the 'Battle of Prague' and 'Copenhagen Waltz'. She used to sing too, in a thin and decorous voice the sweet strains of 'Highland Mary,' so fashionable in that day." [5]

Mrs. Chenoweth speaks of Jerusha's interest in her lineage and of the fact that her family considered her to be an "undisputed authority" on questions of ancestry. The writer refers to a family 'record.' This may possibly be her father's coat of arms, referred to in exactly the same way by the Reverend Joseph Allen in his article in the *Worcester Magazine*. However, Mrs. Chenoweth implies that this particular record is something found or copied by Jerusha herself and not some other family heirloom. This record may have been the one that was sent to the Inn in the Ford era.

In 1938, one of the hostesses at the Inn received some letters from a New Jersey resident, and an old paper, which is headed: "Jerusha How's Record, 1839." This is a fine-inked list of the dates of births, marriages and deaths of members of Jerusha's family, starting with John How and carrying on through the death of Lyman. It purports to be a genealogical listing made by Jerusha herself, perhaps when she was sickly and needed occupation. The person who sent this admitted that she did not know how her family happened to have the paper but felt it was an authentic document as it "does not look cut and dried enough to be a copy. Additions have been made in pencil...." [6]

There are, indeed, pencilled additions made on the face of the paper of the deaths of Adam How, his wife, Jerusha, and their children including Jerusha herself in February 1842

---

*It will be noted that one of these authors speaks of a "piano" and the other of a "spinet." They are writing 14 years apart, Mrs. Lunt in 1880 and Mrs. Chenoweth in 1894. Neither of these ladies would have been likely to make a mistake about what sort of instrument she had seen. However, Mrs. Lunt was familiar with the Inn and its furniture through many visits on many different occasions, both in Jerusha's time and later. Mrs. Chenoweth is writing about a collection of items she saw in the Eaton house in Shrewsbury, some 15 miles west of the Wayside Inn,—the so-called "Eaton Relics" which were inherited after Lyman's death by the family of Ezekiel How, Jr. She may well have seen a spinet and not a piano, which suggests a) that Aunt Abby Eaton got her instrument from the Berry or How farm after Ezekiel junior's death in 1847 and b) that Jerusha's original piano went in the auction in 1860 to Emory Hunt as George Hunt, his son, later maintained in his extensive reminscences about the Inn.

and Lyman in 1861. On the back, in faint pencilled writing, is a note: "Lyman will please pardon the additions made _____ in pencil." It is signed "S.L.B" or "J.L.B."[7]

We have been unable to discover the identity of the pencil writer who must have made the additions sometime after 1861 or between 1842 and 1861. This person could have been Jerusha Balcom, Jerusha How's cousin, whom she mentions in her will and to whom she leaves "the old gold necklace that was my grandmother's." These two women were evidently good friends and had the same grandmother, Adam's wife's mother, who was also a Jerusha Balcom. Or, the pencil writer may have been a member of the Brown family who were also related to the Howes by marriage over several generations.

The validity of Jerusha How's "Record" has not been further pursued as far as we know. It is possible that the record is a copy of information not originating with Jerusha herself but obtained from other sources. Since it arrived at the Inn in the Ford era, as did numerous other items, from someone who did not understand how she happened to have it, its validity is, at best, open to question. The vital statistics could all have been garnered from public records. However, the amateurish and untidy look of it suggests that it is not a careful fake.

Moreover, it is interesting to note that Jerusha, if it is Jerusha, spells her family name as 'How' * all through the Record. Ezekiel How Jr. is supposed to have greatly disliked the addition of the 'E' to the name and continued to spell it in the original way. This man, who was Jerusha's uncle, neighbor and a respected old soldier, was still very much alive in the 1820s and '30s and probably visited the family even after his brother's death, since he himself did not expire until seven years later. His influence on his historically-inclined niece would have been strong.

How much Jerusha knew and how much of it was accurate is not clear. But she was certainly involved in some way with the fabricated coat of arms. Her will, dated February 2, 1842,

*Bezaleel Howe of General Washington's guard was supposed to have been the first to add the "E" to his name, which was then picked up by other branches of the family, but not by Ezekiel Jr. We do not know when or if the name was officially changed from How to Howe. Writers at the end of the eighteenth and beginning of the nineteenth century spell the name both ways and it does not appear consistently as "Howe" until Lyman's time. In England, the two spellings of the name are interchangeable from the sixteenth century.

specifies: "To the Antiquarian Society of Worcester, the other coat of arms of my family name, which I copied from the original held by my father; I direct my executor to furnish it with a frame as near like the original as possible." Also specific: "To my brother Adam, a gilt-framed coat of arms."[8]

This statement implies that at the time of Jerusha's death there were at least three visible renderings of the coat of arms—the "original," which probably remained at the Inn after Adam's death in Lyman's possession, the copy which Jerusha herself painted and left to the Antiquarian Society and which is still visible in Worcester today, and the 'gilt-framed' version which she left to Adam Jr. her brother. There is no record as to what became of this third copy.

From the observations of visitors to the Inn during her lifetime, and from the contents of her will, Jerusha emerges as a genteel, well-educated woman, who held herself and her family a cut above the common travelers who roistered in the old bar room and slept in the chambers under the gambrel roof above.

Not only was she interested in the arts and her own ancestry, but she liked to dress well. At the time of her death, her wearing apparel was valued at $176.11. The old pianoforte and her music books were valued at $115.00 and she owned several pieces of expensive jewelry, including a ruby and pearl ring in the shape of a Maltese cross which she gave to Adeline Lunt.

Jerusha was fond of both her brothers, especially Adam, to whom she once loaned the sum of $6,500. She was precise and careful and, up to a point, generous to relatives, friends and townspeople.

The following bequests are characteristic: "To my mother, Jerusha Balcom How, two flowered coverlets, two large flannel blankets, three white and two striped shoulder blankets...to Jerusha Balcom of Sudbury my old gold necklace that was my grandmother's...my blue bedstead to Libbie Osborne of Sudbury...to the children of Parker Fowle of Boston I give and bequeath four hundred dollars...To the town of Sudbury...to supply the industrious poor...with fuel...."[9]

Jerusha's bequest to Sudbury's "industrious poor" was the victim of some fast political footwork. The bequest in her will, which was witnessed by Dr. Thomas Stearns, among others, is quite specific:

"To the Town of Sudbury, I bequeath the sum of one thousand dollars to be kept as a fund forever, the interest to be applied at the discretion of the selectmen to supply the industrious poor in the town with fuel."

In February 1843 this legacy was formally accepted by the selectmen and shows in the Town Records[10] for that year. But four years later, in March, 1847, when the town was having trouble finding the funds to pay for a new meeting house, the record states: "Article 9. To see if the Town will appropriate the fund left by the late Jerusha Howe to pay for their town house...as they shall think best...."[11] A month later, the town voted to authorize the Town House Committee "to give their notes in behalf of the Town of Sudbury to Nahum Thompson Esq.—treasurer of said town and his successors in office for the sum of one thousand dollars, which sum being a legacy left to the town by the late Jerusha Howe."[12]

This vote is not only in direct conflict with the terms of Jerusha's will which stipulate that the money is to be used for fuel for the poor, but also ignores her directive that only the interest be spent and the capital sum be kept as a "fund forever". Why Lyman Howe, who saw to it that the other provisions of his sister's will were carried out to the letter, did not object publicly is still a mystery.

Another mystery is Jerusha's provision for an elaborate gravestone and lot in the "New Burial Place" (now Wadsworth Cemetery) which was to cause her brother Lyman a great deal of time and trouble:

> My body to be buried in the new burial place...and a monument erected over my grave, of white marble of good quality constructed and finished in a plain, neat style in such form and taste as my brother Adam How, after consulting with the best artists, shall deem suitable and proper, and the monument shall be enclosed with an iron fence...built and superintended by my said brother...for not less than eight hundred nor more than one thousand dollars.[13]

Young Adam, the chosen brother, left it to Lyman to complete the arrangements for the monument and was to lie beside his sister in the new lot at the north end of the cemetery not long after it was finished. The fence was never built, but the white marble obelisk, eroded by the effects of acid rain, remains as testimony to unrequited love and the end of a romantic era.

As she sat alone in her rooms over the old kitchen, penning her last bequests, her frail body racked by illness and her mind embittered by the fact that her English lover had never returned, did Jerusha secretly hope that someday he would come back and find her impressive tomb?

The known realities of her life are slim and sad, but there may be more of Jerusha Howe's story yet to be told.

XI

"A Kind of Old Hobgoblin Hall"

The rumble of the wheels of the New York Mail Coach was suddenly muffled by two inches of mud as the driver turned his team from Boston's cobblestoned streets and headed down the Post Road toward Watertown that April morning in 1826. Amongst the sleepy passengers who had climbed aboard at three o'clock was a young man of 19 from a well-to-do Cambridge family headed to New York to board a steamer for Europe.

Meanwhile, some 23 good English miles away in Sudbury, another young man of 24 slept soundly in the family quarters of the Red Horse Tavern. In a few hours he would be awakened by the bustle of cooks and maids in the kitchen below, as his father made ready to greet the first stagecoach from Boston and offer its passengers a bit of rest and refreshment.

Did Henry Wadsworth Longfellow and Lyman Howe meet briefly that warm April morning and strike up a friendship that would endure for some 36 years? Were they even remotely aware that their chance meeting would be as important to the future of How's Tavern as the ride that Lyman's grandfather, Ezekiel, made to Concord on a similar April morning more than half a century before? These possibilities have fascinated historians, poets and writers of romance for many years.

Lyman Howe was born in 1801, the third child and oldest son of Adam and Jerusha Balcom How, and grew up in the heyday of his father's tavern. Henry Wadsworth Longfellow was born February 27, 1807 in a spacious house in Portland, Maine, the second son of Stephen and Hither Zilpah Wadsworth Longfellow, and grew up in a house built by his grandfather, General Peleg Wadsworth.

Both boys were interested in books and learning. Lyman's diligence is evidenced by a testimonial received at the age of five from one of his teachers. This reads:

> This will certify that Mr. Lyman How has by his good
> behavior in school gained the love and good will of his

instructress and deserves a large rewarde and the name of a faithful, diligent and worthy schollar. And will be remembered by me, with love and affection, so long as he continues to weare this caracter, and it gives me great satisfaction to inform his parents of the same.

Given by me NABBY HOWE
School Instructress
Sudbury, July 17, 1807

(The spelling errors are Miss Howe's.)

At the age of six, Longfellow was at Portland Academy and brought home this "billet", as a mark or note from the Headmaster was called:

Master Henry Longfellow is one of the best boys we have in school. He spells and reads very well. He also can add and multiply numbers. His conduct last quarter was very correct and amiable.

N.H. Carter
June 30, 1813[1]

By the next spring, he was reported as having "gone through half his Latin grammar," and as "standing above boys twice as old as he."[2] Not a bad accomplishment for a lad who would have been just seven years old.

Despite this scholarly bent in common at an early age, it is most unlikely that the two met as young men in any extended way beyond a casual exchange of greetings as the stagecoach passengers stretched their legs or enjoyed a hearty breakfast. Young men just aroused from sleep are not apt to be aware of the touch of history on the shoulder as the first dawn breaks.

It would be more than three decades before their paths would cross again, and then it would only be at second hand. In the intervening years, each went his own way, unaware of destiny.

Lyman and his younger brother Adam appear to have been quiet, bookish boys, more interested in learning than in involving themselves in the day-to-day routine of the tavern and the hard work that it still required. Adam How, Sr. had made the venture a successful one and probably encouraged his sons and daughter Jerusha to pursue the arts and educational things that he himself had been interested in as a young man.

Former generations of Howes had been sturdy yeoman farmers, soldiers and tavern keepers. In the fifth and sixth generations, possibly through the Balcom family, an artistic strain became mixed with the original How stock. Adam How, Sr. was interested in history and genealogy. Jerusha Howe loved music, singing and painting. Lyman was also drawn to music and singing as well as astronomy. He may well have thought that he was born into the wrong sort of business and have wished that he could have made his living as a schoolmaster or a musician. He spent much time as an amateur in both occupations.

Adeline Lunt, sister to Dr. Thomas Parsons and a frequent visitor to the tavern during the mid-1800's, remembers both Lyman and his brother Adam as youths in an article published years later in *Harpers New Monthly Magazine*:

> Lyman and Adam Howe were helpful in the farm work in a moderate degree, but not at all given to hard work of any description. During the winters, Lyman sometimes taught school and there was nothing he enjoyed more than to drill a class of boys in arithmetic....
>
> They were both simple-hearted and extremely good-natured and pleasant and genial in manner. Adam was unpretentious in tastes, and possessed no longing beyond his own home which was to him the only place on earth. Lyman, on the other hand, had aspirations and was fond of the aquaintanceship of superior men and those of higher caste than those with whom he was commonly thrown as the ordinary frequenters of his father's house....[3]

Mrs. Lunt also describes Lyman later in his life:

> Lyman, universally called 'The Squire,' was somewhat looked up to in the town as a person of uncommon capacity for subjects quite above the range of ordinary country minds or occupations. He served on the School Committee, on the Board of Selectmen and in manners of more abstruse character he was interested and well-versed. Indeed, he was a curious mixture. He had natural brightness but he was somewhat vain and overrated himself. He assumed a pedantry with a class that might not know the meaning of the word and yet discerned his boastful sense of superiority, which oftentimes made him their theme for ridicule. With one lofty science he was strangely familiar, that of astronomy....
>
> The Squire was very much afraid of lightning—so much so that during the continuance of any very violent thunderstorms he had the habit of securing what he considered the

safest position by placing his chair in the very center of the bar-room, between two well-polished nails that protruded to the surface. Here, with his feet up on the rounds of the chair, he counted and calculated the distance and the danger of every successive flash and report.

Aunt Margey Carter, who had presided at the births of all Adam Howe's children, and lived into her nineties, and Buckley Parmenter, Lyman Howe's personal manservant, were both well remembered by Mrs. Lunt.

> I never saw so perfect a likeness of one of Macbeth's witches on any stage as she in reality represented...the concerns of the house had now passed, by reason of her great age, out of her supervision and her chief occupation was to sit in the kitchen chimney corner—a looker-on in domestic matters...She was in constant fear that the Squire would be entrapped by some young and frivolous person and it was an agony to her to see him in such company.
>
> Then there was Buckley. Buckley Parmenter—a faithful male servant of the Squire and who had a home with him as long as he lived and who would have laid down his life to serve him. He was near seventy, but nimble as a squirrel and as spasmodic in his movements. He had a remarkable accomplishment which was to take a board nail between his teeth and bite it in two![4]

It would be easy to paint Lyman as an irresponsible dilletante frittering away the fortune gained by years of hard work and thrift by several generations of his family, and many writers of the late nineteenth and early twentieth centuries have done so. He did not marry, had no heirs to carry on after his death, and a place loved and frequented by many people fell, for a time, into disuse and decay. Lyman was a convenient scapegoat, but he was by no means completely to blame.

As he grew older, Lyman involved himself more and more in church affairs. In 1839, a new religious society and a new church were in the making, and Lyman was one of the leaders of this movement. A group of people had been meeting privately in the house of William Brigham, and in March of 1839 the town required Israel How Brown, who petitioned, and all legal voters ''who have congregated the year last past for public worship in a building owned by William Brigham in said Sudbury to meet March 25...for the purpose of organizing, according to law, a religious society for the public worship of God.''[5]

The petitioners for this new cause, which called itself the Sudbury Evangelical Union Society, were leading citizens, including shoemaker Enoch Kidder, E.B. Richardson, Brown, Abel Dakin, Joseph Cutter, Roland Cutler and C.G. Cutler. At the meeting, Lyman Howe was asked to preside in the absence of Cutler. He must have handled a tricky situation well, because he was asked to preside at a second meeting held on April 8, 1839. A separate "meeting house" was apparently organized with greater efficiency and diplomacy by this generation than those attempted by Lyman's grandfather and great-grandfather. Instead of taxing already overburdened taxpayers to pay for the building, as was the case in 1739 and 1779, Lyman raised most of the money by selling pews ranging in price from $40 to $105 to raise a total of $4,705.[6]

While all this was going on, 23 miles away in Boston another event was taking place that would change the way of life at the old tavern forever. A man named William F. Harnden established a long-distance railway express service between Boston and New York. The days of the overland mail coaches were coming to an end.

Lyman's responsibilities at the tavern grew with the sickness and death of his father in 1840, but he continued his interest in the new church, which was dedicated in 1843. His closest friends were members of the Evangelical Society, and they and their descendants remembered him fondly.

"Squire Howe was a man of much dignity, even finer in face than the portrait now at the Inn would seem to show," recalled former South Sudbury Postmaster George W. Hunt, whose general store was a landmark for many years early in the twentieth century. "He was of a strong personality and a musician. My father Emory Hunt was a close friend of Lyman's and they worked together in the notable dedication of the church in 1843 near Sudbury Center.

"At a time when Lyman Howe needed especially the support of another man of strong character and helpful influences, my father felt he had been able to fulfill this need."[7]

This brief comment tells volumes about the life and times of Lyman Howe. As a young man, he was undoubtedly quite lonely and in need of another man of "strong character." Many of the members of his family had died young. His sister, Rebecca, died when he was barely a year old and a few years later, his baby brother, Winthrop, who was born in 1804, followed. He was just beginning to get used to running the tavern following his father's death in 1840 when his mother and sister both expired in the spring of 1842, one in February and the other in April.

Three years later, Lyman's younger brother Abiel Winthrop also died, and barely 12 months later, Abiel's only child, Lyman's three-year-old nephew, Winthrop Adam, died in infancy, leaving Lyman and his brother Adam the sole survivors of a family of nine.[8] A mind already inclined to introspection and melancholia would certainly have taken on a darker hue from these events.

Lyman was especially devastated by the death of Jerusha and spent a great deal of time and trouble carrying out her wishes about her memorial stone. A.J. Goodenough tells of some of Lyman's troubles in a paper read to an audience at the Sudbury Town Hall in 1881:

> The (Wadsworth) cemetery was first enlarged in 1842. Miss Jerusha Howe died in February, 1842. She had provided in her will a sum of money for a monument, which, at that time, seemed an extravagant outlay. Her brother Lyman Howe Esq., wishing to obtain a suitable site for so costly a structure and no satisfactory place within the old grounds being found, he selected the eminence north of the grounds, then a stony pasture, as being more sightly and appropriate.[9]

It took a complex and exasperating series of negotiations with landowner Israel How Brown and another abutter, before Lyman was able to arrange for the enlargement of the cemetery and the construction of the monument which proved to be such a showpiece that the vacant burial lots nearby were quickly snapped up.[10]

Perhaps because the place was associated with his sister, perhaps purely because of family tradition, Lyman Howe continued to maintain an interest in the Wadsworth Cemetery. On a snowy November day, ten years after Jerusha's death, he was a member of a committee of leading Sudbury citizens who officially dedicated the new Wadsworth Monument.[11]

His Excellency, Governor George S. Boutwell, military bands, speeches and a solemn procession through a steady snowstorm paid tribute to those 29 men who were killed in April, 1676 in a fierce fight with the forces of Philip of Pokenocket. On that November day Lyman may well have remembered with pride that among the "remains of the ancient dead"[12] were those of his great-great-uncle, John How Jr., the brother of Samuel How.

Lyman would have had plenty of time for this civic work, for things were slowing down considerably at the Red Horse Tavern. Now the railroad whisked passengers from Boston to New York and beyond in less time and with more comfort than the massive coaches that once pulled up outside his door. One coach a day ran from Boston to Marlborough and back, and its passengers had no need for food or lodging.

It was sometime during this period that Daniel Treadwell, Rumford Professor at Harvard College, embarked on a carriage trip with his family to the interior of the state and chanced to spend the night at Howe's Tavern. Like so many travelers who have followed in the 150 years since his visit, he was so charmed "with its seclusion and rural beauty that he resolved to spend some time there during the heat of summer."[13] He not only kept his promise, but he brought a circle of his friends from the Cambridge intellectual community. Among them were Dr. Thomas Parsons, Luigi Monti and Henry Ware Wales. Later Longfellow would immortalize them, along with Lyman Howe, as the main characters in his *Tales of a Wayside Inn.*

"Accordingly, with a little circle of intimate friends, he secured a sort of home at this old place, which, with every passing year became more dear and delightful," recalled Mrs. Lunt. "Indeed, the place with its surroundings—the whole lay of the land about it—was a little nook of peace and natural beauty."[14] Outwardly, Mrs. Lunt's observation may have been true, but behind the scenes all was not tranquil. Young Adam Howe became engaged to a young lady of good family in a neighboring town and built a modern house in the Greek Revival style within sight of his old home (it still stands on the north side of the Post Road just before the turnoff to the Inn). When everything was finished and the house ready for occupancy, the young lady grew sick and died.

"Thus were blasted the fond hopes of Adam," wrote Mrs. Lunt. "A blow from which his mind never fully recovered. The vacant house, conspicuous on a prominent slope, was a sad and constant monument of all his worldly dreams of happiness."[15]

Many years later, Adam married one of the housekeepers at the tavern. He died in 1854 of consumption, leaving his older brother with the task of managing a declining business and a staff of domineering and competing housekeepers, cooks and servants. Mrs. Lunt sets the scene:

The Squire, now left alone to preside over the house, had not inherited any capacity for keeping a hotel, and the moderate ripple of business that came in those days to the house was almost too much for his faculties. Was he not a star gazer, a mathematician, a philosopher? How could he consider the vulgar daily food of such a class as claimed his special consideration?

And now began struggles with housekeepers. It was easier to combat one helpless bachelor than two, and although Lyman had thus far escaped the matrimonial meshes, he was none the less a target for domestic broils. Oh! the wars of words that sometimes rose up in that homely old battlefield, the old inn kitchen! After some grand scena and aria from some prima donna of that lively department, philosophically shaking his head, he would retreat, repeating to himself those consoling words: 'All women are warriors.'

A strange life it was, those days of the decline and fall of the old tavern. With summer came its guests—a quiet coterie that brought a certain life and air of indolent ease and leisure to the old place, which for the time was as their own domain.

The old, low, beam-browed parlor glowed with a fresh domestic charm and the old piano sent out astonishing bursts of sound after long silences—they perhaps more musical than its sound; the open fire blazed on the hearth in the chill evenings with a color that seemed like none else and the conversation and bon-homie and the abandon of all hearts to the genuine spirit of the place itself were undisguised and natural. The range of the house and the grounds was the guests' prerogative. The Squire and his servants occupied a portion somewhat removed and the main body of the house was given up to the guests. The chambers were large and airy and one of these that had formerly been a dancing hall with lights hanging from the ceiling, a musician's stand at one end and seats placed for the dancers all around the sides....

There was, of course, a freedom of the house and a management and direction of its affairs by the guests, that under different circumstances would not have existed. The Squire regarded their wishes as paramount and perhaps it was through this very deference he paid to them that the jealous differences grew up in the kitchen department. The housekeepers too often proved refractory and took advantage of his weak, pacific nature. Someone said that each one came with a determination to marry him, and finding this a failure, she avenged herself by torturing her difficult victim.

They treated him at times as if he were a little, unruly boy...Seizing his telescope, his ever-constant solace, he would retire saying, 'By Jupiter! I'll have a look at Mars!' and in this way he philosophically soothed his ruffled dignity.[16]

Mrs. Lunt, a friend to many of the tellers of Longfellow's *Tales*, is a major source of information about the Inn in the time of Lyman Howe and Longfellow. Of all the authors of the period who wrote of the Inn, she was probably closest to the inner circle of Longfellow's friends, yet she makes no mention of a meeting between the poet and the landlord.

Ernest Wadsworth Longfellow, in an article written for the *New York Times* after his father's death, insists that Longfellow did not visit the Inn in his youth.[17] The poet's brother and biographer, Samuel Longfellow, has this to say:

"It has been suggested that as the Red Horse Tavern was the stopping place for all stage coaches going west from Boston, the author of the *Tales of a Wayside Inn* must at this time have made acquaintance with that ancient hostelry. He, however, makes no mention of it."[18]

Samuel Longfellow is possibly implying that since his brother did, in fact, mention several other places which had struck him in his letters to his parents—Northampton, Philadelphia, New York—he would have mentioned the Red Horse Tavern if it had particularly gripped his youthful imagination. It is more probable that as a young man on his first trip to Europe he had other things on his mind or was fast asleep.

The only recorded visit of Longfellow to the Inn is the one mentioned in his own journal for October, 1862.

Alfred Salerno Hudson, whose *History of Sudbury* was published by the town in 1889, just 28 years after Lyman Howe's death, gives us a first-hand and sympathetic account of the man:

"Squire Lyman Howe, the last landlord of the inn and the one of Mr. Longfellow's poem, was a man rather imposing in appearance, somewhat dignified and grave. He was at one time a prominent singer in the Congregational Choir, a school committee man, and justice of the peace. Years ago he was a familiar sight to the villagers of South Sudbury, riding in his chaise with the top tipped back, as he went to the post office or to visit the district schools; and he fitly represented in his younger and more prosperous years, the family of Howe. He lived as a bachelor and was the last link of an illustrious lineage. As a tavern keeper, he did less and less business as his years increased."[19]

Lydia Maria Child paints a similar picture as she tells of a visit from Jerusha Howe shortly before Jerusha's death in 1842.

> Years afterward, Jerusha made me a visit. Her father was dead and I knew she had troubles although she tried to hide them. A shadow had long since been coming over the sunshine of her home: the shadow that has enveloped so many homes in utter darkness. Travelers who stopped there to rest their teams were accustomed to call for strong drink; and the brother on whom she depended to maintain the reputation of the old establishment paid the penalty to which so many tavern keepers have fallen due to familiarity with the accursed thing. Everything about him degenerated from its ancient thriftiness and began to wear a shabby and disconsolate aspect....[20]

The various chroniclers of the times agree that in Lyman's day the Inn *did* fall on evil times, whether because the landlord indulged in 'strong drink', whether he was just lazy or disinterested or whether simply because trade declined as the railroad took over mail and long distance passenger service from the stagecoaches. Undoubtedly, it was a bit of all three.

A more endearing account of Lyman "as his years increased" is that of Caroline Morse, who, in the late 1920's, wrote retrospectively of a Thanksgiving visit to the old tavern in 1860 (Lyman's last Thanksgiving), when she was a child of three and on her way to see her grandfather in Shrewsbury. Her father, Stephen*, had boarded at the Inn as a district school teacher when Lyman was landlord, and her great-grandmother, Rebecca

---

*This Stephen is almost certainly the Stephen Morse who served as executor of Jerusha Howe's will, and a year after the scene described by Caroline, was one of those asked to appraise Lyman's debt-ridden estate. There had been close contact between the Howes and the Morses for a long period of years. Caroline Morse's great-grandmother was the Rebecca Howe born August 20, 1766, tenth daughter of David How, Junior and Abigail. She left Sudbury on November 1, 1786 to marry a Stephen Morse of Marlborough. Her father was Ezekiel How's older brother, born in 1717, and often mentioned in town records during the period before, during and just after the Revolution. He lived on adjoining property and helped his brother with the innkeeping business during Ezekiel's military service and later. This would have made it possible for his youngest daughter, Rebecca, to have been married from the Inn as Caroline Morse explains. (Daniel Wait Howe, p. 39)

How, had once lived there. Caroline Morse writes about this incident:

> Cousin Lyman...expectant of Stephen and his family, stood in the open doorway, regardless of November's chill. With simple dignity he welcomed us and ushered us into the warm parlor, where apples were roasting on the ashes and mugs of cider were on the hearth...Cousin Lyman piloted us through the great, untenanted, bewindowed rooms...he opened with reverence his sister Jerusha's piano...When at last we reached the worn stairs and had climbed with him into the great, open attic with its huge chimney and uneven floor, my heart bounded with delight. There were hornets' nests and bunches of herbs hanging from the weather-stained, hand-hewed beams. Near the chimney was an enormous four-poster with a huge, fat, tempting feather bed on it. Cousin Lyman told us that in the old stage coach days it was used for all the 'left overs,' even eight or nine travelers had slept in it at the same time...The call 'Come children' brought us hurriedly forth. Cousin Lyman swung us one after another to our seats and stood bareheaded waving us goodbye. [21]

As her father's wagon turned the bend in the road towards Marlborough and Shrewsbury, and little Caroline Morse watched the landlord's bareheaded figure disappear, she probably didn't realize that she would never see 'Cousin Lyman' alive again. One April morning in 1861 Buckley Parmenter found Lyman insensible in his bed. By nightfall the last in the line of Howes lay dead. Dr. Thomas Parsons, Longfellow's "poet" of the *Tales*, penned his funeral dirge in his 'Old House at Sudbury:'

> Thunder clouds may roll above him
> And the bolt may rend his oak;
> Lyman lieth where no longer
> He shall dread the lightning stroke.

> ———

> On the broken hearth a stranger
> Sits and fancies foolish things
> And the poet weaves romances
> Which the maiden fondly sings.

> All about the ancient hostel
> And its legends and its oaks
> And the quaint old bachelor brothers
> And their minstrelsy and jokes.

No man knows them any longer
All are gone; and I remain
Reading as it were, mine epitaph
On the rainbow colored pane.

Some are in their graves and many
Buried in their books and cares;
In the Tropics, in Archangel:
Our thoughts are no longer theirs.

Fetch my steed, I can not linger,
Buckley, quick, I must away!
Good old groom, take thou this nothing
Millions would not make me stay."[22]

Interlude: English Origins
1576–1642

Map by Sir William Dugdale, 1654.

XII

"The Woodland of Warwickshyre"

Histories are founded on facts which can be documented, proved and itemized. Old records are searched, old handwriting is deciphered, quests are undertaken into musty archives, vaults and storage boxes; courthouses full of deeds, wills and inventories are invaded; journals, letters, diaries, account books and maps are unearthed and perused with care. But when all this is accomplished and the evidence bristles tidily from the page, and certain conclusions have been drawn from tabulated data, there is still much which must be left to speculation, imagination and question.

In this chapter we raise some questions. Questions which have been pursued in the course of the research but which have not been fully answered. Where did John How come from in England? How did the coat of arms originate? How and when did the Red Horse Tavern get its name? Where was Adam How at the end of the eighteenth century?

These are questions at the point where research leaves off and informed imagination takes over, questions at the borderland of fact and fancy.

Where did John How come from in England? There is a tradition that he came from Warwickshire and specifically from Ladbroke. But it is far more likely, for reasons we shall show, that he came from the village of Brinklow, if he came from Warwickshire at all.

We explored John How's county on foot. In Warwickshire, as in most of the counties of England, the villages are close to each other and most are less than a day's hike away from wherever one happens to be. Brinklow, Church Lawford, Coventry, Monks Kirby and Stretton-under-Fosse form a circle one can cover in a day at a brisk pace. Nuneaton and Chilvers Coton are a bit further away. Southam, Ladbroke, Wormleighton, Itchington and Warwick are another day's saunter. Kineton, Tysoe and Edgehill are a lengthy expedition. In the seventeenth century Coventry and Warwick were major towns, both central. Anyone who was growing up in this period would have been mobile and would have known all these places well, especially if he moved around on foot and could not afford a horse.

Villages like these do not change greatly over the centuries. Distances of travel, as the crow flies, or as old Public Footpaths run, remain roughly the same. So it is possible to re-trace a walk someone might have made three hundred years ago or more.

Village people in England have, from a very young age, strong loyalties and traditions. At least some members of each family are apt to remain in the same village for generations, as old churchyards bear witness. If someone moves, by reason of marriage or profession, it is often to a neighboring village. Hence a fabric of relationships forms and endures.

If someone moves a long way off, even to another country, friendships from the past remain durable. A person can be recognized as 'Hodge from Gloucestershire,' or even 'Hodge from Snowshill' when he arrives in Massachusetts. He will be called 'Haines from Worcestershire' or 'Haines from Wickhamford,' or, in this case, 'How from Brinklow,' or 'Coles from Warwickshire.' In a foreign country such ties are especially honored. If peoples' families had known each other in neighboring villages of the same county, even many generations earlier, any traveling member of such a family would have been welcomed in the New World.

Where is this speculation leading? To the possibility that John How, the first of the family who ran taverns in the colony of Massachusetts, and John Coles, the first painter of a family of painters, were both from the county of Warwick and possibly knew each other as boys.

Here, to be sure, fact mixes enticingly with fiction. But it is not all misty obscurity.

We do not know and cannot prove with certainty where precisely John How came from nor on what ship he sailed. In spite of the Warwickshire family tradition, he may have come from one of the East Anglian counties. An authority on emigration to New England has said: ''Two thirds of the early settlers of New England came from the Eastern counties of England, one sixth from the Southwestern counties of Devonshire, Somerset and Dorset, and one sixth from other parts of England.''[1]

If John How came from Warwickshire, he is included in "one sixth from other parts of England" and "other parts" includes Warwickshire.*

Banks, in his lists of emigrants to New England, shows only seventeen people from Warwickshire who were recorded in all. But if his estimate of the number of ships' lists which have survived is correct—one eighth of the total—we can assume that roughly 136 came from Warwickshire in actuality.[2] Even this estimate is probably far below reality since many people came without listing their home county or village. After 1639 there are at least four known instances of passengers being taken aboard in groups of fifty to two hundred and more with no listings of places of origin and no names. They appear to have taken the oath of allegiance en masse, being sworn by an officer appointed for this duty to save time.[3]

For even in King Charles' England some lingering sense of mercantile priorities seems to have remained, especially when the country was on the brink of war and tempers and purse strings were fraying. The tedious and time-consuming task of checking, individually, hundreds of passengers' allegiance to the Crown, would have delayed ships beyond season and beyond the patience of ships' masters. So there was compromise. And who is to say if the officers at the major ports chose to turn a blind eye to the large numbers of human beings who left the country listed in exactly the same way as other cargo: "125 passingers...150 barrells of beefe...40 hogsheads of mault...2 tonns of wine...500 weight of small shott...20 pounds worth of iron tooles...150 dozen of shirts..."[4] No more and no less important.

John How may have walked from Brinklow to the coast. He may have left England as one unidentified man among the crowd of people in these ships' lists.

---

*Along with English evidence which points to How's having come from a county other than Suffolk, Hertfordshire, Hampshire, Dorset, Essex, and Wiltshire—from which came the majority of Sudbury's early settlers—one can glean from the record of John's life in Massachusetts that he came from a different background. He was a loner. He was not part of the "in group" in Sudbury. He worked hard, kept his own counsel, kept the peace and trod carefully. He seldom spoke out but when he did, did so with conviction and without fear—as in 1655 on the issue of syzinge the common land. His personality and behaviour suggest he came from a county distant from the other settlers.

Why Brinklow and not Ladbroke?
To begin with, why Ladbroke?
And further, why Warwickshire?

What evidence has been presented about John How's origins up to now? Search reveals that the discussion, ranging over almost one hundred and seventy years, about where this Sudbury settler came from in England, is founded almost entirely on a chapter written by the Reverend Joseph Allen in the *Worcester Magazine and Historical Journal** in the year 1826. In that chapter, Allen states:

> According to a tradition handed down in the family, the first English person that came to reside in Marlborough was John How, son of a How of Watertown, supposed to be John How, Esquire, who came from Warwickshire in England and who, as appears from a record in the possession of Mr. Adam How of Sudbury, also a descendant of John, was himself the son of John Hull of Hodinhull, and connected with the family of Lord Charles How, Earl of Lancaster in the reign of Charles I.

This reference to John How is part of a chapter on the history of Northborough and adjoining towns. Rev. Allen concludes the chapter with the following disclaimer:

> The preceeding sketches have been made up from material collected from various sources. The aged fathers of this and some of the neighboring towns have been consulted...several descendants of the early settlers of Marlborough have kindly furnished many valuable papers relating to the events of former days and which have been handed down from father to son for three or four successive generations....The writer has aimed for accuracy but fears, where so much rests on mere tradition, or memory not less treacherous, that many errors besides those of the press, have become incorporated in the history. For these, he craves the indulgence of his readers. [5]

The important point here is that subsequent historians *all* take their information about John How from this one rather slim source, which the author himself admits is open to error.

*This *Journal* contains "topographical and historical sketches of the towns of Shrewsbury, Sterling, Leicester, Northborough, West Boylston, Paxton, Lancaster and other papers illustrating the past and present condition of the County of Worcester."

No attempt was made to track primary sources. Farmer in 1829, Barry in 1847, Savage in 1860, Temple in 1887 and Banks in 1937, one after the other, and without exception, cite the *Worcester Magazine* and those who have cited it previously, as the earliest and sole source of information on the subject. Where did the Reverend Allen obtain his information? Probably from a coat of arms which he saw hanging on the wall of the parlor at the inn. And from a conversation with Adam How, the landlord in 1826.

Several other historians of the nineteenth century, writing about ships' lists and known emigrants to the colonies, either do not mention John How at all, or say they cannot ascertain his point of origin. These include Hotten in *Licenses to Go Beyond the Seas*, Bond in his *History of Watertown*, and Ward in his *History of Shrewsbury*.

Barry throws doubt on John How stopping at Watertown, whereas Savage suggests he was there 'a long time.' Temple is the first writer to date to record that John How was a glover by profession but there is no stated authority for this statement. (See Appendix B.)

Judge Daniel Wait Howe, in his *Howe Genealogies*, published in 1929, efficiently summarized information known at that date:

> Every reasonable effort has been made by me and by various others of the descendants of John How, to ascertain something definite about his English ancestry and these efforts have been aided by genealogists in England and others there. So far very little progress has been made....
>
> Of the ancestry of John Howe of Sudbury and Marlborough nothing seems to be known, except that he was an Englishman. From the painting which used to hang upon the wall of the old Red Horse or Howe Tavern of Sudbury and from vague family traditions it has been conjectured that the father of John was John How Esq., that the latter was of Warwickshire, England, and was a son of John How of Hodinhull and was related to the family of Lord Charles How, Earl of Lancaster in the reign of Charles I.
>
> ...Hodinhull, in Warwickshire, was merged in Hodnet...In Dugdale's *England and Wales* (ed. of 1835, Vol. II p. 967) Hodnet is mentioned as being in Warwickshire, three miles from Southam, nine from Warwick, and seven from Kineton,

and as having a population in 1835 of only nine. It lay between
Ladbroke and Itchington* and is now depopulated...[6]

Another authority has said more recently: "'The whole
area—Hodnell (or Hodinhull), Wills Pastures, Chapel Ascote
and Watergall were all depopulated by the sixteenth and
seventeenth centuries and, in fact, the ruin of the parish
church was disused by 1635...Wormleighton is an adjoining
parish...these places were inhabited by sheep and a very few
shepherds...''[7]

The Spencer family, whose arms are adapted to the How coat
of arms, *did* live near Ladbroke. Sir John Spencer of Althorp is
mentioned in a local book about the village.[8]

Judge Howe, drawing on Dugdale,† was the first person to
mention Ladbroke. This was almost certainly the source from
which Charles Edward Banks, writing his *Index of Emigrants
to New England* in 1937, ten years later, arbitrarily picked
Ladbroke as the village from which John How came.[9]

Banks cited Farmer as his source, but Farmer did not mention Ladbroke. Only Judge Howe did and one wonders why
Banks did not choose Southam, Kineton or Itchington as
equally likely points of origin for How if he had read the Judge's
statement correctly. Judge Howe was merely saying that Hodnet, or Hodinhull, was a dead village, lying near three other
villages. For some reason best known to himself, Banks picked
Ladbroke, or Ladbrooke as he called it, and the uncertainty
about John How's village was compounded.

But regardless of how Banks arrived at his conclusion, the
idea that Ladbroke was How's village arose from the coat of
arms and *not* vice versa. The painting named only Hodinhull
and Wormleighton; other nearby villages in that area were
gradually mentioned by other people. Rev. Allen, to his credit,
did not mention a specific village. He simply quoted direct
from the coat of arms—i.e. 'Hodinhull'—and the place names

---

*Judge Howe also raises the possibility that St. Nicholas parish in the city
of Warwick might have been the point of origin for the How family. We
discuss this theory in detail in Appendix B.

†Sir William Dugdale was an 'antiquarian' who lived in Warwickshire and
is one of the most important sources for events in his part of the country
before, during and after the Civil War...."*The Antiquities of Warwickshire*
(1656) by William Dugdale was one of the most professional of seventeenth
century county studies and the product of over twenty years work...."
Hughes, *Politics, Society and Civil War in Warwickshire, 1620-1660.*

followed in a haphazard manner over the next hundred and ten years.

Having assembled these facts from all available sources, we began our own search in Warwickshire by investigating the village of Ladbroke firsthand.

'Lod Broc'—The Village of Ladbroke

Ladbroke today is a dead village, built around an old stone church and an even older village green. It has a population of just over two hundred people. It was once a prosperous farming community but is now mainly a place where retired people or commuters live.

The village itself goes back at least as far as Saxon times and Saxon farmers probably pastured their cattle on the village green. Ladbroke in Saxon is *Lod Broc* and means to *draw water*, from the large, clear brook which still runs along the side of the green.

After the Norman Conquest in 1066 the land was split among four great overlords—Robert, Count of Meulan, Turchil of Warwick, Hugh de Greatmaisnil and William, son of Corbuchion. This is recorded in Domesday Book, twenty years after King William won the battle of Hastings against the Saxons.

Land was measured in "hides." Ten hides was equal to roughly twelve hundred acres.* A man's standing in his area was directly related to the amount of acreage he controlled. The amount of produce a man could expect from his serfs also depended on how much land he had under cultivation.

In the twelfth century, the Norman family, De Ladbroke, who must have inter-married with the Saxons, is recorded as possessing five hides worth of land or approximately six hundred acres. These large tracts were usually sublet to a number of tenants who farmed the lands and paid annual dues to the overlord.[10]

The village Church of All Saints dates from the end of the thirteenth century and the first recorded rector is John de Pavalay, from 1298 to 1303. This ancient grey stone structure, with its tall tower against the skyline, dominates the village. In the churchyard a search was made for Hows. Legible names on the oldest gravestones are Hewitt, Palmer, Turner, Chebsey,

---

*"The extent of the hide has been much controverted. The general conclusion is that a hide was normally 120 acres but the size of the acre itself varied after 1066..." *Oxford English Dictionary*, Vol. 5 p. 268.

Allibone, Glover and Mortiboy. Some are too faded to read or have long ago been allowed to fall apart. Moss and ivy grow over everything.

Many names which appear on the old gravestones also appear neatly inscribed in the earliest church records of baptisms, marriages and burials; these are in the County Record Office in Warwick, date from 1558, and carry on to 1762. During the incumbency of Rector Roger Inforbie, who presided from 1586 until 1626, no record of births, marriages or deaths of any member of the How family could be found. Parish names which predominate are, in additon to those mentioned above, Bafford, Stanton, Garrett, Clarke, Talbot, Pratt, Treadwell, Throckmorton and Spencer.

Oral history is an important element in English villages, but present day residents of Ladbroke, including the oldest living person, two church wardens, and a town official, could remember no How in the village recently, or in former times. The local pub is the Bell Inn and goes back to the 1600's. In the "early days" before the Civil War it was known as the White Horse Tavern. After 1646 it became known as the Bell, "in the house of Chebsey." Again there was no flicker of recognition of the name How by the present owner or his varied clientele.

This evidence is further confirmed by two intelligent, articulate old gentlemen, who were once rectors of Ladbroke. Canon George R. Fishley and Canon Ronald T. Murray, now retired and living in Kenilworth, are historians by hobby and can remember "no Hows in Ladbroke."

An old map of Ladbroke for the year 1639, which shows the principal land owning families, includes most of the names visible on gravestones and in the early church records. There is no How.

The absence of the name of How as a land owner is not in itself surprising. As far as we know the How family were not land owners. But the significant point is the total absence of *any* record of a How from Saxon and Norman times to modern public records, church registers, maps, gravestones or hearsay.

There are two notable exceptions. The major source of historical information about Ladbroke in early centuries, apart from public records, is a book by Reverend S.A.H. Hervey, *Ladbroke and Its Owners.* Rev. Hervey was a retired minister who had been Rector of Ladbroke and had spent much of his life studying the history of his village. He wrote his book in retirement and knew his subject as well as anyone could.

In the entire book there are only two mentions of Hows. The first is the so-called "Palmer Evidences." Sometime before 1637, a certain William Palmer distressed his neighbors and family by settling "all his recent purchases in Ladbroke on his second son" [11]. After his death "an Inquisition was taken at Warwick on June 18, 1637 before Robert Harvey, General Escheator of the King in the County of Warwick, through the oaths of several leading citizens. Among those listed is "Richard Howe." [12]

No further reference is made to this Richard Howe—where he lived, how he earned his living, and so on. The date of the inquisition is suggestive, but we have not been able to discover that it in any way relates to John How's departure from England nor to the dissensions of the oncoming Civil War.

Hervey's second reference to a Howe is equally unenlightening. The author describes the library at Ladbroke Hall, which contains over six hundred books printed between 1600 and 1700 and is a valuable seventeenth century collection. On the flyleaf of one of these books, Camden's *Britannica*, printed in 1637, there is an inscription: 'Pretium, 30s. Wm Howe. Fili die miserere mei, 1651.'

The author goes on to say: "One may wonder what wrung this prayer from William Howe. I find a William Howe who...was born in 1620, the son of William Howe of London; he went to Merchant Taylors School and St. Johns College, Oxford. Then he practiced medicine in London. When war broke out he took up arms for the King and had command of a troop of horse..." [13]

There is no way to determine if either of these two men is connected with John How. It seems most improbable since Ladbroke is not specifically noted as the home of either, much less any association with a John How. Since the book collection at Ladbroke Hall is a general collection of books of the period, not relating to Ladbroke per se, the fact that it includes a *Britannica* once owned by a William Howe is probably pure coincidence.

There is a great deal of interesting material in Rev. Hervey's book, which certainly establishes the fact that Ladbroke is a very old village going back to Domesday Book and further "with a population—more or less—of 235 inhabitants." This history also demonstrates that Ladbroke was once a thriving farming community.* But none of this pertains to Sudbury Hows as far as we can determine. This information, or lack of information, about Hows, shown in Hervey's book, tallies with the evidence of the churchyard and vital statistics examined in Warwick. There are no Hows buried in the churchyard with gravestones legible. There are no baptismal or marriage records for Hows. Hows simply do not appear in Ladbroke.

"John how, sonne of John how, November, 1600"

In Brinklow, twenty miles away, the picture is quite different. Hows are thick on the ground, both figuratively and literally. What led us to Brinklow? After drawing a blank in Ladbroke and nearby villages, we made a systematic study in the County Record Office of *all* parishes in Warwickshire.

We looked for Hows in general and John Hows in particular—baptisms and marriages—in the relevant periods. There are, for Warwickshire, more than fifteen pages of Hows and one and a half pages of John Hows. Of these, there are eighty-five recorded John Hows, christened or married in the 1600's, 1700's and 1800's, the great majority in Brinklow or adjoining parishes.

Without precise dates, such isolated statistics, of course, prove nothing. But there are, in fact, precise and relevant dates. In the year 1576 a "John How, sonne of Edward How" was baptised the sixth day of January. He may have been the father of our John. For in the year 1600, a "John how, sonne of John how," was baptised November [date illegible]. On the same page as this John How is a record of the birth and baptism of a John Bolton, the son of the Pastor of that day, Pastor John Bolton. So it would seem to be a particularly reliable record. [14]

---

*Ladbroke is on record for a dramatic happening in June 1607, the Great Ladbroke Enclosure Riot. This involved four hundred protesters against the policy of enclosing arable land for sheep farming, a common practice of wealthy landowners in the late sixteenth and early seventeenth centuries. Warwickshire was once "the heartland of the common field system of farming," and a major grain growing area. As sheep farming increased, grain prices rose simultaneously and people rioted in protest against hunger. Enclosure for sheep runs in Ladbroke put eighteen 'houses of husbandry' [farms] out of business. No wonder this particular protest was spectacular. It was well organized, led by a Captain and a pipe and tabor player, drew participants from twenty other villages, and its effects "reverberated across the country-side." (Roger Manning, *Village Revolts, Social Protest and Popular Disturbances 1509–1640*).

This christening in Brinklow in 1600 is the only record of a John How baptized in the county of Warwickshire in the first ten years of the seventeenth century.* This is by no means proof positive, but it is at least specific evidence.

This baptism is preceded and followed by numerous other baptisms and marriages of Hows. Common family names are Thomas, Sarah, Samuel, Rebecca, Mary, Jonathan, Elizabeth, Daniel, David and Susanna. There are also many Hows baptized and married in the nearby villages of Church Lawford, Priors Hardwick, Nuneaton, Fillongley, Bedworth and Stretton-under-Fosse. These villages are all within a twenty-mile radius of each other and contact among families would have been easy.

There is more. We don't know when John How left England for America nor on what ship he sailed. Nor how old he was. Our first specific record of him in Sudbury is in 1639, sometime before the twenty second day of the last month, when 'rates' were instituted based on land—he was then allotted two acres and an acre and a half for allowance.'' So he must have left England, at the latest, sometime in 1638 or early 1639, whether he stopped in Watertown or not. He died in 1680. So he was in his early thirties when he arrived in Massachusetts, no matter when he was born. We know little of his wife except that her first name was Mary. There is no marriage record with her surname in the colonies.

Put against this dearth of information another entry in the Brinklow records: ''1635, John how, filius of John how and Mary. Baptized January [date illegible].'' [15]

It was unusual for a young man in the early part or the seventeenth century, when life expectancy was far less than today, to marry as late as thirty-eight or forty. He would be more apt to marry in his twenties. John How may very possibly have married his Mary in *her* parish in Warwickshire sometime in the 1620's or early 1630's. In which case her surname would show in England and not in Massachusetts. The John how baptised in Brinklow in 1635 could equally possibly be John and Mary How's first son.

---

*Not all parish records are available. Some have been lost or destroyed, some are illegible, some have simply vanished over time. Because it is the ''only record'' does not mean it is the only John How born in the county between 1600 and 1610. It is the only John How we can find *recorded* in that period.

If so, this son may have died soon after birth or died at sea. The first recorded birth in Sudbury is John How, 24 August 1640. This boy may have been named for a dead brother. It was the custom then to name brothers and sisters for siblings who had perished in infancy. John and Mary How had two other children we know of who died young.

There is, of course, no absolute proof that 'John how, filius' in the year 1635 is the son of the John How who founded the line in Massachusetts. Nor is there proof indisputable that the John how baptised in 1600 is our man. But these two records are fact and not supposition.

Moreover, How family history can be traced fairly clearly in Brinklow. In the old churchyard are four How graves still legible:

"To the memory of Robert Howe who died February 20, 1780, aged 74 years. Also of Mary, his wife, who departed this life March 20, 1781, aged 67 years."

"Here lies the Mortal remains of Robert Howe who exchanged worlds on the 4th of July 1827 in the 29th year of his age. Blessed is the memory of the just."

"Sacred to the Beloved Memory of John Howe, who died July 21, 1874 aged 84 years." [An imposing gravestone].

"Sarah Howe...beloved daughter of John and Martha Howe, died August 23, 1932"

All these people were traced in an effort to connect them with the rest of the family in Brinklow and with each other. A Robert Howe was christened in Brinklow on September 1, 1706, the son of Robert and Margaret Howe. This man is almost certainly the one who died in 1780 at the age of 74. The dates fit exactly. He lived and worked in Brinklow all his life.

Similarly, the Robert Howe who died at the young age of 29, is probably the son of John and Sarah Howe, christened May 28, 1798 in Stretton-under-Fosse. (Stretton is the very next village to Brinklow). Again, the dates fit exactly. We don't know his relationship to the man born in 1706.

A John Howe was christened in Wolston, a nearby village to Brinklow, on July 3, 1781. This is probably the man who died in Brinklow in 1871, three weeks after his eighty-fourth birthday. This man is also, almost certainly, the father of the Sarah Howe who lived until 1932.[16]

The local undertaker, Mr. Harry Johnson, whose family has lived in the village for four hundred years, has a record of Miss Sarah Howe dying at the age of 88 in August 1932, as the gravestone shows. He was a young man then and recalls the funeral. His is a family business.

From Mr. Johnson and other older residents there is living evidence that the Hows have lived for a long time in Brinklow. In 1932, as the gravestone and the undertaker's books record, a Miss Sarah Howe died at an old age. She was the daughter of one man named John Howe and the sister of another. The younger John Howe ran the family business, a candle factory, as his father had before him. This he later sold to a certain Mr. Pudmore* and moved away. His sister Sarah, who ran a boarding school for young ladies, Dunsmorc Housc, remained for life. Miss Sarah Howe, 'Sally' as she was called, was a "tartar to work for"[17] but nonetheless respected and a leader in the limited society of the village, as her family had been for generations. She is well remembered by local residents.

Foremost among these is Lucy Cryer, aged ninety-four. Cryer, like How, is an old and respected name in the village that goes back a long way. The present-day Miss Cryer, when she was a young girl, was a friend of the school mistress Howe and remembers riding with her in a donkey trap. Miss Cryer also recalls Miss Howe "walking very sedately and slowly up the main street, in the middle of the road, long dresses sweeping the flood..."[18]

According to Lucy Cryer, Miss Sarah Howe was distantly related to a John How who had lived in the village hundreds of years before. She recalls "being taught in History lessons about John How going to America in the sixteen hundred...it was like Cromwell, Nelson and Napoleon, everybody remembers them. John How was history in our village. So we were taught about him along with the others...The Howes were a very religious family..."[19]

From the evidence of gravestones, statistics in the County Record Office as well as this living testimony from present residents in the village, we were convinced that the How family has lived in Brinklow for many generations. There is a continuous record at least from 1576 until 1932. (Sarah Howe

---

*Interview with Mrs. Edna Walker Hallam, an old lady, who has lived in Brinklow all her life.

died unmarried and left no direct descendants.) The Robert and Margaret Howe whose son, Robert, was born in 1706, were living in Brinklow sometime in the last half of the seventeenth century; they probably married about 1680 or a bit earlier in the bride's parish. This elder Robert, the father in the christening record, could very possibly be the son of a brother or a cousin of the John How who, by the deposition of one still living, "went to America in the sixteen hundred..."

With these facts established, the history of the village of Brinklow was more closely examined, especially the period just before the English Civil War, in an attempt to connect the How family in Massachusetts more closely with their English origins and to find specific reasons why a young man might have emigrated sometime in the first forty years of the seventeenth century. Conditions in Warwickshire during John How's boyhood, as well as events that took place on the national stage, both of which would have formed the backdrop to a decision to leave for the Colonies, are discussed in some detail.

'Brynca Low'—The Village of Brinklow

Brinklow, like many villages in England, dates back to Roman times. The Fosse way, originally a Roman road, runs straight through the center of town. Authorities disagree about how the name came about. Some think an Anglo-Saxon warrior by the name of '*Brynca*' chose the '*low*' or hill which lay in the Fosse Way, and which may have been a burial ground around which the Romans diverted their road, as the site for his earth and timber fortress. Others maintain with Sir William Dugdale, that "this place hath its name doubtless from that eminent Tumulus* whereon the Keep or Watch Tower of the Castle which long ago was there...did stand...because this little hill termed by our ancestor a '*low*' stood there upon the edge or '*brink*' of the natural ascent, overtopping the rest of the country thereabouts..." [20]

Brinklow, in its early forms, Brinchelawa and Brinchelau, is not found in any records before 1173 a.d. However, it is known that it was combined with the parish of Smite in the 1086 Domesday Book after William the Conqueror took over the

---

*It is worth noting that a recent definition of the name How, reads as follows: "How or Howe, also spelled Haugh, means a natural hill or hillock and often an artificial mound, tumulus, or barrow (burial mound)...it is an English name..."

country. This accounts for the high Norman rating of six hides worth of land and enough area for twenty five ploughs. The overlord was Robert of Meulan, as in Ladbroke.

In the days of King Stephen, a Norman system of fortification, called the motte and bailey, was built by the Mowbray family. This is still visible behind the church and is "one of the best surviving defensive earthworks in England." The overlordship passed from Robert of Meulan to the Earl of Leicester, who is on record in 1275 for holding a court there twice a year and providing bread and ale.

Even before this, in the year 1218, Brinklow was large enough to be given a grant of weekly market, and as with any main road village where markets were held it accumulated a large number of ale houses.

In the sixteenth and seventeenth centuries, Brinklow's history emerges from what can be gleaned from old fortifications, feudal land records and other scattered remnants, into a clearer sequence.

In 1539 the manor of Brinklow was granted to Mary, Duchess of Richmond and Somerset and later divided between the Dawes and Gregory families. [21]

The keeping of church registers was made obligatory in the mid 1500's and in 1557 the records of births and deaths in Brinklow begin. Soon after that marriages are also recorded. These old lists are available in the Warwick County Record Office. Church records of a sort had been kept in previous centuries because there is a list of Rectors of Brinklow starting in the year 1252 and carrying on to the year 1966. The original Patrons of the Church of St. John the Baptist were the Prior and Convent of Kenilworth. John Williams was Rector in 1524 and John Bolton in 1584. In 1583 Queen Elizabeth became the first of the Royal Patrons.

Village life in places like Brinklow in the last years of the reign of Queen Elizabeth I would have been relatively peaceful and uneventful. After the Queen had successfully repelled the threat of invasion by the Spanish Armada in 1588, and had silenced the threats against her life from her Catholic first cousin in Scotland, Queen Mary Stuart, the nation breathed a collective sigh of relief. People were able to get on with their own jobs and were glad to let 'Good Queen Bess' get on with hers. But when Elizabeth died without an heir, in 1603, and the son of her Scottish rival became James I of England, a new and disquieting era began in Warwickshire and throughout the land.

LADBROKE AND SURROUNDING AREA

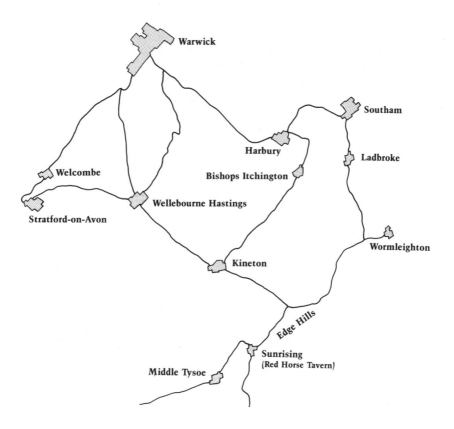

Scale: One inch equals two miles.

BRINKLOW AND SURROUNDING AREA

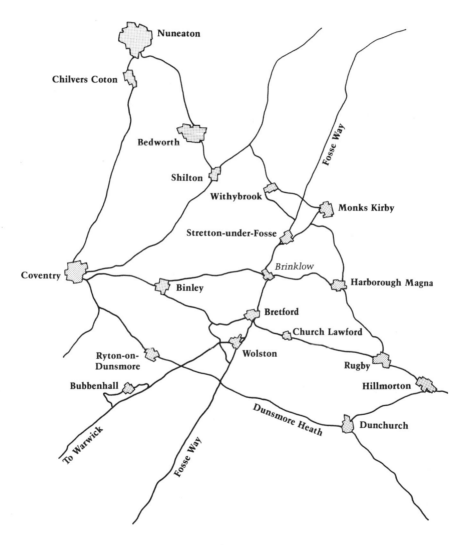

Scale: One inch equals two miles.

What would it have been like to have been a boy and a young man growing up in Warwickshire in the early part of the seventeenth century? It was a period of unrest, hardship and danger. Old values were being challenged and the old fabric of life under the Tudors was in jeopardy. The How family were almost certainly tenant farmers to William Dawes or the Gregory family, who by 1557 owned the manor and all its holdings. They would have been dependent on one of these two large landowners for a meager agrarian living unless they were working as coal miners in the nearby village of Bedworth. (The "coals of Bedworth" were well known in the area). The Hows would have been tenant farmers because at that time there was a law that unless a person owned property worth 40 shillings, was heir to property of that value, owned goods worth £10, or belonged to certain identified groups—gentry, clergy, scholars, miners or colliers—he was not free to dispose of his own labour." Between the ages of 12 and 60 he was required to work as a farm labourer and fined for vagrancy if he refused. [22]

The hated Stuart doctrine of "divine right of Kings," on which much of their arbitrary policy was based, would not have been directly felt in Brinklow or by the Hows, but villagers would have perceived that all was not well when it became too risky to hunt for an occasional partridge or hare in the royal forest of Arden,* as the How family had done for generations to supplement their boring daily fare, or when they heard gossip about a heated quarrel about the best church pew between two members of the gentry in the neighboring village of Wolston. (Archbishop Laud's high church policies emphasized social distinctions and caused a lot of local friction).

More alarming was the news of the Guy Fawkes Gunpowder Plot to blow up the King and the Houses of Parliament in 1605, not because this King was so much loved, but because the plot was hatched by Catholic conspirators. In those days the distinction between a Protestant and a Catholic was a profound and frightening part of a man's daily life. There were men living in Warwickshire whose family members had died in

---

*The Game Laws passed in 1603 and 1605 restricted the dogs, guns and nets that could be used and made it illegal for anyone to hunt in the royal forests except under very limited conditions.

the fires of Smithfield* not long ago, and the memories died hard. "Papist plots" were suspected everywhere and the Gunpowder Plot gave substance to suspicion.†

Planned by wealthy Catholic landowners like Robert Catesby in Ladbroke, the plot may have distressed the governing body in London and made it aware of long-term peril, but its immediate results in Warwickshire were arrests of property owners upon whom large numbers of poor people depended for employment, and confiscation of property which took arable land away from farmers. This reduced the amount of food that could be put on the How family table. [23]

Between 1625 and 1628 several events occurred which undoubtedly affected the How family along with other villagers.

*Smithfield was an area outside London where Elizabeth's older sister, Catholic 'Bloody Queen Mary,' burned three hundred people during her short reign.

†Ever since King Henry VIII wrested control of the Church of England from Rome, and for more than half a century the prevailing royal winds shifted uncomfortably from Protestant to Catholic and back again during the reigns of his three children—King Edward VI, Queen Mary I, and Queen Elizabeth I—there existed a deep and lasting fear of Catholicism in England. Elizabeth was succeeded by King James I, Mary Stuart's son, who was fortunately married to a Protestant. But when King James' son, Charles Stuart, became king in 1625, and married the French Catholic princess, Henrietta Maria, the possibility that the nation might revert to Catholicism once more became alarming. (The fact that King Charles was the grandson of one Catholic Queen Mary and married to another did nothing to improve his image).

War between Catholics and Protestants broke out on the continent of Europe in 1614 and continued for thirty years. When England failed to go to the rescue of French-Protestants in La Rochelle, and most of them were brutally massacred in 1627, there was strong reaction: "It was the greatest dishonour the nation ever underwent."

Fear of Catholic interference from abroad was not lessened by the fact that King Charles' favorite minister, Thomas Wentworth, Earl of Strafford, was ruling in Ireland. There he had gained control of a large Catholic army. It was feared—and rightly—that this gave the King a standing force that he could call on to invade England across a few short miles of sea if his relations with Parliament and people became too strained. (Hill, *Century of Revolution*, pp. 49–61.)

The unrest between Protestants and Catholics in England as a whole was exacerbated in Warwickshire by the dangerous combination of many influential Catholic families and an "important body of Puritan opinion for further reformation." Radical Puritans, like Lord Brooke, firmly cited the 1588 Armada and the more recent Gunpowder Plot of 1605 as evidence of continuing threats from Catholics, attempting to put local religious disagreements into a wider and more sinister context and thereby unite contending Protestant factions in Warwickshire. (Hughes, p. 62 and p. 154.)

In the early seventeenth century religion was not a polite conversational topic. If you said the right thing in the wrong place, or vice versa, you were in danger of being burned alive or having your head chopped off.

A rich London merchant, Mr. Thomas Wale, left the income from property in Brinklow and other parishes to provide a schoolmaster in the school at Monks Kirby, this school to be free to the children of Monks Kirby, Stretton and Brinklow. Education would have improved. [24]

In the same year a young cleric, William Clarke, a graduate of Magdalen College in Oxford, was appointed to the Church of St. John the Baptist as its twenty-ninth rector. His family were wealthy landowners in the vicinity and Sir Simon Clarke, who was probably William's father, appears in the records for 1633 as High Sheriff of the county. [25] The Clarke family used much of their own money for church repair and upkeep. In those days care of the church and charity were very much a private enterprise and good works did not hurt the chances of a family member being preferred for service in this world as well as the next. Rector Clarke came to his pulpit under good conditions.

Rector Clarke was a member of the wealthy gentry and although we can only surmise what he was preaching to his flock in the 1620's and 1630's, Magdalen College, where he received his training, was, like most of Oxford University, strongly Royalist. Clarke's sermons probably supported King Charles' policies.

The clergy had a profound influence on the thinking of their villagers but so did the views of powerful laymen. The Hows would have been listening not only to Clarke but to forceful opinions from another quarter. In the year 1628 a young man named Robert Greville became the Member of Parliament from Warwick and a dominant figure in the area. Greville was a radical Puritan who believed in the separation of church and state and in the authority of the individual conscience. [26] He would not have approved of a minister in Brinklow who told his flock, as most ministers did after 1626,* that it was a sin to refuse to give money to the Crown. When Greville succeeded to his cousin's title in 1631, and became Lord Brooke, a member of the House of Lords, his revolutionary and anti-monarchical views became an even stronger influence on the people of his county.

Many residents of Warwickshire agreed with Brooke's opinions. This county was a center of Puritanism long before the outbreak of the Civil War in 1642. Warwick Castle became a

---

*In 1626 King Charles ordered the Church of England clergy to instruct their flocks that it was a sin to refuse financial support to the Crown.

refuge for harrassed Puritan ministers, as Thomas Dugard's diary tells us. Dugard was a local schoolmaster and a friend of Lord Brooke. [27]

Conflicting opinions—expressed by one man in the pulpit every Sunday and another on frequent public occasions in the city of Warwick—would have been confusing and disturbing to the How family. The Rector urged support of the monarch and traditional obedience, while Lord Brooke opposed his arbitrary policies and taxes. Discussion would have been cautious but it would have been a daily reality as men moved closer to the brink of war.

To men and women of that time religion was the meat and drink of conversation, much as domestic politics and world affairs are now.

It was not unusual for a family to go to three sermons on a single Sunday in different places. Ministers traded off their own duties in various parishes so they could hear outstanding sermons. [28]*

But the villagers of Brinklow—the Hows along with others— had more immediate problems than religious debate. Right on their doorstep poverty and drunkeness were on the increase. A local history records this incident:

> Trinity 1632. One Thomas Smyth...who lately inhabited Brinklowe...and there did fall lame...is now lately come from thence to one John Smyth, his father who liveth at Harbo-rowe...did now endeavor to discharge from their parish the said Thomas Smyth fearing that...being now lame...he may become chargeable to them as a poor...

The parties were summoned in front of the local Justice of the Peace with the expectation that the unfortunate Smyth would be returned to Brinklow "there to remain." [29]

Smyth's plight was shared by many others because there was a great fear that the poor and unemployed would become a burden to parishes which were not responsible for them. Strict

---

*Two villages very close to Brinklow, Rugby and Nuneaton, had notable Puritan ministers—James Nalton and Richard Vines—to whose sermons "multitudes resorted." The Hows probably attended some of these sermons, which had all the flavor of a movie or a stage play today, especially since people were doing something naughty in leaving their own parishes to go elsewhere for a different view from the pulpit. Clarke's parishioners, if they thought like the Hows, would certainly have skipped town from time to time.

laws had been passed to prevent bands of beggars from roaming the countryside at will as they had done in the sixteenth century. What began as a necessary Poor Law in 1563 was extended to people in general in 1621, when a law was passed which prohibited a person without property from coming to any city or town to dwell."[30] Anyone who tried to disobey was hauled before the Justices of the Peace and sent home.*

People were thus locked in place. And there was no effective means of protest.

Men were beginning to see that the House of Commons only represented a fraction of the people of England, the prosperous gentry and the richer merchants. "We be the gentry" said a member of this body in the year 1610. Unfortunately he spoke the truth. No wonder the number of disputed elections trebled between 1604 and 1624.[31]

The political situation in which men found themselves had not altered much since it was described a few years earlier by one of Queen Elizabeth's ministers: "Day labourers, poor husbandmen, yea merchants or retailers which have no free land...copyholders and artificers...have no voice nor authority in our commonwealth and no account is made of them but only to be ruled..." How senior would probably have fallen into the category of "poor husbandmen."[32]

"Poor husbandmen" had to hold their tongues and get on with their daily round. Fear of reprisals from the King's men kept them silent. And the reprisals were fearful. The Hows had before them the example of William Prynne, a lawyer, who had protested in London against a certain church appointment. He was dragged through Coventry in chains with both his ears chopped off, on his way to prison, and although he was roundly cheered by a large crowd of enthusiastic onlookers, this did not

---

*Poverty and vagrancy gave rise to an increase in ale houses. Brinklow had trouble with this issue also. A few years after Smyth had been sent packing a record tells us:

> For as much as it appeareth to the court...that there are seven ale houses in the said town of Brinclow, by means whereof the children and servants of the inhabitants are often drawn into many inconveniences and so neglect their callings to the great trouble and grief of their parents and masters...it is therefore ordered that six of the seven ale houses shall from henceforth be suppressed and put down...

The seventh ale house which was allowed to remain was to be carefully chosen and vouched for by the Rector and at least five substantial citizens. It was also to be licensed by the Justice of the Peace.

mitigate his sentence nor the fear it inspired. His punishment would have effectively quelled any stirrings of resistance from poor people—Prynne was a professional man, a gentleman—if this could happen to him, who would be next?

But harsh reprisals did not intimidate Lord Brooke. He was a peer of the realm and he made his views known, as he rapidly became "one of the King's most irreconcilable enemies."[33] It was his his custom to spend every summer in Warwick during the Summer Assizes (cases of law), before returning to his duties in London. But in the summer of 1636 he left his constituency in a hurry on August 15th, because he learned that King Charles would pay the city an official visit five days later on August 20th. This action was a clear demonstration of his opprobrium for the King; it was a protest the "townspeople could not fail to notice."[34] Nor the poor farmers in the country outside Warwick.

Brooke had great skill as a rallier of confused men.[35] Shortly after his hurried departure from Warwick, he concluded a speech with these stirring words: "Lord, fight thou our battles...strengthen us and give us heart, that we show ourselves men for the defence of thy true religion [Protestantism first and Puritanism second]...and our own and the kingdom's safety ...God Almighty will arise and maintain his own cause, scattering and confounding the devices of his enemies...not suffering the ungodly to prevail..."[36]

Despite this fiery eloquence, there was every chance that in the short run, at least, the ungodly *would* prevail by arresting, imprisoning and torturing people who resisted them. Prynne was one example. There were many others. King Charles' relations with husbandmen like How and noblemen like Brooke—who were at the extreme opposite ends of the English social order of the time—were equally deplorable.

When Charles dismissed Parliament in 1629, for the second time in a few years, and embarked on a precarious eleven years of personal rule, he was strapped for money and tried all sorts of desperate expedients to raise funds. He continued to collect customs dues on imports; he raised new forced loans and fined, imprisoned or impressed into the army those who refused to pay; he borrowed extensively from the London Corporation; and fined anyone caught poaching in the Royal Forests. Worst of all, he re-introduced Ship Money, which rapidly became his most detested and most controversial tax.

Ship Money was an old feudal tax which was originally imposed on coastal towns for money to build ships to protect their shores and ships from pirates. But King Charles extended it to inland towns as well. In Warwickshire, far from the sea, reaction was immediate and sharp: "Unto my...Lord Lieutenant of Warwick...gentlemen gave a flat denial..."[37]

In 1635 Warwickshire was assessed for the great sum of £4,000. Constables refused to collect the money by force. Coventry, particularly hard hit by an assessment for £500, sent representatives to London to protest. In the Brinklow area, as in many others, officials had to send their own servants to collect the hated tax, and Justices of the Peace often had to choose between the King's orders and their neighbors' ire. The general reaction in Warwickshire and elsewhere was: "No man alive ever knew or heard the like."[38]

Ship Money was the last straw to a straitened people. It destroyed the old order in the English countryside and made common cause between lord and commoner. How and Brooke were on the same side. And for more or less the same reasons. To any Englishman of that time the issue was a political hot potato. Neither lord nor commoner could permit the King to collect, in perpetuity, a tax without the consent of Parliament. This controversy highlighted, for the first time, the question of 'no taxation without representation,' which would later become the rallying cry for a larger and more famous revolt in the New World.

Events moved swiftly after this. The Ship Money issue came to a head in London after years of bitterness, and Warwickshire men watched the ensuing drama closely. Their own people were heavily involved. In 1637 a wealthy Puritan, John Hampden, refused to pay the oppressive tax, brought a test case against the King and went on trial amid a blaze of publicity. Leading Puritans supported Hampden with all the force at their command. The Providence Island Company, of which Lord Brooke was a prominent member, backed him to the full. His case was defended by one of Oliver Cromwell's cousins.[39] Unfortunately, the judges decided against Hampden and he lost the case, but not before he became a dramatic symbol of royal injustice. The nation was horrified.*

---

*The judges tried to argue that the whole realm should pay for national defence and not just the ports. But that was not the issue. The best known contemporary historian of the period, Edward Hyde, Lord Clarendon, himself a Royalist, said: "When men heard this demanded as a right in a

The Hows shared the nation's horror. But they probably kept silent and hoped that matters would not get worse. Their way of life was seriously threatened and it was hard to know whom they could trust. Laws against the poor and lame. Gentlemen mutilated in public. A village that had faithfully paid its tithes to support its church unsure how to react to its Royalist Rector's teachings. And a bold, local nobleman who spoke out eloquently against the King's policies. For Lord Brooke did not limit himself to leaving Warwick in protest against the King's presence nor to radical speeches. He went further.

As war drew nearer and a Scottish army was massing on the northern borders of England at Berwick-on-Tweed, Brooke was asked, in 1639, with other gentry, to send a force of Warwickshire men to help defend the country against invasion. He refused point blank. He also refused to take the oath of loyalty to the King. King Charles arrested him [40] and threw him into prison in the city of York.*

Brooke would be vindicated in the long run. When the Civil War began, Parliamentary forces took all of Warwickshire soon after the first battle, Edgehill, was fought on its borders in the autumn of 1642. Within weeks the old stained glass windows in the Brinklow church would be destroyed and altar ornaments and other valuables would be stolen. Medieval relics would disappear for good into forest or thicket. And in these years just before the war, as men like Brooke and How searched their consciences for answers to questions never before asked, history was in the making not only in London but in this remote corner of Warwickshire's green farming country, just as it was all over England.

---

court of law, and found it adjudged so by sworn judges of the law, upon such grounds and reasons as every stander by was able to swear was *not* law...they no longer looked upon it as the case of one man but the case of the Kingdom..." Moral victory went to Hampden and the King's grip on his people weakened again.

*Brooke's sentiments grew more radical before and during the war. In a speech made two years before his premature death in 1643, he spoke to a large crowd in Warwick: "we behold the beauteous face of this kingdom overspread with the leprosy of Civil War...in defense of God's true religion which has been invaded by the practices of Papists and Malignants...I doubt not each of you will play your part in that noble resolution and Christian courage as the greatness and meritoriousness of the work does challenge..."

It is probable that John How was influenced in his statement to the townsmen of Sudbury, in the quarrel over the sizinge of the commons in 1655, by Lord Brooke's style of oratory. "If you persecute us in one city we must fly to another" has the ring of an accomplished speaker.

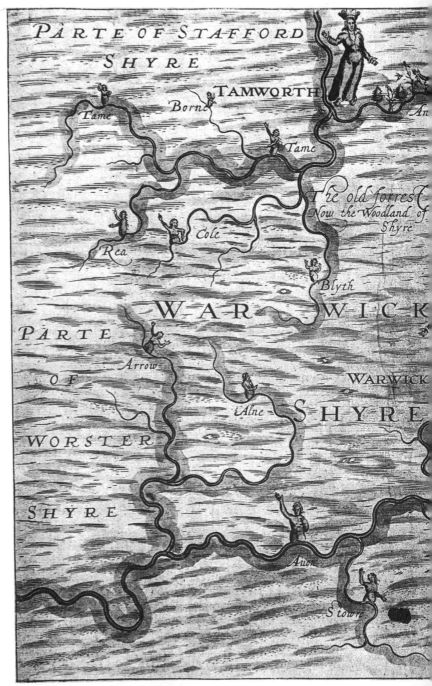

From Polyolbion *by Michael Drayton, 1612.*

The Woodland of Warwickshyre

Enclosing "Poor Man's Commons" vs.
"The Benefit of Planting in New England"

Daily life in Warwickshire and other counties was deeply affected by all these events. In a century when men took it for granted that their time on earth would be "nasty, brutish, and short" and life expectancy was roughly 35 years,[41] the margin for disaster in the life of a poor farmer was very narrow. There was no insurance, no unemployment compensation, no protection against acts of God or acts of man.

Warwickshire was especially affected by the enclosure of farm land. Enclosure of "poor man's commons" had been going on, slowly but surely, since Queen Elizabeth's time. But its effects were felt more sharply in the 1620's and 1630's because of other misfortunes. Between 1621 and 1623 there were bad harvests three years running. In 1631 there was a widespread famine during which the customary food of the poor, rye bread, was unobtainable and the best that could be hoped for, if one was lucky, was occasional barley bread.[42]*

Inevitably there were strikes and protests. Desperate, hungry people took the law into their own hands in the days before a police force existed. In one year bands of poor people went from house to house asking for alms and in some cases seizing provisions by force. Warwickshire—which was a farming county—was especially hard hit by the enclosures for sheep runs. The high price of grain was a major bone of contention.

One eloquent spokesman for farmers insisted: "We do feel the smart of those incroaching Tyrants which would grinde our flesh upon the whetstone of poverty so they may dwell by themselves in the midst of theyr heards of fatt weathers..."[43]

Matters came to a dramatic head in Warwickshire with the Midland or Diggers Revolt of 1607. (See map, p. 149.) The term 'digger' meant exactly what it said. Poor farmers, robbed of the earth of England from which they traditionally, over centuries, had wrested a meager living, dug up enclosing hedges in visible and violent protest.

Hillmorton, a few miles from Brinklow, was the center of one of the first riots. A contemporary account of events in Warwickshire in April and May of 1607 says:

*Bread, or the lack of it, was a crucial issue in the seventeenth century. Old Sir Edmund Verney's famous saying before the outbreak of war, when men were choosing sides, that he had "eaten the King's bread" for many years and would therefore stand with him, was practical as well as idealistic. (Hill, *Century of Revolution*, p.25)

...A great number of persons suddenly assembled them-selves...they violently cut and broke down hedges, filled up ditches, and laid open all such inclosures of commons and grounds as they found inclosed, which of ancient time had been open and employed to tillage. These tumultuous per-sons...grew very strong, being in some places men, women and children a thousand together, and *at Hillmorton in Warwick there were three thousand*...and wheresover they came there were...relieved by the the near inhabitants, who sent them not only many carts laden with victuals but also good store of spades and shovels for speedy performance of the present enterprise... [44]

John How's father was certainly a "near inhabitant" and may well have been a participant in this revolt. If he was not, he would definitely have been in agreement with what the group was trying to do. No small farmer was safe from encroachment, and an inquiry made a few years later into the most distressed villages mentioned, in addition to Hillmorton, several other places a few short miles from How's home— Shilton, Withybrook, Ryton on Dunsmore, Church Lawford, Chilvers Coton and Nuneaton. The whole eastern part of the county suffered.

This band of determined people issued a proclamation: 'From the Diggers of Warwickshire to all other Diggers,' entreating others to join their crusade "...better it were in such case we manfully die than hereafter to be pyned to death for want of that which these devouring encroachers do serve their fat hogs and sheep withal..." [45]

The countryside as a whole intensely sympathized with these "poor delvers and day labourers," but that did them no good. Such revolts were swiftly and sternly suppressed. The troops were called out and there was a "sharp skirmish." The Diggers' leader, John Reynolds, was captured and cruelly exe-cuted. He was hanged, drawn and quartered, according to the custom of the day for traitors and other dangerous criminals. So were many of his followers, no doubt including relatives and friends of the Hows.*

*This large-scale protest was followed by several others in the next eight years as John How was entering his teens. In 1609 a band of women rioted in Dunchurch, and a few years later, fifty rioters in Escott destroyed an enclosure on which corn was struggling to grow. They made "great braggs and used most vile and lewd speeches sayeings they would overthrow all inclusures in the countrye..."

In 1614 there occurred the famous Welcombe case near Stratford-on-Avon. The opponents were an encloser, William Combe, and members of the

This whole dramatic and searing episode would have made a profound and lasting impression on the mind of a seven-year-old boy. He would never forget the events of the spring of 1607 and would, later in life, strongly oppose any measure which took common pasture land away from poor men.

All this activity had social as well as economic implications. People who owned no land of their own, like the How family, were thinking of levelling social ranks as well as hedges. There were threats of violence against both gentry and clergy: "They will accompt (settle accounts) with clergie men and counsell is given to kill up gentlemen and they will level all states (social estates) as they levelled banks and ditches..."[46]

Against this background of revolts, reprisals and hunger, the How family would have heard reports of colonization in the New World which had begun to trickle back to Warwickshire. Jamestown had been founded in 1607, Plymouth in 1620 and the Massachusetts Bay Colony in 1630. Letters from friends and rumors from other sources highlighted opportunities across the ocean, especially for an able-bodied, ambitious young man like John How.

In constrast to the unpleasant conditions of life at home, where a man was stuck in a rut if he had not been born to money and property, the possibility of making one's way through hard, individual initiative must have been appealing. Rather than wait to be "harried out of the land," many were finding their own way out and chancing an uncomfortable three months voyage instead of circumstances with no hope of betterment.

The colony Sir Walter Raleigh had started in Virginia had taken firm hold and ironically, in the same year as his execution, 1618, "a hundred young boys and girls that lay starving in the streets of London" were shipped to Virginia to a new life. The settlements in Massachusetts had paved the way for a new group of emigrants seeking to escape from harsh conditions and

---

Stratford Corporation, who resisted, led by Thomas Green. But the case is remembered not because Green won his case, which he eventually did when the Lord Chief Justice ruled aginst Combe some years later, but because one of those who protested with him was a leading citizen of the town of Stratford named William Shakespeare. Shakespeare, who was an old man at the time, owned a half share in a lease of tithes on the land in question and undoubtedly used his influence and prestige to help Green, who was his friend. The playwright is on record for saying that he "could not bear the enclosing of Welcombe." (Manning pp. 89–92).

when the Massachusetts Bay Colony began to flourish, colonizers spread the word about "the benefit of planting in New England."[47]

One of the keenest of these colonizers, and one of the most influential, was Robert Greville, Lord Brooke. He had helped to organize the Providence Island Company, which did a brisk trade overseas, and was one of its "most committed members." He cooperated in several property transactions in New England in the decade of the 1630's and at one point seriously contemplated emigrating there himself. Thomas Dugard's diary notes a wave of emigration to New England during the difficult eleven years of King Charles' personal rule.[48]

Brooke's accomplishments would certainly have attracted attention in Brinklow. He was powerful enough in Colonial affairs to help a man find a way around obstacles and may have assisted John How, directly or indirectly. In the days before newspapers, radio or television, the opinion in small towns and villages was shaped, to a great extent, by the attitudes of leading local figures. And the fact that a local man of great prestige and power was a Puritan who turned his attention to new lands across the Atlantic would, without question, have made a strong impression on a young man farming in Brinklow.

The other strong influence on How was the parish church. He had to attend services on Sunday and was fined if he did not. Rector William Clarke, as previously noted, was a Royalist. He would have put strong pressure on his congregation to remain loyal to the King and old obedience to established customs. (Rector Clarke was forced to leave his pulpit in 1644 and was threatened with "Sequestration," (defrocking) as were many ministers of the day who would not preach Puritan doctrine.)*[49]

---

*After the Civil War began a minister's opinions were open to review. County Committees were appointed by Parliament to conduct investigations of parishes, and ministers who did not toe the correct line were summarily dealt with. Clarke was ejected from his pulpit "upon supposition that he received letters from and gave intelligence to his Sacred Majesty's Committee for Plundered Ministers..." In other words, he remained a Royalist and lost his job. He was not allowed to return until after the restoration in 1660. Ironically, when Clarke died in 1671, eleven years after he returned to Brinklow, he was again a respected member of his parish, because he and his wife are buried in the chancel of the church, two of the six graves in this place of honour.

With Rector Clarke at one end of the argument about kingship and mens' rights and Lord Brooke at the other—both of them powerful influences on local residents—no one living in Brinklow in the years preceding the war would have been unaware of tension or unaffected by the general unrest. It was a good time for a young man to think of emigrating, and his ability to do so would have been stronger if he was inclined to Puritan beliefs.

Puritan doctrine and the ownership of land were two controversial and closely allied issues. Certainly How would have favored the definition of Puritanism which taught that "Doers shall be saved and by their doing..." [50] This view of religion was a strong motivation to grapple with the conditions in the wilderness of the New World, where hard work and unremitting struggle were essential to survival and qualified a man for eternal salvation by this "Doing."

In England if you did not have property you had nothing and were treated accordingly. "No goods...to be whipped," was a frequent ruling of the Justices of the Peace in handing down decisions. [51] John How would have been well aware that English society required land or other property as the basis for any kind of freedom or advancement. But a Doer in a new country could acquire such property by the sweat of his brow and win both freedom and salvation simultaneously. And so he set sail.

By what means John How made his way from Brinklow to the coast, on what ship he sailed and from what port we do not know. Much of our speculation about How's place of origin is still conjectural. Eventually someone may come forward with a missing piece of the puzzle—a letter, a diary, a journal or other personal history—which will clarify, once and for all, the entire mystery. Until they do, readers can continue to accept various possibilities and invent others—that John How refused to take the oath of supremacy and left in disguise, under another name, or as someone's servant, all of which were frequent practices in those time of fines and arrests; that How had the help of a powerful man who owned ships, such as Robert Greville; that he came from somewhere in a southwestern county or from Suffolk; that his family came to the colonies well before 1638 and resided in Watertown.

All these ideas are possible and plausible. Without a much more extensive investigation of parishes all over England, there can be no absolute certainty as to John How's place of origin.

In the absence of such proof, one can take all the available evidence, as we have done, and build a theory that How came from 'The Woodland of Warwickshyre.' If so, based on facts discovered at the date of writing, the case for Brinklow is far stronger than a similar case for Ladbroke.

The Midland Revolt of 1607

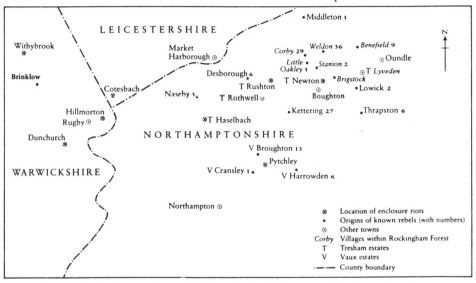

Map adapted from Roger B. Manning's Village Revolts, Social Protest and Popular Disturbances, 1509–1640 (Oxford: Clarendon Press, 1988), p. 243. Used by permission.

The How Coat of Arms which hangs over the fireplace in the parlor of the Wayside Inn.

The How Coat of Arms

What role did the coat of arms play in the story? How and when did it first make its appearance? What happened to it after Lyman's death? On these points there is interesting and sometimes conflicting evidence.

Some of this evidence is discussed in Chapter IX—the reasons John How could not have brought it with him in the 1630s; its absence from How wills and inventories until 1796; the ably enunciated opinion of William Prescott Greenlaw regarding the heraldic painter, John Coles; the fact that the coat of arms was appraised as worth $4.00 in Ezekiel's will, an amount almost exactly equal at that time to John Coles guinea fee.

But there are more facts which are relevant. For some reason Greenlaw's letter, an important piece of research, has not received much attention until now. We have not been able to discover why this letter has languished more or less un-noticed in the Archives at the Inn, unless it is that in Ford's day and later, people were anxious to preserve a halo of dubious nobility and antiquity—the "pale light of tradition" carried to excess.

Greenlaw's letter to his "Cousin Littlefield," a hostess at the Inn, after submitting detailed and convincing proofs, concludes by saying:

> The writer is quite familiar with Coles' 'heraldic paintings' many of which he has examined and two of which hung in his grandfather's hall for half a century...we have kept a copy of one of his arms framed in our library to show to people who bring in specimens of his work, believing they are genuine arms. The similarity is so great that people usually acknowledge his handicraft...I may add that in many cases where I have examined the blazon in detail the arms were not correct even for the family in England of the same name. Coles did not seem to have heraldic knowledge enough to correctly emblazon arms from a description...[52]

Mr. Greenlaw's opinion, put forth more than sixty years ago is ably supported by the present day Archivist in the County Record Office in Warwick. M.W. Farr, consulted several times in the last decade, had this to say about the coat of arms:

> The coat of arms and accompanying text at the Wayside Inn have all the appearance of having been written circa 1780–1800 and it seems almost certain that the writer came from Warwickshire. The noble descent of the family is, however,

quite untrue and a complete fabrication, compiled by someone with considerable knowledge of the Wormleighton region.

The reasons why I am sure it is a fabrication are as follows:

1. Henry V had the title of Duke of Lancaster until 1413, but when he became king his honours were merged in the crown, and there have been no Earls or Dukes of Lancaster since.

2. There is no Baron How of Wormleighton created in 1606. There is, however, Baron Spencer of Wormleighton created in 1603.

3. The office of Treasurer was put in commission for the first time in 1612, but the chief commissioner or first lord was Henry Howard (not How), Earl of Northhampton.

4. Among the favourites of Edward II the best known, apart from Piers Gaveston, were the two Despensers, father and son, both named Hugh, and both executed in 1326. When the Spencers of Wormleighton became great landowners in Elizabethan times, some Tudor herald compiled a pedigree linking them with these Despensers, which was believed until the last century.

I am sure the titles Knight of the Garter and Gentlemen of the Bedchamber are equally spurious.

The coat of arms itself is impossible heraldically, or at least very unlikely. Without the wolves' heads it would be all right, and exists for a family named Holden of Erdington in N. Warkwickshire in 1730. Several families named How have a wolf's head as a crest, so the writer is right in linking wolves with the name, but no herald would have placed them like that on the shield. The Spencers of Wormleighton have a wyvern for a supporter. The animal drawn for the crest here is actually a wyvern, not a dragon, and no doubt is borrowed from the Spencer coat of arms.[53]

Mr. Farr was writing without knowledge of John Coles, nor of Mr. Greenlaw's letter. He was reacting simply to a photograph of the Wayside Inn coat of arms, sent to him recently. Without any prior knowledge, he confirmed Mr. Greenlaw's opinion. Equally important, he pointed out, which no one else had done to date, that the person who fabricated the How coat of arms had a detailed knowledge of Warwickshire which he used to advantage. This raised new possibilites.

The Coles family is a large and important one in Warwickshire. There are, in the County Record Office, more than forty pages relating to Coles family members, three and a half of these specifically 'John Coles.' The chances that the family of the Boston heraldic artist came from the same county as the Hows are exellent. The Archivist in Warwick is certain that the 'fabricator' of the How coat of arms was a Warwickshire man with an intimate knowledge of the geography and history of that county. He also must have had an awareness of families like the Spencers from whose arms the How arms are adapted.

Three entries in the Warwick records merit particular attention.

A John Coles was christened 30 December 1752 in Stretton-on-Dunsmore and another in Harbury (near Ladbroke) in December 1762. Both places are near the area where the coat of arms was placed—Wormleighton. If either of these two Coles emigrated to the Boston area he could have been in business by 1796, a young man of 34 or 44. Since he came from Warwickshire, he might reasonably have sought the company of Ezekiel and Adam How, and was probably welcomed as a fellow 'county man.' And his knowledge of the history and geography of Warwickshire was ideal for his purposes.

The third entry about a Coles is even more intriguing. In December of 1600, a John Coles was christened in Brinklow, almost exactly a month after John How. These two, without too great a stretch of the imagination, could have known each other as boys growing up in the same village and have explored the countryside together. They could have talked and dreamed of the future—one of freedom for those who till the soil to live and worship and own more land without having to pay unfair taxes, and the other of knights and banners and crests from the Middle Ages. They could have left for the Colonies in the same decade.

This theory, we admit, is pure supposition. It is impossible at the present time to discover exactly when John Coles, sign painter and heraldic painter of a family of painters, came to America. He may have been a recent emigrant in the second half of the eighteenth century. Or his family may have come to Massachusetts long before. It is worth noting that a recent consolidation of ships' passenger lists shows a John Cole* as one of those who took ship in April 1634, on *The Confidence*.[54] This man would have been a fellow passenger of Peter Noyes, John Bent, Walter Haynes and others who first settled in Sudbury.

*Coles and Cole are spelled interchangeably in England.

But excluding speculation, the known facts strongly suggest that a John Coles made an agreement with the How family in the years just before Ezekiel's death, either by a visit to the tavern or a meeting in some other setting. He talked with Ezekiel or Adam or both about a coat of arms, persuaded the two that they were entitled to Warwickshire crest based on the Spencer arms, and was paid his fee. He then proceeded to create the How coat of arms.*

Any number of assumptions can be made as to why either Ezekiel or Adam, would have authorized a coat of arms by the noted 'fabricator.' Adam may have convinced himself that it was legitimate. Ezekiel, soon after helping win a war against the British, may have felt he was just as entitled to a crest as any of the 'rascals' he had beaten. Both landlords would have been in favor of putting on the wall a colorful conversation piece which would be good for business. Whatever picture one's imagination paints of Coles declaiming to the older or younger How by a fireside in winter or under the oaks in spring, the indisputable fact is that by the fall of 1796, at latest, the coat of arms *was* on display somewhere in the inn. And it remained there until 1826† when Reverend Allen of Northborough saw it and wrote about if for posterity and all later historians of the nineteenth century.

That Jerusha was aware of the fabricated coat of arms is a surety. Her will, dated February 2, 1842, specifies: "To the Antiquarian Society of Worcester, the other coat of arms of my family name, which I copied from the original held by my father; I direct my executor to furnish it with a frame as near like the original as possible." Also specific: " To my brother, Adam, a gilt framed coat of arms."

This statement tells us that at the time of Jerusha's death there were at least *three* visible renderings of the coat of arms—the 'original' which presumably remained at the inn after Adam's death in Lyman's possession, the copy which Jerusha herself painted and left to the Antiquarian Society and

---

*There is always the possibility that Coles merely paid for a night's food and lodging with the coat of arms, as itinerant artists frequently did in that time, and that it was never commissioned by the Hows at all. In which case the whole business is a magnificent accident!

†The date 1826 is not a hard and fast one. Rev. Allen may have visited the Inn and talked to Adam years before that. The story in the *Worcester Magazine* article was published in 1826 but the topic was one of general interest and could have been written earlier.

is still visible in Worcester today, and the 'gilt framed' version which she left to Adam junior, her brother. There is no record of what became of this third copy.

But if one puts Jerusha's copies to one side and concentrates, as we have, on Coles, one must assume that the coat of arms came into the Inn between 1796 and 1826, and hung there through the stewardships of both Adam and Lyman. What happened to it after Lyman's death in 1861? There are many conflicting stories and rumors which we have tried to piece together and discuss in Appendix C.

The Red Horse of Tysoe (Adapted from an aerial photograph in The Five Red Horses of Tysoe *by W.G. Miller).*

The Red Horse of Tysoe

The third major conjecture in 'The Woodland of War-wickshyre' concerns the name of the Red Horse Tavern. We don't know exactly when or why How's Tavern was renamed the Red Horse. There is a tradition that Ezekiel How christened the inn in 1746 and hung out a sign with a prancing red horse in the same year. But there is no clear evidence of this. In fact, the tavern continued to be called 'How's Place' or ''Howe's Tavern' in the mid to late eighteenth century, throughout the Revolution and afterwards. And there are at least two known instances of a sign of a black horse instead of red.

The name 'Red Horse' may have originated in Warwickshire and have been a legend in the How family. The Vale of the Red Horse of Tysoe was, and is, within walking distance of both Brinklow and Ladbroke. One can see it on James Drayton's topographical map of the county and a representation of the Red Horse for whom it was named. Red Horse Hill at Tysoe was, and still is, ''famous both for a huge, ancient figure of the Red Horse, cut in the turf, and for one of the best known inns in Warwickshire, variously known as Sunrising and the Red Horse Tavern.''[55]

Recently a pamphlet* was published in Warwick recounting the story of the five red horses of Tysoe. This describes, in detail, how the horse came into being on the hillside about a thousand years ago and how it changed through the centuries. The first horse was ''an enormous solid figure, nearly an acre in extent, and was 'scoured' by the Saxon farmers every year as a spring jollification, a magic ritual to ensure a fine summer and good crop.'' Tysoe means a spur of land dedicated to the Saxon god Tiu. Red Horse Hill is magnetically dead east of Tysoe Church, hence, the name Sunrising.[56]

This first red horse, a huge, galloping animal nearly one hundred yards long and seventy yards high, was a landmark in the countryside for generations. It is mentioned by Camden in his last edition of *Britannica* in 1607:

> Of the ready soil here comes the names of Rodway and Rodley; yea, and a great part of the very Vale is thereupon termed the vale of Red Horse, of the shape of a horse cut out

*This pamphlet is called *The Red Horse of Tysoe* by W.G. Miller and K.A. Carrdus, published in 1965. Miller is known in Warwickhsire as 'Red Horse Miller' because he has devoted a great part of his life to the riddle of the changing red horses.

in a red hill by the country people hard by Pillerton.

This horse is also described by Sir William Dugdale who first saw it at the Battle of Edgehill in 1642:

> Within the precinct of that Mannour of Tyshoe now belonging to the Earl of Northampton (but antiently to the family of Strafford...) there is cut upon the side of Edgehill the proportion of a Horse in very large forme; which by reason of the ruddy colour of the earth is called the Red Horse, and giveth denomintion to that fruitful and pleasant country thereabouts, commonly called the Vale of the Red horse; the trenches of which ground where the shape of the said Horse is so cut out, being yearly scoured by a Fee Holder in this Lordship, who holds certain lands there by that service.*

Camden saw the horse from Fosse Way as he travelled. Fosse Way, the old Roman road, was five miles from Pillerton. Dugdale saw the horse first at Edgehill and a second time when he came back to record the nation's treasures soon after 1642, in case the Puritan soldiers started smashing them. The horse was visible to these two travellers—Camden and Dugdale—at a distance of several miles and would have been similarly visible to anyone walking the countryside before the year 1800. In that year a certain Simon Nicholls bought Sunrising from the Marquess of Northampton and ploughed under the ancient horse as a symbol that the peasant obligation to scour it annually was at an end. (This scouring was later re-instated on a volunteer basis because the profits at the Red Horse Tavern suffered on the Easter weekend with no farmers quenching their thirst and no visitors coming to watch the ceremony).[57] John How, in the early 1600's, at a young and impressionable age, could have seen this great unforgettable red horse. A long yearly tramp to Tysoe for the spring festival would have been for the How family the equivalent of a modern-day trip to the circus. The family would have stopped to refresh themselves at the Red Horse Tavern, which was a popular, bustling inn for travellers on the road.[58] This inn goes back at least to the beginning of the seventeenth century; the present owner tells of Cromwell and his soldiers having breakfast there.

---

*Miller goes on to tell us: "We may be sure that Dugdale was given this information by the Earl of Northampton and that it is authentic...it is also probable that Dugdale was the last to record the ancient Great Horse which did not survive the Civil War and all future references are to the smaller horse which was only 55 feet long."

John How would have been struck by the size and color of the horse and an outing of this sort would have remained in a young man's memory. He would have told his children and grandchildren about the Red Horse of Tysoe and the story would have been kept alive in the family.

John's great-grandson, Ezekiel,when his own tavern became successful and well-known, remembered the story of the Red Horse across the sea which had been handed down through the generations and decided to revive the old tradition. If Ezekiel had just commissioned and paid for an English coat of arms, he might have thought that this red horse, along with the crest, would be a fine additional flourish and good for business on their own Sudbury road.

An alternative theory is that Adam How, Ezekiel's third son, made a trip to England sometime between 1780 and 1790.

Some years after the Revolution travel to England was once again possible and fashionable. Ezekiel was doing well enough to have afforded to send his son abroad. He might have enjoyed boasting to his cronies that the 'antiquarian of the family' had gone to investigate his Warwickshire roots for himself.

This conjecture is supported by several facts. First, Adam had two older brothers, Ezekiel, born in 1756 and Eliphalet, born in 1761, both of whom would have been in their twenties in the decade in question, and both of whom appear often in Town Records. They would have provided enough man power to help Ezekiel in the running of the family business.

Second, unlike these brothers and other members of the How family over many generations, who began town service in their teens or very early twenties in such minor posts as swine keeper or constable, there is absolutely no record of Adam How until the year 1790 when he would have been 27 years old. This may be a significant gap.

Third, Adam married unusually late for a man of his time. His marriage to Jerusha Balcom did not take place until December 3, 1795, when Adam was 32 years old.

Fourth, the name of Adam's oldest son, Lyman, suggests that his father may have visited Warwickshire and examined some old records there. Lyman is an unusual name which does not show in Sudbury Howe family records until after Lyman's birth. What caused Adam to give this name to his son? We touch on this in our discussion of the parish of St. Nicholas, Appendix B.

If we suppose that Adam How, between the ages of 17 and 27, *did* return to the mother country and visit the county of Warwickshire, he may have met Coles or his family there and have suggested to Coles that he emigrate to Boston at the turn of the century, assuming this Coles was the first member of his family to come to America, which, as previously discussed, he may not have been. Adam could also have become acquainted with the family of the Englishman, who later visited the tavern and became acquainted with Adam's daughter, Jerusha, and engaged to marry her.

Jerusha's life and personality also give color to the theory that Adam How may have gone to England as a young man. Jerusha was born just after Ezekiel's death in 1797. Adam brought her up to love the things he loved. She was devoted to the history of her family and to English associations. She painted a copy of the coat of arms and made a careful pen and ink family tree. She fell in love with an Englishman and refused to consider local swains after he jilted her. She was musical and artistic and a cut above country society in Sudbury, yearning for refinement and aristocracy. She had wistful delusions of grandeur. She was the apple of her father's eye. "We are the music makers, we are the dreamers of dreams..."

Whether or not he met Coles in England or not, if Adam *did* visit Warwickshire in a quest for his ancestry, he would have returned to Sudbury full of enthusiasm about his travels and things English. Whether he was gone six months, a year or longer, his impressionable mind would have been affected.

The coat of arms must have been painted, copied or otherwise obtained before the fall of 1796 when it is first mentioned. The next mention of it is in 1826 when Rev. Allen wrote about it. We suspect that Adam How figures in both these incidents, first as a young man just back from England, second as an established innkeeper of middle age.

Regardless of whether Adam How went to England and met Coles there, travelled in the Vale of the Red Horse and examined old records for St. Nicholas parish, Coles himself, who was an expert on Warwickshire, unquestionably knew the Vale of the Red Horse well. He would have seen the Red Horse of Tysoe on more than one occasion and probably drunk ale at the Red Horse Tavern, or Sunrising, which was in its heyday in the eighteenth century. Coles started his professional life as a painter of signboards, and it is not hard to imagine that

Ezekiel or Adam might have asked him to design an appropriate new signboard for the inn at the same time that he created the How coat or arms. What could be more appropriate to an artist than the combination of a Warwickshire crest and a signboard with a proud horse, straight from the ancient red earth and folklore of the same old county? All three men would have been pleased.

There is no record of a red horse swinging in the wind before the end of the eighteenth centry, and the one that Ezekiel put up may have looked very much like the Red Horse of Tysoe. The tavern may never have been *officially* named. A sign with a red horse was put up one day and How's place was recognized by travellers along the road as 'at the sign of the Red Horse.' And so it remained.

Everyone must draw their own conclusions about the theories discussed and the questions raised in this chapter. Bits of knowledge, individual imagination and personal approaches to history will come into play.

If one examines Drayton's seventeenth century map closely, as part of this chapter, one enters an Alice-in-Wonderland world where speculation and wild surmise are one's travelling companions in a journey through the 'Woodland of Warwickshyre.' Why is there a river named Cole? Was the name 'Dunsmore' from Dunsmore Heath transferred to a boarding School for young ladies, run by Miss Sarah Howe in the nineteenth century? Did a young boy wander as far as the Edge Hills on a fine summer day, not realizing his countrymen would be at war there a few years later? Did the How family walk from Brinklow to Tysoe to watch the ceremony of scouring the Red Horse at the Palm Sunday festival every year and remember this huge animal on the hillside over centuries? Did a new generation of Hows in the New World take the name of their tavern from this Vale of the Red Horse? In a county circled with rivers, did a young man's imagination follow their path to the sea?

XIII

"Alas, No Longer An Inn!"

Henry Wadsworth Longfellow was still in mourning that bright October day in 1862 when his publisher James T. Fields suggested a drive in the country to the Red Horse Tavern. His wife had burned to death in a tragic accident at Craigie House the previous spring, and he hadn't written a word since that time.

Fields and many of his other friends were trying to get Longfellow's mind off the tragedy by encouraging him to pick up his pen once more, and they appeared to be succeeding. The poet's curiosity was stirred by the tales his friend Luigi Monti told of spending summers at this run-down hostelry surrounded by colorful country characters and many of his Cambridge friends and neighbors.

Longfellow tells of the visit in his journal:

> 31st. October ends with a delicious Indian summer day. Drive with Fields to the old Red Horse Tavern in Sudbury— alas, no longer an inn! A lovely valley; the winding road shaded by grand old oaks before the house. A rambling, tumble-down old building, two hundred years old; and til now in the family of the Howes, who have kept an inn for one hundred and seventy five years. In the old time, it was a house of call for all travellers from Boston westward.[1]

It was indeed an inn no longer, although Orin Dadmun, who rented the property from the heirs of Lyman Howe, and lived there as a widower until 1878, maintained a hostess and appears occasionally to have put up guests for a time. Dadmun may have been responsible for changing the dates on the signboard—the 1716 following David How's initials to 1686. Frank Noyes put forward a theory that Dadmun may, in barn or attic, have run across a faded copy of Peter King's deed of sale to Samuel How for Lot # 50 of the New Grant in the year 1676, mistaken the date for 1686 and had it painted in error on the sign.[2]

A few days after this visit to the Inn, Longfellow wrote a postcard of thanks to a Miss Eaton, who was living at the Inn and serving as a hostess at that time:

> Dear Madam, I delivered safely into Professor Treadwell's hands the cane which you gave me and he seemed much gratified at your kind remembrances. Speaking of the old Inn, he said that on one of the parlor window panes were written some verses with a date. Would you be so kind as to copy them for me? Or any names and dates written on the windows. At Mr. How Brown's* we saw the Coat of Arms and the old clock. I remain, Dear Madam, Yours truly. Henry W. Longfellow.
>
> P.S. Both Mr. Fields and myself feel much obliged. [3]

There are two other entries in Longfellow's journal for the fall of 1862 that indicate that the poet had the title of the poem in mind long before it was finalized in print just prior to publication. On October 11 he writes: "Write a little on the Wayside Inn. A beginning only."

And on November 18: "A lovely day—the latest Indian summer. Finished the 'Prelude' to the Wayside Inn." [4]

Longfellow was an accomplished poet, sensitive to atmosphere and his observations found their way into his poetry. The Prelude to the tales, which he finished on November 18, 1862, gives us a picture of what the Inn must have looked like a year and a half after Lyman Howe's death:

> A kind of old Hobgoblin hall
> Now somewhat fallen to decay
> With weather stains upon the walls
> And stairways worn and crazy doors
> And creaking and uneven floors,
> And chimneys huge and tiled and tall....
>
> ———————————
>
> A region of repose it seems,
> A place of slumber and of dreams,
> Remote among the wooded hills!
> As ancient is this hostelry
> As any in the land may be,

---

*This "Mr. How Brown" is undoubtedly Israel How Brown, who was a well-known figure in the town of Sudbury and lived opposite the Wadsworth Cemetery. Barbara Eaton Deveneau, Assistant Innkeeper at the date of writing, has told us that her great-grandmother, Alice Howe Jones Parmenter, remembered meeting Longfellow at the home of her grandfather, Israel How Brown, at the age of nine, on the occasion when Longfellow came to see the clock and the coat of arms on the same October day he visited the Inn in 1862.

> Built in the old Colonial day
> When men lived in a grander way
> With ampler hospitality... [5]

The writing of the tales was accomplished against a background of mental anguish. The first part was written in the fall of 1862 while Longfellow was still mourning his first wife. The poem was finished in the summer and fall of 1863 in the midst of the Civil War. Longfellow told of new personal troubles in a letter to a friend in England:

> December 28, 1863. Since I wrote you, I have been through a great deal of trouble and anxiety. My oldest boy, not yet 20, is a lieutenant of cavalry in the Army of the Potomac. Early in the summer he was taken down with camp fever, and did not rejoin his regiment until September. In the last battle on the Rapidan, he was shot through both shoulders with a rifle ball and had a very narrow escape of it...The two anxious journeys to the army to bring him back and the watching and waiting have not done me much good or left me much time for other things. However, I have managed to get a volume of poems through the press and have requested the London publishers to send you a copy.... [6]

That volume of poems was *Tales of a Wayside Inn*, which was very nearly published under the title *The Sudbury Tales*. After a discussion with his good friend Charles Sumner, Longfellow wrote to his publisher James Fields on August 25, 1863, while the book was at the printers:

"I am afraid we have made a mistake in calling the new volume 'The Sudbury Tales.' Now that I see it announced, I do not like the title. Sumner cries out against it and has persuaded me, as I think he will you, to come back to the Wayside Inn. Pray, think as we do." [7]

Longfellow and Sumner prevailed, and the book was rechristened and released on November 25, 1863. Longfellow marked the occasion in his journal:

"November 25, 1863. Published today by Ticknor and Fields, *Tales of a Wayside Inn*; fifteen thousand copies. The publishers dined with me, also Sumner and Greene." [8]

The book received a favorable review in the *New York Times* of December 5, 1863: "The pleasant fiction of a company of guests at a village inn, which has been a favorite framework with so many eminent writers of narrative both in poetry and prose, is here turned to excellent account by the dainty pen of Mr. Longfellow.'' Just after Christmas the same year, Dr. Thomas Parsons, the poet of the *Tales*, wrote Longfellow in great excitement from the Inn, which he had already rechristened:

> Wayside Inn
> Sunday after Christmas
> December 27, 1863

> Carissimo Poeta,
>   Ecomi quia! In my old house again, which even amid this gloom and wreck of winter seems now so pleasantly associated with your name that it is greatly relieved of many sad memories—such as all inns are liable to on this sad wayside of life....I could not forbear the pleasure of sitting down in Miss Eaton's chamber and asking for a pen and paper that I might tell you with what delight she had read your new volume—much of which she has repeated to me by heart—I can...assure you that in Howe's Tavern the book is an overwhelming success...I say so in Sudbury at the 'Red Horse.' [9]

In March of the following year, some four months later, Parsons wrote his friend again: ''Letters from Luigi [Monti] tell me that he has received a copy of the 'Wayside Inn' which my sister [Frances Parsons Monti] had sent by the Govt. Despatch Bag. He is full of delight and has written to you, he says, to express his admiration....'' [10]

Longfellow's little book of poems not only delighted readers all over the world, it also aroused their curiosity. Who were the tellers of the tales? Were they real people or figments of the poet's imagination? Had they actually met at the old inn? Soon after the poem's publication, Longfellow wrote to a friend:

''The Wayside Inn has more foundation in fact than you may suppose. The place is just as I have described it...all the characters are real...the Musician is Ole Bull....'' [11]

The Musician may have been modeled on Ole Bull, but this famous Norwegian violinist never visited the Inn. Neither did Isaac Edrehi, the Spanish Jew. But these were the only two. Thomas Parsons, the Poet of the Tales, Luigi Monti, the Young Sicilian, and Henry Ware Wales, the Student, had all visited the tavern many times in Lyman Howe's day. Professor Treadwell, the Theologian, was the member of the Cambridge group that first discovered it and brought the others to Sudbury for summer sojurns.

The most complete, and probably the most valid account of how this group formed and was interrelated, both personally and professionally, came from the pen of Elena di Majo, the daughter of Luigi Monti. On August 29, 1923, she wrote William M. Emery of New Bedford from Rome:

Dear Sir:
   The person who really discovered the Wayside Inn, if one may say discovered, was Prof. Treadwell, who one summer was hunting for a quiet place for his invalid wife, and he came to the Wayside at Sudbury. He was a long-standing friend of the Parsons family, so that year my mother Francis A. Parsons, then not married but engaged to my father, and her two sisters passed the summer at that spot and were so happy and pleased that they went there every summer.
   My father spent the Saturday to Monday at the Inn, going back either to Cambridge or Boston, where he kept up giving lessons at Harvard. He went regularly once a week to drive with Mr. Longfellow, and thus he told him of his happy gatherings, and the stories which were told in the evenings at the Inn.
   My uncle, Dr. Thomas W. Parsons, as you of course have heard, was a great lover of Dante, and dedicated most of his life to translating part of the *Divina Comedia.*
   My mother was born in Boston and was a true Bostonian. My parents were married June 21, 1855. I was born in Boston at 1 Beacon St., then called the Albion. My father was still professor at Cambridge. During that summer, my mother went to the Wayside Inn as always, and the year after, my father being nominated U.S. consul at Palermo, they sailed for Sicily.
   I am the only child living. My two sisters died in early youth. The happy days my father spent at the Wayside Inn were often told me by my mother who was a guest there with her sisters and father as often as possible—the vacations, of course, he passed them there.
   In my mother's family, there were Ellen Parsons who married Dr. Parks and died three weeks after the wedding, Frances A. Parsons, my mother, and last, Adeline, who married Mr. George Lunt. My cousin Francesca Lunt and I are the only surviving offspring. Francesca married in New York, twenty five years ago, an Englishman.
                                          Very Sincerely Yours,
                                          Elena di Majo. [12]

At the time of his visits to the Inn, Monti, a Palermo refugee, was teaching Italian in the Department of Modern Languages at Harvard, a job which Longfellow helped him obtain. George Lunt was a well-known Boston publisher. He and his wife, Adeline Parsons Lunt, both wrote about visits to the Inn during Lyman Howe's time. Ole Bull was a personal friend of Longfellow and a frequent guest at Craigie House.

Dr. John van Schaick, Jr., in his book *The Characters in the Tales of a Wayside Inn*, reveals the real identity of the musician who played for Treadwell's group at the Inn by quoting from this enlightening letter to the *New York Times* of July 24, 1923, from J. William Fosdick of Gloucester, a friend of Monti and his wife:

> On cool autumnal nights the Inn family used to gather about the old fireplace, where they would roast apples and pop corn, tell stories or listen to the fiddling of a farm hand whom they invited in to make things lively. Upon his return to Cambridge, Monti graphically described all these incidents to Mr. Longfellow, and the poet settled upon the idea of the convivial storytellers, the great fireplace, the fiddler etc. and set about writing the famous creation of the Wayside Inn...the real musician of the Wayside Inn was the humble farm hand who used to help them roast their apples and pop their corn. [13]

Henry Wadsworth Longfellow would not cross the threshold of the Wayside Inn again in his lifetime, but his two brief visits and his little book of poems accomplished a great deal. The days of the old place being "alas, no longer an inn," would be short indeed.

XIV

"Into The Hands of Strangers"

The November 16, 1861 issue of the *Mass Ploughman* signalled the end of an era. In a terse announcement in its advertising section was the following item: "To be sold by Public Auction in pursuance of a license from the Probate Court for the County of Middlesex as much of the Real Estate of Lyman Howe, late of Sudbury, deceased, as will raise the sum of sixty-six hundred and sixteen dollars and one cent for the payments of the debts of said deceased and charge of administration...."[1]

Lyman Howe, the last of four generations of his family to run the How Tavern, lay dead and buried in the Wadsworth Cemetery which he had helped enlarge and dedicate, leaving behind a financial nightmare. He had made no will, was deeply in debt to Warren Nixon, and the old building that had been started by his great-grandfather David How and enlarged by each successive generation, was badly in need of repair.[2]

Nixon, anxious to make sure he got the money due him as speedily as possible, petitioned to be appointed administrator of the estate on April 23, little more than a month after Lyman's death. On May 1, 1861 Stephen Morse of Marlborough, James Moore, and Ephraim Stone of Sudbury were appointed to appraise the estate. The total inventory came to $12,885.

The sale was to start on December 16 and continue the following day if necessary. In addition to the contents of the house, certain lots of land on the property—pastures and shed lots—and sizeable amounts of firewood were to be sold. More than 100 acres of these "lots" were involved with their sale scheduled for the following March. There is an ominous addition to the notice: "If further sales should be required, they will be made of parts of the homestead...."[3]

Further sales did not prove to be necessary. The property sold for $161.87 over its appraised value, more than enough to satisfy the petitioner Warren Nixon.

Although legends of rare and unusual items being gavelled down to wealthy fanciers of antiques still persist, most observers at the time saw the sale as only an ordinary one. Sudbury historian A.S. Hudson, whose *History of Sudbury* was published 29 years after Lyman's death, adds this insight:

> ...marvelous stories have already been told of the auction that followed the death of Squire Lyman Howe, but these stories are extravagant. A few articles that were rare or relic-like may have been sold, but, for the most part, it was only a commonplace sale at the inn where the landlord died. Probably the house was largely depleted of what it once contained. The family was never one of great wealth and the circumstances attending the life of the last landlord would naturally scatter many of the furnishings of the old-time inn. [4]

With Lyman's debts finally settled, the property was inherited by Rebecca Balcom Puffer, sister of Jerusha Balcom Howe, Adam's wife and Lyman's aunt. She was a very old lady at the time of Lyman's passing and died herself soon afterward, leaving the property to her two sons, Winthrop and Freeman Puffer. It remained in possession of various branches of the Puffer family until 1893, when Lucy Ann Puffer (Mrs. Augustus) Newton sold it to S. Herbert Howe, former Mayor of Marlborough, and Homer Rogers of Sudbury, who functioned as joint owners for four years before selling the entire property to Edward R. Lemon, who opened it once more as an inn. [5]

During these 34 years and throughout the many changes of ownership, the old house was rented to a procession of tenants, several of whom opened up the building for dances, tours and sleighing parties, but did not accommodate overnight guests on a regular basis.

The first of these was Orin Dadmun, a local man and a widower who moved in shortly after the sale in 1861 and remained until 1878, when he married Mary Parmenter and moved to his mother's old house with his new wife, making way for his nephew Lafayette Dadmun and his family.

For eleven years, Mr. and Mrs. Dadmun, their children, Archie and Hallie, a mastiff named Tige, several teams and a carriage horse named Woodchuck held forth at the old house, upon occasion taking in boarders. They were followed by Mr. and Mrs. H.C. Seymour, who functioned as caretakers from 1889 until 1897.

There are a few scant reminders of the quiet days when the Dadmuns were living at the Inn in the 1870's. In April, 1929, Edward Bennett wrote his recollections as a young man:

> In 1871 or 1872, Mr. Frank Bowditch of Framingham and Mr. Edward Bennett of Southborough, while going over the Inn , found the old ballroom filled with broken furniture...they cleaned the room and for the next two or three years had all their parties and dances there...then it became too popular and they dropped it. At that time, the floor was so worn that the nails were driven down and the floor planed. [6]

Cyrus Felton, writing about "Remarkable Events in Marlborough and Neighboring Towns," adds this reminiscence:

"On September 1, 1871, many persons by the name of Howe and relatives of the Howe family, visited the old Howe Tavern. It was the day after the great Howe Gathering at Harmony Grove, Framingham." [7]

Gilman Howe, the editor of Judge Daniel Wait Howe's book, *Howe Genealogies*, refers to this event in his Preface. He explains that the family gathering, which numbered more than 1,000 people, was the original impetus for Judge Howe's "stupendous task" of compiling the Howe family tree which took more than 40 years. Soon after the gathering, Judge Howe wrote the following preface to an early effort:

> On August 1, 1871, a meeting of the Howes in this country was held at Harmony Grove, Framingham, Mass. Everyone bearing the name of Howe was invited to be present and to bring any ancient records or relics pertaining to the family, which they might possess. A very large attendance was the result of this invitation and it was at this meeting that the project was started of having a genealogy of the Howe family published and an effort was made to collect the material necessary for that purpose, but after about a year, the work ceased, principally due to lack of funds. [8]

A large amount of material was obtained as a result of the Howe Family Gathering and was preserved by Willard Howe of South Framingham, Mass. Mr. Willard Howe later placed these records at the service of Judge Howe, who declared them to be "really the beginning and foundation"[9] of his work.

In 1874, Samuel Adams Drake published his *Old Landmarks, Historic Fields and Mansions of Middlesex*. This included an eloquent chapter on the Wayside Inn, which prompted Edwin

Mead to tell his readers years later that Drake was "the most sympathetic guide to the...inn after the poet himself...."[10] Drake is not only recalling the Inn as he saw it in Orin Dadmun's time, but is writing a nostalgia piece about an earlier era:

> It stands in a sequestered nook among the hills which upheave the neighboring region like ocean billows. For nearly two hundred years, during the greater part of which it has been occupied as a tavern, this ancient hostelry has stood here with its door hospitably open to wayfarers.
>
> In the olden time the road possessed the importance of a much-travelled highway. At present the house is like a waif on the seashore, left high and dry by some mighty tide, or a landmark which shows where the current of travel once flowed. Its distance from the capital made it a convenient halting place for travellers going into or returning from Boston. Its reputation for good cheer was second to none in all the Bay Colony.
>
> Coming from the direction of Marlborough, at a little distance, the gambreled roof of the Wayside Inn peeps above a dense mass of foliage. A sharp turn of the road, which once passed under a triumphal arch composed of two lordly elms, and you are before the house itself. On the other side of the broad space left for the road are the capacious barns and outhouses belonging to the establishment and, standing there like a blazed tree in a clearing, but bereft of its ancient symbol, the sight of which gladdened the hearts of many a weary traveller, is also the old sign-post.
>
> Everything remains as of old. There is the bar in one corner of the common room, with its wooden portcullis, made to be hoisted or let down at pleasure but over which never appeared the ominous announcement 'No liquors sold over this bar.' The little desk where the tipplers' score was set down, and the old escritoire, looking as if it might have come from some hospital for decayed and battered furniture, are there now. The bare floor, which once received its regular morning sprinkling of clean white sea sand, the bare beams and timbers overhead from which the whitewash has fallen in flakes, and the very oak of which is seasoned with the spicy flavors steaming from pewter flagons, all remind us of the good old days before the flood of new ideas. Governors, magistrates, generals, with scores of others whose names are remembered with honor, have been here to quaff a health or indulge in a drinking bout.

In the guest's room on the left of the entrance, the window pane bears the following recommendation, cut with a gem that sparkled on the finger of that young roysterer, William Molineaux, Jr., whose father was the man that walked beside the king's troops in Boston to save them from the insults of the townspeople—the friend of Otis and John Adams:

What do you think
Here is good drink
Perhaps you may not know it;
If not in haste, do stop and taste
You merry folk will show it.
Wm. Molineaux Jr. Esq.
24th June 1774 Boston

The writer's hand became unsteady at the last line and it looks as though his rhyme had halted while he turned to some companion for a hint or, what is perhaps more likely, here gave manual evidence of the potency of his draughts.

A ramble through the house awakens many memories. You are shown the travellers room which they of lesser note occupied in common, and the state chamber where Washington and Lafayette are said to have rested. In the garret, the slaves were accommodated and the crooknecks and red peppers hung from the rafters. Unfortunately the old blazonry and other interesting items have disappeared under the auctioneer's hammer.

Conducted by the presiding genius of the place, Mr. Dadmun, we passed from room to room and into the dance hall, annexed to the ancient building. The dais at the end for the fiddlers, the wooden benches fixed to the walls, the floor smoothly polished by many joyous feet, and the modest effort at ornament, displayed the theatre where many a long winter's night had worn away into the morn ere the company dispersed to their beds, or the jangle of bells on the frosty air betokened the departure of the last of the country belles... The place is silent now and there is no music, except you hear through the open windows the flute-like notes of the wood thrush where he sits carolling a love-ditty to his mate. [11]

Apparently some of the tenants at the Inn between 1862 and 1897 made extra money by conducting tours and letting out the ballroom for dances and parties. Alfred Williams Anthony of Providence, Rhode Island writes of a drive to the Inn from Concord in 1880 when he was a sophomore at Brown University. He was travelling with a friend, Howard W. Preston:

At two o'clock Dodge was harnessed and waiting. Sudbury is seven miles off and we know that somewhere in its vicinity is the 'Wayside Inn' made famous by Longfellow's pen...the road to Sudbury is very good though grass-grown, appearing but little used...in South Sudbury we drew up before a large gambrel roofed house, unmistakably an aged settler. The veritable 'Wayside Inn' was before us!

We hitched Dodge beside the barn across the road and having drawn a draught of water from the long-handled pump, approached the door no longer left open for travelling guests, but kindly opened by the lady of the place, for it is now used as a farm house...the woman took us first into the tavern sitting room...the windows are low and the panes of glass small, the size which is usually found in houses of great age...two panes of glass have been removed and framed.

We passed into what used to be the bar-room, now used as a kitchen...the timbers show overhead and this is the only room which did not have a smooth ceiling...the woman conducted us all over the house from attic to cellar...over the dining room on the second floor is the old guest chamber where, we were told, Washington and Lafayette had slept-...the walls are covered by a very old style of paper, figured with the blue bells of Scotland...

The attic is mostly unfinished showing the rafters of the roof...one of the rooms was used for suspicious characters, those who looked seedy and unclean so our guide informed us...next beyond is an unfinished room where slaves used to be quartered when travelling with their masters.

We were accommodated with bread, crackers, milk, cake and berries in the old dining room...on settling our bill the charges were ten cents apiece for being shown around the place and ten cents for the milk, a total of thirty cents....[12]

Four years later, a schoolmistress named Lucie Welsh boarded at the Inn for a winter term during the tenancy of Lafayette Dadmun and his family and later wrote vividly of her experiences in Sudbury. Her account was discovered by her niece Mrs. Henry Sewell, and published in the *News Enterprise* in October, 1952.

Fresh from Framingham Normal School (now Framingham State College), Miss Welsh eagerly accepted a teaching post for the winter term in Sudbury's Southwest District, because it gave her the chance to live at the Wayside Inn "with its historical and literary background," for two dollars and a half a week.

"It was the Dadmuns who lived at the Inn in those days," she recalled. "And it was simply a private house with perhaps a dancing party on Saturday nights to which Mrs. Dadmun would serve an oyster stew...Mr. Dadmun was a teamster and had several horses in the barn opposite the house.

"The Dadmuns were kind and friendly people doing all they could to make me comfortable. It was no fault of theirs that the Inn was a cold storage plant and the Lafayette room with its open fireplace was a cold freeze compartment in which the hot water brought me in the morning was promptly frozen and covered with ice...."[13]

On the first day of the term, Miss Welsh breakfasted with Archie and Hallie Dadmun who would be her pupils later on that day, and then walked with them to the schoolhouse on Peakham Road a little more than a mile away. On the way, the boys told stories of how tramps often snuck into empty rooms of the Inn on cold winter nights and started fires in the old fireplaces to ward off the chill.

Miss Welsh had eight students and put in a long day from 8 a.m. to 4 p.m. She walked to and fro from school except in very bad weather, when Archie Dadmun, the older son, would fetch her with a small rig drawn by his horse Woodchuck. She was met at the door by Mrs. Dadmun each night.

"The doors at either end of the broad hall were kept bolted, locked and barred at all times," she recalled. "The ritual of admitting me to the inn was followed each night of my residence there. I would hear the bolt toward the upper panel of the door as it slipped back, then the heavy key...and finally the oak bar across the door was removed...the door opened to disclose my hostess with Tige, the big mastiff, at her side. Larger than an ordinary calf, he was distinctly Mrs. Dadmun's dog and was treated with respect by the rest of the family including Mr. Dadmun himself.

"In those days the public road passed directly in front of the house and the well and pump by the doorstone was used by teamsters, stragglers, tramps and passers-by of all sorts. Mrs. Dadmun was alone all day and was naturally a timid soul...in a short time she imbued me with her own fears.

"I remember walking alone from school one night with three tramps behind me and two more only a short distance ahead of me. Worse yet were the occasional droves of cattle being driven to Brighton to the slaughter houses. They did frighten me terribly...the bars, bolts and heavy keys are still on the doors of the Inn. They are...still in use."[14]

After an old-fashioned hearty dinner, Mrs. Dadmun took her lodger to Miss Jerusha's sitting room "away from the boys and the rest of us" and warned her that her husband occasionally got together with his cronies and drank too much hard cider. "When he comes home he is not always quite himself," she said. "He is all right if you do not cross him." Miss Welsh made it a point to comply.

"Miss Jerusha...was company for me during those solitary evenings," she wrote. "I liked to think of Miss Jerusha who had sat here for so many years, helping her brother to manage the affairs of the Inn. I visualized her as a tall, well-built woman, dressed in figured silk or cotton and wearing a hoop skirt...if the moon shone into the room it was filled with eerie shadows. On a dark night, anything or anybody might be just behind waiting for me...."[15]

Miss Welsh's association with the Inn was a short one. By the end of winter, she had succeeded well enough in quelling a variety of insurrections with her small and unruly class to be asked to continue. During the spring term she lived with widow Lorenzo Parmenter whose home was closer to the schoolhouse. The following year she was asked to take on the school in the center of town.

Mr. and Mrs. Horace Seymour replaced the Dadmuns as tenants in 1889 and stayed on until 1897 when S. Herbert Howe and Homer Rogers, who had bought the property from Lucy Puffer Newton in 1893, sold out to Edward R. Lemon. They continued the tradition of showing visitors around the house for a ten cent fee and used the old ball room as spare sleeping quarters for the hired men of the neighborhood. An article appearing in the September 4, 1892 edition of the *New York Tribune* sets the scene:

> From whichever direction you approach the house, be it from east or west, the Inn is the most conspicuous object in your view...yellowish-brown sides and gambrel roof, well-shaded by an enormous elm tree from which, in the old days, the sign of the red horse hung to tempt the travellers.
>
> The woman who greets you on your immediate entrance is by no means a typical English landlady. She is plain Mrs. Seymour, the wife of a most estimable farmer who 'lows that 'them poets and fellers havin' once been in their house don't

help keep the wind out in winter nor buy beef for the family...' If Mr. Seymour were wiser in his methods the fact that he lives in the Wayside Inn would help him materially to buy beef for the family. But the ridiculously small price of ten cents is charged to be 'shown round,' and Mrs. Seymour, who does the showing round, confines herself to gospel facts which, in themselves, are too few and if it were not for talks with some of the old men in the adjacent town one would go away rather sparsely informed as to the various traditions which centre in this famous tavern.

But Mrs. Seymour knows the special history of each room well and has apparently committed it to memory to judge by the easy and voluble manner in which she rattles it off.*

The bar-room, although now made use of as a paltry modern kitchen, is eminently suggestive...what can not a man with keen imagination picture to himself...on the great iron staple were thrown the chains of a prisoner whenever a constable had one in his charge and had occasion to stop there for refreshments and while thus loosely confined, some cakes and a mug of ale would be thrust into his hands....

Perhaps the most interesting thing in the reception room is the How coat of arms†, the original copy of which, gaudily engrossed on linen, rests carelessly on the mantle...That more people do not come to see the house seems strange for it is easily accessible from Boston and Worcester...There surely could be no more interesting or charming place...than the old Red Horse Tavern of Sudbury....

---

*Henry Ford's Inn manager, Mr. Earl Boyer, arranged for Mr. and Mrs. Seymour to give him an exact room by room description of the Inn during the years of their tenancy, prior to any of the changes made by Mr. Lemon. This was done early in Ford's ownership and was an important source for those who were restoring the Inn for Ford. Mrs. Seymour had indeed learned all the history and local gossip.

†This is the first mention of a copy of the How coat of arms being in the Inn since the auction of Lyman Howe's estate in December of 1861. Drake makes a point of its *not* being on the premises when he was preparing his book in 1873. Whether Seymour found it in the attic or cellar, or was given a copy we do not know, but evidently he didn't consider it significant enough to mount on the wall. One clue as to when this might have happened is Alfred Williams Anthony's observation in 1880 that the two panes of glass inscribed by Molineaux had been removed from the window and framed. Drake remembered them still *in* the window frame in 1873. Perhaps Orin Dadmun, late in his tenure, or Lafayette Dadmun and his wife, decided to play up the building's historic interest for visitors sometime in the seven-year period between 1873 and 1880. They framed the window panes and replaced the coat of arms as talking points for tourists.

Atherton Rogers, the father of Mrs. Forrest Bradshaw of Sudbury, purchased the property from Mrs. Newton in 1893 for S. Herbert Howe of Marlborough and Homer Rogers and helped run it for four years. In 1917 he wrote down his recollections of the town during the preceding sixty years, which included several interesting periods in the Inn's history. He starts out by describing the building as it looked in his boyhood:

> The rooms had fireplaces and were low with the big beams encased and sides sheathed up part way from the floor. Squire How was there and had a housekeeper and Buckley Parmenter was the man of all work. The old bar room could tell of wonderful times if it could speak...I purchased the Inn in 1893 of Mrs. Newton, one of the original Howes, for Ex-Mayor S. Herbert Howe of Marlborough and Hon. Homer Rogers of Boston, a Sudbury boy.
>
> I had charge of the place one season and we changed the old driveway barn so the hill in front of the house might be seen...Parties from Concord, Marlborough, Framingham and other places would come and dance in the old hall and Mr. Seymour and I would set the tables and serve the lunch they would bring with them. We had tables, chairs, linen, crockery, but no food only what was brought by parties.
>
> Over the old bar we served soft drinks and cigars...also ...the book, *The Tales of the Wayside Inn*. Over four thousand registered between May and December, people from all over the world.[16]

In the last decade of the nineteenth century a flood of nostalgic articles about the Inn began to appear in books and magazines. Among the authors was Edwin D. Mead, previously mentioned, who expressed anxiety about the old building's future in a long and impassioned article in the *New England Magazine* which included the following plea:

> How beautiful and fitting and wise a thing it would be for the sons of Sudbury as they celebrate their two hundred and fiftieth birthday of their historic town, to secure their most historic and interesting building for the public use and enjoyment!...It is a thing in which lovers of our sweet Cambridge poet, and all lovers of what is historic and what stands for true and beautiful sentiment in New England should be glad to help; and no memorial could be conceived so fitting, so fortunate, so attractive and so impressive as this restored Wayside Inn would be in the old town of Sudbury!

"Clearly the Wayside Inn is not without proper appreciation in Sudbury itself, and we do not doubt that the Sudbury people can be trusted to properly preserve their precious possession, and in due time put it to the highest and most beautiful use. The time will certainly come when the sign of the Red Horse will swing before it once again, and pilgrims from near and from far, from Boston, Sicily and Alicant, students, musicians, theologians, poets, shall gather in the autumn evenings around its blazing fires, enjoyers of a finer hospitality than any known of yore."[17]

Mead's message did not fall on deaf ears. Not long after his article appeared in print, he received a letter, forwarded from the magazine's Boston office. It said in part:

...That old Wayside Inn and my furniture ought to go together. I wondered if the place could be bought at any reasonable price and went up to see. I bought it and am moving up my furniture.[18]

It was signed Edward Rivers Lemon.

XV

"A Finer Hospitality than Any Known Of Yore"

House Which Longfellow Made Famous to be Re-Opened. The Ancient Structure in Sudbury Has Been Purchased by E.R. Lemon of Malden....He Will Restore Every Nook and Corner in Detail....Many Historic Relics to be Added," joyfully announced the *Boston Herald* on page one of its January 29, 1897 issue.

The rumors that had been spreading around the town for most of the winter were finally confirmed. On January 27, 1897, the Middlesex County Registry of Deeds records that Edward R. Lemon purchased "'a tract of land with buildings thereon, known as the 'Wayside Inn Estate' situated in the westerly part of the town of Sudbury in the county of Middlesex, containing 32 acres and 14 rods more or less...'" from S. Herbert Howe of Marlborough and Homer Rogers.

Whether he was motivated by Mead's turn-of-the-century articles, his own love of history, art and antiques, or by pressure from friends, Lemon's move to give the old tavern a new lease on life could not have come at a better time and caused great excitement in the press and among the public.

"The first of April it will again be opened as literally a wayside inn and restored in every nook and corner to such a detail that should the ancestors of many a prominent Boston family or suburbanite accidentally drop in there, they would welcome the sight with unfeigned delight," the *Herald* continued.

"The structure has been purchased by Mr. Edward R. Lemon of Malden, a descendant of old New England families and a collector of articles of historic value," the *Herald* account went on. "Mr. Lemon will add many features of historic interest to the inn and at the same time all the old features will be observed. He has the old Howe coat of arms which will be hung as originally....Mr. Lemon has hundreds of old curiosities which he will place in the tavern...the old Wayside Inn...

promises to be one of the greatest places of historical interest in New England...."

Lemon was a man of his word. A wealthy wool merchant connected with the Sawyer Woolen Mills of Dover, New Hampshire, he instantly hired workmen to begin the task of renovating and repairing the old building in anticipation of an early spring opening. Evidently he succeeded, as the following article appeared in a Sunday edition of the *Herald* the following July under the headline: "The Famous Wayside Inn is Becoming the Mecca for Literary Pilgrims."[1]

"The old Howe Tavern is becoming a veritable Canterbury for literary pilgrims. Reopened as a summer resort, it has made the town of Sudbury a very popular place. Though the season is still young, over a thousand pilgrims have found their way to the Wayside hostelry...

"A great transformation has taken place in the inward appearance of the tavern. The rooms are now enriched by countless examples of antique furniture and china, paintings and bric-a-brac worth several thousand dollars. The present host of this tavern, Mr. Edward Lemon, has been collecting these articles for a number of years.

"Among those of historic interest are the Howe coat of arms alluded to in the 'Tales of a Traveller' [one wonders where the *Herald* came up with that title for Longfellow's poem], a mirror owned by Squire Lyman Howe, the landlord in Longfellow's time; a window pane written on by Major William Molineaux and now carefully framed; a bureau used by Squire Howe, a thimble of Miss Jerusha, sister to Squire Lyman Howe...."[2]

Through the next 26 years, Lemon labored long and hard to live up to these tributes. He became a resident landlord, moving his family into a suite of rooms in the rear of the house. One of his first decisions was to have a large woodshed to the east of the Inn connected to the old kitchen and converted to an art gallery to display some of his most precious paintings which included a portrait of his grandfather painted by Gilbert Stuart. We know it today as the Ford room.

Many items in Lemon's furniture collection were of great historical value in their own right. There was a chair once used by President John Adams and others from Admiral Farragut's flagship *Hartford* which sailed up the Mississippi River to bombard Vicksburg in 1862.

Lemon may have been an antiquarian by avocation, but he was also a businessman, and a good one at that. He attracted people to the Inn by emphasizing its age and centuries-old history and tradition. He changed its name to Longfellow's Wayside Inn, but also stressed its ties with the Howe family and the heritage of Colonial times. In the quarter century following the Civil War older roots were cherished. The War of Independence and families connected with it had immense appeal.

That appeal was enhanced on June 17, 1897 when the Society of Colonial Wars gathered several hundred strong on the grounds of the Inn to hear historian and orator Samuel Arthur Bent. Bent chose as his topic: "The Wayside Inn—Its History and Literature."

Bent's well-documented speech* dwelt on the long and colorful history of both Sudbury and the Inn. Bent had a sense of both scholarship and legend as well as a keen imagination for recreating a lost era. His description of the Inn in Ezekiel How's time is vivid and unusual—both accurate and intensely real.

Bent's preparations for his oration must have begun at about the same time as Lemon's purchase of the Inn. He was certainly aware of the background of events that led to that purchase and took it upon himself to fulfill an earlier prophecy. Looking out over the multitudes sitting in the shade of the great oaks near the Inn, he drew attention to Mead's article in the *New England Magazine* some seven years before:

> In these later years...hither began to wend their way pilgrims from this land and from all lands, until their number was swollen to thousands...many of whom had never heard of the Red Horse Tavern, but to all of whom the Wayside Inn has become a household word," he said. "And one wiser and more prescient than the rest wrote: 'The time will surely come when the sign of the Red Horse will swing again...and pilgrims from far and near...shall gather around the blazing fires, enjoyers of a finer hospitality than any known of yore.'
>
> And lo, the prophet's words fall true, and again the doors of the Wayside Inn fly open to the expected guests; the descendants of the men of earlier days recall around these tables 'the good old colony times'...Mr. Governor and fellow members, let me be your toast master today. Representing

*To those interested in the history of the How family or Sudbury's role in the Revolution, we recommend reading this address. It is available at the Sudbury Library.

indirectly four generations of worthy hosts, let me wish 'renewed prosperity, long, aye, a still longer life, to the Red Horse Tavern of ancient Sudbury!'[3]

As the five hundred members of the audience, including the Governor of the Commonwealth of Massachusetts, rose and cheered mightily as they realized they were taking part in the revival of a legend, Edward Rivers Lemon may have allowed himself a smug smile. The reputation of his new venture was assured.

Bent's address had wide coverage and crowds swelled the grounds and the rooms throughout the summer. Among the guests from all over the country and abroad were Mr. and Mrs. Henry Howard of Brookline. They recalled their October, 1897 visit some 29 years later when they returned to the Inn in 1926.

> In October, 1897 when we were living in Brookline, Massachusetts we came here in the first automobile ever seen at the Wayside Inn. It was a steamer car, built by George E. Whitney in South Boston. The car was well-built and reliable. It was exhibited in the winter of 1896-97 at the Bicycle Show in the Mechanics Fair Building, Boston, and gave the Stanley Brothers their inspiration to design and build the 'Stanley Steamer'—the first of which came out two years later.[4]

By the summer of 1898, the fame of the restored Wayside Inn had reached Europe and one of the principals of the *Tales*. In early August, Lemon received the following letter from Luigi Monti.

> Rome, July 4, 1898.
> I am delighted to learn that you have purchased the dear old house and 'carefully restored and put it back in its original condition'...It is very sad for me to think that I am the only living member of the happy company that used to spend their summer vacation there in the Fifties; yet I still hope that I may visit the old Inn once more before I rejoin those choice spirits whom Mr. Longfellow has immortalized in his great poem.
> I am glad that some of the old residents still remember me when I was a visitor there with Dr. Parsons [the Poet] and his sisters, one of whom, my wife, is also the only living member of those that used to assemble there...'The Musician' and 'the Spanish Jew', though not imaginary characters, were never guests at the Wayside Inn.
> Luigi Monti,
> The Young Sicilian[5]

This letter is quoted in Lauriston Bullard's book, *Historic Summer Haunts* which devoted a chapter to the Wayside Inn and concludes as follows:

> You may reach the inn by railroad train, stopping off at the little Wayside Station or you may motor from Boston or from Worcester, a few miles away. The walk from the station, a little more than a mile, is a more satisfactory approach than is the helter-skelter of the usual automobile trip. The walk takes you over a winding country road and through groves of oaks, pines and chestnuts, until, a few rods from the Inn, you emerge upon the oiled road, and soon sight the new Red Horse sign which swings before the hostelry. The splendid oaks near the house have been remarked by nearly all its guests. Dr. Parsons was in a special sense the poet of the inn, and of these trees he sang:
> "Ancient Druid never worshipped
> Beneath grander oaks than these;
> Never shadows richer, deeper,
> Than have cast these ancient trees."[6]

Guests of a cultural bent were what Lemon wanted. Actors, artists, students and professional people were welcomed and encouraged. The Paint and Clay Club, a group of artists, poets and writers which included Edward A. Filene, Quincy Kilby, Abbott Graves and Alfred Ordway, met there regularly; a group of Unitarian ministers calling themselves the "Fraters" held an annual retreat which still takes place each January.

Lemon was an admirer of Longfellow and he and his wife planned and created the Longfellow garden, which looks today much as it did in Lemon's time, with the famous bust of the poet copied from the one in the Poets Corner in Westminster Abbey.

Lemon did more than just repaint and erect a new Red Horse sign with the initials of all the How innkeepers and his own name on a supporter at the bottom. He also initiated construction of a gatehouse straddling the driveway to the east of the Inn using timbers said to have been salvaged from the old Sun Tavern in Watertown. Henry Ford later moved this building to its present location across the Boston Post Road from the Inn.

Lemon's restoration efforts continued with vigor, but the cost of the project, combined with fluctuations in the wool business, began to put him in a financial pinch. In June of 1902 he took a full-page advertisement in *Country Life in America*

Magazine offering the property for sale. The advertisment said in part:

> The Wayside Inn estate in its location twenty miles from Boston on the old County road now a macadamed boulevard, from which a fine private driveway runs in front of the Inn in its natural beauty and in its imperishable tradition offers an opportunity for a gentleman's country place that can nowhere be matched. It is not a place for a mere 'Money Bags' for he would have no appreciation for those memories which cluster about it, but for a gentleman of means and patriotic sentiment it is a place of all others.
>
> Correspondence or personal visit is invited by the owner Edward R. Lemon, the Wayside Inn, South Sudbury, Mass. or the Edward P. Hamilton Co., 96 Broadway, New York.
>
> "NOTE: Until sold, the Inn will be maintained as it has been for the past five years as a quiet and refreshing country inn for the entertainment of guests.
>
> E.R.L.

Whether he got any serious responses to his advertisement, we do not know, but evidently Lemon had a change of heart. Barely a month later he deeded the property to one Adolph F.A. Schulz, who, the very same day, made it over to Lemon's wife, Cora E. Lemon, who held it for the next 21 years.

Outwardly the Inn seemed to continue placidly and prosperously. The *Boston Herald* reported that 6,000 guests had been entertained in 1904 with all 48 states and several foreign countries represented on the guest register. As many as 50 automobiles a day were making the Inn their objective.

Joseph S. Seabury wrote up the Inn in the July 1914 issue of *House Beautiful*, saying that: ''There are few old New England houses and probably no early country taverns so faithfully and splendidly preserved as the Wayside Inn. Neither is there a country house hereabouts richer in history and tradition.''

In October, 1916, C.A. Lawrence added his accolades in *Arts and Decoration Magazine*, calling the Inn: ''One of the few unspoiled mansions built in rural New England during the seventeenth century,'' and telling of Lemon's finding sacks of potatoes stacked in the How dining room ''where both Washington and Lafayette had sat at meat.'' The only sticks of furniture Lemon found in the great rooms were an oil portrait of Lyman Howe, the tall tavern desk, and the massive and bolt-studded family safe that still sits beside the door leading to the Ford room.

But behind the hustle and bustle of a busy inn, Lemon's money problems continued. He had mortgaged the property soon after he purchased it in 1897 in order to finance restoration. In the four years that followed, 1897, '98, '99 and 1900, receipts exist for interest due on this mortgage which was held by Sarah Bailey. Her son, R.M. Bailey, was a Boston architect who had built Lemon a house in Malden and was a friend and colleague of some years standing.

The sums due were for small amounts—$112, $65 and similar sums, all carefully labelled "interest on mortgage." We have not been able to find a record of the exact amount of this mortgage but it would not appear that the interest owed, by itself, was a major source of financial trouble.

For several years, starting only a year after he bought the Inn in January of 1898, Lemon was engaged in defending himself in a lawsuit brought against him by Charles F. Jones, a builder, for bills incurred in work done at the Inn between March and May of 1897. Lemon had agreed to pay Jones $1,000 plus an additional $500 for work requested later. Jones billed Lemon for $3,635.67. Lemon paid him $1,300.

The suit dragged on for years, putting a lot of money in the pockets of the attorneys involved. There are detailed records of testimony from numerous witnesses—carpenters, masons, lumber dealers, auditors, builders, book keepers, and the architect Bailey. It appears that Jones had been overcharging Lemon, listing a $5 charge every time he spent a day or part of a day at the Inn. He also built in profits on payments he made to different workmen.

The case turned on the verbal agreement for $1,000 plus $500 extra, with no written contract and no daily rate specified. Another vital point was whether mistakes that were made, such as dormer windows on the third story, (removed when the Inn was rebuilt following the 1955 fire), were the fault of Jones or of the architect Bailey. Bailey appears to have been slow and imprecise about when he gave "plans" to Jones, and Jones is even more imprecise as to what plans he was following.

Since Lemon owed Bailey's mother a large sum of money, he was not in a position to press the architect on responsibility for errors he may have made in the restoration process. Lemon testified he had to hire additional workmen at his own expense to finish things that were incorrectly or poorly done by Jones and his men.

That the mortgage became an issue in the suit seems likely. On December 13, 1909, more than 11 years after the case was brought to court, Lemon signed a release to Bailey which stated: "In consideration of one dollar and other legal considerations to me, paid by Robert M. Bailey, I do hereby release him from any and all claims I may have against said Bailey as contained in a certain action at law now pending in the Superior Court, which action is to be entered 'Neither Party.'[7]

Just what the final settlement was and whether or not Jones received additional money is not clear. The important point is that the transcripts of the trial provide a picture of the changes Lemon made, which included remodeling the dining room (today's tap room) and adding a piazza; installing four single and one double dormer windows and a new staircase on the third floor; removing the flight of stairs leading from the old bar room to the drivers and drovers room and replacing it with a closet; rebuilding five mantlepieces and installing a dado (bay window) in place of the outside door in the How dining room.

In the meantime Lemon had other problems. He seems to have been in constant need of funds. On May 28, 1900 he had the contents of the Inn appraised by Leonard and Company of Boston. Total value of the goods and chattels was $4,426.45, with the How coat of arms appraised at $15. Three years later, shortly after his insurance bill on the Inn property had jumped 25 percent to $374 a year (for $12,000 worth of coverage), he mortgaged them for $900 to Walter Woodman of Cambridge.[8]

Lemon's financial worries continued until his death of pneumonia on December 19, 1919. He was buried in Malden, leaving his wife and her sister-in-law Miss Lemon struggling to carry on alone. When it became known that the struggle was becoming too much for the aging ladies and "the widow did not feel able to hold the property," a group of concerned and well-to-do Boston citizens led by L. Loring Brooks, formed a trust which aimed to protect and preserve the Inn. Other trustees included Charles Francis Adams, Speaker of the Massachusetts House of Representatives B. Loring Young and distinguished lawyer and businessman E. Sohier Welch.

An appeal was sent out to people to become shareholders of the Wayside Inn Trust "which has been organized under an agreement and declaration of trust to acquire and hold the Wayside Inn at Sudbury...so well known through the song and story of Longfellow and Hawthorne and its patronage by

Washington and Lafayette and other great men of past generations...the purpose of the Wayside Inn Trust is two-fold: to
preserve the Inn with its priceless antiques as nearly as possible
in their original condition, and, second, to maintain and
operate the Inn as an inn."

This appeal was sent out above the names of Charles W.
Eliot, Allan Forbes, Henry Cabot Lodge, Dr. Myles Standish
and other notables. Its aim was to raise $200,000 for the
undertaking with shares priced at $100 apiece. It informed
interested parties that: "The trustees will proceed with the
plan when, in their opinion, sufficient capital has been
secured." [9]

Mrs. Lemon was favorable to the idea and gave the trustees
an option on the entire property. The crusade was widely
acclaimed and endorsed by numerous prestigious organizations
including the Boston Society of Architects, the Sons of the
American Revolution and the New England Genealogical Society. Governor Cox approved it and called for its support. A
well-known innkeeper, Robert P. Peckett of Peckett's at Sugar
Hill, Franconia, New Hampshire, announced himself ready
to take on the innkeeping responsibilities and ensured the
backers that the old Inn would, in fact, still function as a
hostelry.

Newspapers in Boston and elsewhere were caught up in the
spirit of historical salvation. They spread the news of the plight
of the old inn. The *Boston Transcript* of June 14, 1922 ran the
headline: "Historic Place to be Saved for the Future....In-
formation Asked as to How to Take Part."

But progress was too slow. The option was renewed after a
year. Then, suddenly, after more than two years of uncertainty
and anxiety, the whole picture changed almost overnight. A
new landlord appeared on the scene.

The *Worcester Telegram* got the scoop. On the morning of
July 10, 1923, it broke the first news in big, bold headlines:
"Henry Ford buys Wayside Inn at Sudbury; May Maintain it for
Public as Historical Museum. Buyer Negotiates for 145-acre
Bright Estate Near Tavern. Plans Veiled in Secrecy."

The Telegram had jumped on a rumor and luckily was
correct. *The Herald*, taking no chances came out with a
headline the following day that prudently stated: "Rumor Says
Ford Buys Wayside Inn...Owner and Neighbors Are
Non-Committal..."

By July 12 it was a secret no longer and newspapers throughout New England had a field day. "Ford's New England Agent To Convert Old Wayside Inn Into a Shrine Set in a Magnificent Park Covering a Mile," proclaimed the *Worcester Gazette*. "Trustees of Earlier Project Yield to Auto Magnate's Representative."

"What Will Ford Do With Wayside Inn?" queried the *Boston Post*. "Wayside Inn Saved! Longfellow Shrine...300 Year Old Tavern Rich in Memories of Other Days..." trumpeted the *New York Times*.

A new era had just begun. And money would be no object.

XVI

"A Trustee For The Nation"

Loring Brooks couldn't help thinking of the incongruity of it all as he rode up Boylston Street that early July morning in 1923. The instructions he had received from Dutee W. Flint in the lobby of the Copley Plaza Hotel the day before seemed more fitting for a spy thriller than a business deal, but then, Henry Ford wasn't exactly your everyday businessman.

In his position as Chairman of the Wayside Inn Trust, which held an option on the property from Cora Lemon, the widow of Edward R. Lemon, Brooks had had dealings with Ford before. Earlier that year he had traveled to Dearborn, Michigan, at Ford's expense to discuss the sale and preservation of the old tavern and the surrounding property but returned home disappointed. It appeared that his more than two years of work to find a suitable buyer for the Inn would have to continue.

Flint, Ford's business agent in the New England area, had called two days before. Yes, he said, Mr. Ford was interested in the Wayside Inn property and wanted to meet Brooks the next day at the Copley Plaza. But when Brooks showed up as scheduled, he was buttonholed by Flint in the lobby.

Any kind of publicity must be avoided at all costs, Flint said. Brooks was to return to the Copley Plaza Hotel the following day, enter by the front door on Copley Square, walk through the lobby and exit by the side entrance on Dartmouth Street. He was then to enter an automobile that would be parked there.

Brooks, a Boston investment broker with a summer home not far from the Inn, did what he was told. After mingling with the guests in the Copley lobby for a few minutes, he walked out the side door where a Lincoln sedan was waiting. Inside beside Flint sat the trim lanky figure of Henry Ford.

Ford nodded to driver John W. Burke, who threw the Lincoln in gear and proceeded west by a circuitous route to confuse any curious reporters who might be following. Upon reaching

Sudbury, Ford asked Brooks to show him every property upon which the Trust held options. As they talked, Ford busily scribbled down acreages and prices.

The final stop was at the Inn itself, where Brooks and Cora Lemon, widow of Edward Rivers Lemon, showed him through the house. As he prepared to leave he turned to Mrs. Lemon. "I'll take it all," he said.

"He fell in love with it at first sight," driver Burke was to tell the *New York Times* some 33 years later. "And so did I." Burke retired in 1956 after 42 years as the Ford family chauffeur. [1]

By the time the Lincoln dropped Brooks off at his office at 53 State Street late that afternoon the task of the Wayside Inn Trust had been completed. Henry Ford's name would soon be added to the list of Landlords of the Wayside Inn.*

Flint did his job well and swiftly. By the time the *Worcester Telegram* broke the story on July 10, 1923, he had not only closed the deal on the Lemon property but also secured an option on the 140-acre William Bright estate immediately to the west and made inquiries about several other pieces of property near the Inn. Ford's decision to shun publicity had been a practical one, designed to foil real estate speculators.

The July 12th edition of the *Worcester Evening Gazette,* one of the country's oldest newspapers which first saw the light of day as the *Massachusetts Spy* in the years before the Revolution, spelled out Ford's plans in words of one syllable. "Auto magnate will come in on the purchase, which includes estates on both sides of the Boston-Worcester Road, stretching for a mile and a half...will be preserved as an unmarred highway to provide a fitting approach to a museum for preservation of American colonial antiquities. The trustees of the earlier project [Brooks's Wayside Inn Trust] have yielded to the auto king's representative."

Ford paid $60,000 for the Lemon property, which included the Inn and 60 acres of land. By October 1924, when the historic Parmenter Garrison Farm to the east of the Inn became the final piece in his initial real estate puzzle, his investment had ballooned to $550,000, and he held title to more than 1,300

---

*This incident was recounted by Frank Noyes in an article in the *Boston Herald* in June 1956 as told to him by Charles Hovey Pepper who heard it from Brooks himself.

acres "To provide a fitting frame for the picture and keep hot dog stands and peanut wagons out of the front yard."[2]

While Ford's action was hailed by many who loved the old Inn, it received mixed reviews among the residents of Sudbury, some of whom viewed the takeover as a threat and an insult. Ford didn't help his public image with the locals when he returned to the Inn in February of 1924 to host a gala party for Boston society that left most of his neighbors-to-be, including the local newspapers, on the outside looking in over the shoulders of burly security men.

Ford himself was as cheerful and carefree as a schoolboy. He went skating several times on Josephine Pond, danced until midnight, carved a goose, exchanged Ford car jokes with his guests and chopped wood. While his spurned Sudbury neighbors fumed in silence, the newspapers took up the cudgel for them.

"Ford at Wayside Inn as Silent as Historic Walls," said the *Boston Traveler*, "Denies Interviews as he Arranges Party for Tonight." "Town Folk on Outside Looking In," added the *Boston Post*, "Henry Ford Dance Is Exclusive in Extreme."[3]

Ford hinted the next day that he was planning another party for his real South Sudbury neighbors, as this one was strictly a family and business affair. One item of business was a $100,000 offer to John D. "Jack" Pearmain for his land and buildings on Nobscot Mountain. Pearmain at first refused the offer, but Ford eventually succeeded in obtaining the land, which he developed into an orchard.[4]

Ford kept his promise in a big way the following winter with an old-time dancing party for Sudbury residents who had lived in town 50 years or more. Among the guests who danced the old reels, waltzes, schottishes and quadrilles to the strains of Ford's old-fashioned orchestra were Atherton Rogers, William "Bill" Rice and Francis E. Bent, all descendants of original Sudbury settlers.

The previous August, Ford had played host to 4,500 members of the Middlesex County Farm Bureau and Extension Service on the grounds of the Inn. He made a speech, accepted a grub hoe made by Ben Boyden in 1794 from young Bill Loring of Wayland in an impromptu ceremony in the Longfellow Garden, shook innumerable hands, picnicked with his guests, and watched horseshoe pitching, tugs of war, and a baseball game between married and single men.

The chance to see Ford's 1,000-acre estate and hobnob with the auto magnate swelled the annual Farmers Picnic to more than four times its normal attendance, and Chief of Police Seneca W. Hall and other traffic officers were kept busy directing and parking more than 1,000 automobiles. His one-minute speech, delivered from the tailboard of a covered Ford pickup truck, was remembered long after the addresses of the major speakers of the afternoon were forgotten.

Unnoticed by the multitude, Harvey Firestone quietly enjoyed the occasion. The following day he and Ford were joined by Thomas Edison. The three men walked all over Ford's growing estate, talking business and politics, admiring the groundwork for Ford's new grist mill, and later enjoying a demonstration of jigs and reels given in the 1800 Ballroom, where they were joined by Lieutenant Governor Fuller.[5]

This meeting was also the planning session for the trio's annual summer vacation, which included a visit with President Calvin Coolidge in Plymouth, Vermont. There Ford was presented with a wooden sap bucket made by the President's great-great-grandfather.[6] All the notables present signed the bucket which is still kept at the Inn. It was later signed by Edward, Prince of Wales* when he was a guest of Ford's at a Detroit lunch party.

The *Boston Post* couldn't resist a dig at Ford and his party in its August 21, 1924 edition, noting that he, Edison and Firestone left only a dollar tip after spending several days with their entourage at the Okemo Tavern in Ludlow, Vermont.

In Sudbury, thanks primarily to the Farmers Picnic, Ford's public image was considerably brighter. ''Henry Ford has taken the 'Rube' out of ruralist,'' said the *Christian Science Monitor* in a report on Ford's intention to turn his newly acquired property into an experimental farm. ''He has broken through the isolation of the farm family; the automobile has taken civilization to the farm...''[7]

One of the main reasons that Ford was so easily able to win the confidence of farmers and the working class was the fact that he manufactured a car that they could not only afford to buy but also repair themselves. They respected the fact that he had started his career in a machine repair shop and built his

---

*After the abdication of Edward VIII in 1937, the bucket became a curiosity for sightseers at the Inn. It was shipped to Greenfield Village in Dearborn before the 1955 Inn fire and was later returned to Sudbury.

first engines with his own hands. His chatty, informal style was something that farmers could understand and respond to in a genuine way.

Ford's attitude towards history was equally down to earth. "The only way to show how our forefathers lived and to bring to mind what kind of people they were, is to reconstruct, as nearly as possible, the exact conditions under which they lived," he said in the lead article in the July 1926 issue of *Garden and Home Builder**:

"The younger generation knows a good deal about automobiles and airplanes and the radio and the movies, but it has nothing to go on when it comes to comprehending the pioneers and what they stood for. There is no use talking about colors to a man who is color blind."

Ford's agents had already set about collecting old farm implements, furniture, wagons and tools that would have been used at the Inn in early times, which soon filled the barns and sheds on the property to overflowing. His famous and oft-misquoted statement that "History is bunk"[8] applied only to written history. "The doings of kings and princes do not properly mirror how people lived," he rightly observed.

The public enthusiastically agreed. Letters and articles from all over the country descended on innkeeper E. J. Boyer and Frank Campsall, Ford's executive assistant in Detroit, asking for information about the early Howes or purporting to be related to the Howe family. This led to the employment of Mrs. Gladys Salta, who was given the task of looking up all available information about the early Hows.

Mrs. Salta spent some months in the East Cambridge Courthouse and other places, patiently recording in longhand what was known about John, Samuel, and David. She suggested a "very interesting story"[9] could be made about them and about the Inn. For some reason, her advice was not followed and after a careful labor of some two years her research efforts ceased.

Ford quickly discovered that acquiring the common household goods and tools of Everyman could be an expensive proposition. By 1925 his acquisition costs alone were projected to top the million dollar mark, and his agents were incessantly deluged by letters from people who were convinced that they

---

*This article was entitled "Why I Bought the Wayside Inn and What I am Doing With It."

had something of interest to the new landlord. These ranged from antique dealers offering "a mahogany grandfather clock" or an "old candelabra" or "a trammel crane" for sale, to individuals who wondered if Mr. Ford would be interested in a "Brewster Chair," a "very old piano," "a cradle"[10] and so on.

Many of the offers were from those who hoped to make a fast buck from the millionaire, but some were genuine offers of important How memorabilia. One of these was from an old man, David Howe of Taunton, Mass., who proved to be the sixth generation in direct descent from David, the original innkeeper. He voluntarily donated many deeds and other documents to the Inn, along with a cane belonging to his great-great-great-grandfather, the first innkeeper.

Howe's gesture was evidently a breath of fresh air to Campsall, who sent him a personal letter of thanks that said in part:

> Your interest and courtesy are much appreciated in comparison with the attitude shown by some of David How's descendants...you are the only one who really appears to have understood Mr. Ford's ideas in regard to the Inn...Mr. Ford wished to restore all that was possible of the original How furnishing but it is to be rather regretted that he placed any particular reliance upon possible aid from How descendants in this connection. Immediately after this was known, tables that might have brought $100 in some antique store jumped forthwith to $6,000 and other objects in like proportions. ...You can now understand what a relief it was to have you volunteer your own possessions in your courteous way.[11]

No matter what their intent, all letters and requests to Ford, Boyer, or Campsall were investigated and answered. The administrative burden became so onerous by the late 1920s that a Mr. William W. Taylor was employed on a regular basis to deal with the purchase of antiques. Taylor's quest took him as far away as Kansas, where he purchased an old trunk that had long belonged to the Howe family, but other treasures were closer at hand. Longfellow's "Sombre Clock" was tracked down locally, taken to Dearborn to be repaired, and returned to the Inn. The worn-out parts were saved and placed in a small box fastened inside the clock's cabinet. In the same room was placed the old How family Bible, which was refurbished and provided with an authentic Bible box. Both items survived the 1955 fire. The Abbott and Downing stage coach, which is still on display in the barn across from the Inn, was purchased by

Taylor on August 19, 1924 from E.E. Mitchell of York Beach, Maine. It was refurbished under the supervision of the Sudbury Companies of Militia and Minute in 1974.*

Ford reopened many of the fireplaces that had been bricked up in Edward R. Lemon's time, and by 1930 had converted the woodshed that had been Lemon's art gallery into his own private apartment, with a fireplace set into an alcove on the north side for use during his frequent visits to Sudbury.

"We went about getting the Inn back into its original condition," he told the *Garden and Home Builder.* "All except one bedroom. This we have named the 'Edison Room' and have furnished it as of the time of Mr. Edison's birth.†

"The lighting gave us a good deal of trouble. The old inn was lighted by candles in wall sconces and in candlesticks. These had been replaced by ordinary electric light fixtures. We could not, as a practical matter, go back to candlelight as the fire risk would have been too great. We finally managed to get sconces such as must have been used in the Inn and to get candle-shaped electric lights which very well imitate the old candles."

Asked by another reporter if he had consulted Edison on the electrical changes, Ford replied "You bet I did."[12]

By 1925, the collection was attracting large numbers of vacationers and, according to one reporter: "The old Inn looks younger than when the characters of the *Tales* went away ...Longfellow remarked that it was a kind of hobgoblin hall which had somewhat fallen to decay...it has been rescued and restored. Fireplaces croon and crackle all over the house ...thanks to the wisdom, foresight and generosity of the new owner the generation of the future will contribute its own story to the accumulated treasures of this ancient and storied edifice...."[13] Henry Ford had quickly made up for a bad beginning. And bigger and better things still lay ahead for the Wayside Inn.

---

*Bill Cossart of the Sudbury Troop of Horse arranged to have the coach transported to Louden, New Hampshire where it was restored to to its original factory specifications by Edward and Barbara Rouse and Harry Fellows. On September 30, 1974 the coach was assigned a special five-day star route mail run from Louden back to Sudbury under the supervision of retired Sudbury Postmaster Forrest D. Bradshaw. The restoration cost $5,000.

†The Drivers and Drovers room in today's Inn.

Henry Ford's

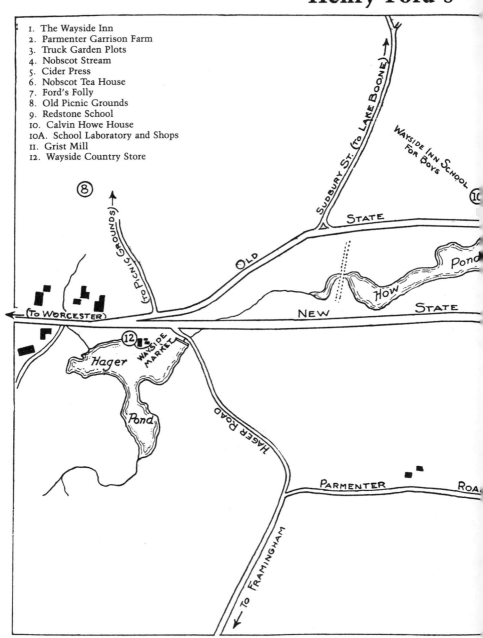

1. The Wayside Inn
2. Parmenter Garrison Farm
3. Truck Garden Plots
4. Nobscot Stream
5. Cider Press
6. Nobscot Tea House
7. Ford's Folly
8. Old Picnic Grounds
9. Redstone School
10. Calvin Howe House
10A. School Laboratory and Shops
11. Grist Mill
12. Wayside Country Store

Wayside Inn Estate

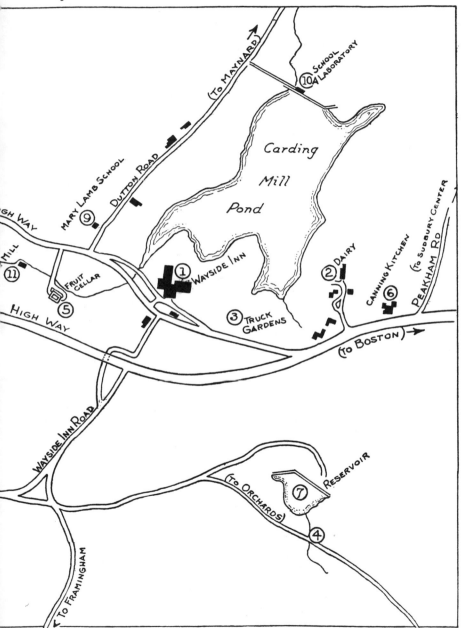

XVII

From The Three R's To Ford Cars

Tobacco is a filthy weed
And from the Devil sprang its seed
It dirts your hands
Scents your clothes
And makes a chimney of your nose."[1]

Young David Bentley had rehearsed his lines well. His was the lead role as the Sun in the Redstone School Play "The Day the Sun Didn't Get Up" and his words would have brought a satisfied smile to the lips of Henry Ford. The Wayside Inn's new landlord wasn't much for cigarettes or liquor, and the little morality play that Miss Martha Hopkins and her 16 students were performing was an excellent object lesson.

Ford had opened the one-room schoolhouse for grades one through four on January 17, 1927, barely six months after discovering it being used as a garage and storage shed at the Baptist Church Parsonage in the town of Sterling. It had stood for 60 years on Redstone Hill and gained instant fame when Mary Sawyer brought her lamb to school, inspiring young John Roulstone to write the first three stanzas of the famous nursery rhyme.*

Work crews from the Inn began dismantling the building on June 17, 1926, and by November 1 it was rebuilt on a little knoll across the brook from the Inn and ready for occupancy, complete with the original teacher's chair, some old school desks and benches of the period, an outhouse and a 30-foot-deep well. The workmen had salvaged as much of the original material as possible and supplemented it with boards and timbers cut locally and sawed in the Inn sawmill.[2]

---

*The controversy about who wrote the poem is not relevant to the story of the Inn, but interesting nevertheless. In summary, Mary Elizabeth Sawyer, later Mrs. Columbus Tyler, was the little girl whom the lamb followed to school. She had nursed the animal back to health after it had been forsaken by its mother. The teacher, Polly Kimball, turned it out of the schoolhouse. The incident was witnessed by John Roulstone, a young divinity student. He rode over the next day with the first three verses of the poem and gave them to Mary. Many years later, the well-known Sarah Josepha Hale completed the poem in its present form.

Ford had explained to the Sudbury School Committee that he needed a school to "accommodate children in the families of his employees at the Wayside Inn and that he would take in some others." He offered to pay the teacher and transportation costs for the pupils. The School Committee agreed and the Redstone became part of the Sudbury School system.

Ford was present at the ceremonial opening, posing for pictures with the students and the obligatory lamb, as the parents of the 16 lucky children looked on. After the ceremony, the children were immediately dismissed as five cases of scarlet fever had been reported in Sudbury schools and all had been ordered closed.

Members of that first class included Thomas Winship, who went on to become editor of the *Boston Globe*; Edith Laberee; Ruth, Caroline, Eleanor, Ivan, and Ralph Stone; Evangeline McDonald; Parker Bartlett; Donald Bowry; Ernest Little; Jane Way; Betty Harrington; Alice Cowern; Frederick Christensen; and Charles Whitworth. [3]

The Redstone was to be only the first of Ford's Wayside Inn schools. In 1928, 31 underprivileged boys between the ages of 16 and 18, all of them wards of the state who had been carefully screened for aptitude and intelligence, began to gather at the old Calvin Howe house opposite the mill dam. The Wayside Inn Trade School, later to become known as the Wayside Inn Boys School, was born.

Ford's stated aim was to combine a standard curriculum which included English, history, economics, biology, general science, physics, chemistry and mathematics with practical training for a trade in life, and he wanted his students to learn to live financially independent of others.

But there was also a practical side to the venture. The Inn estate was a working farm, just as it had been in the heyday of the Hows, and labor was needed to run the dairy, poultry, orchard, mill, machine shop and carpentry operations. Ford was offering a high school education, a chance to learn a trade and a fair wage, but the students were expected to earn it.

"Henry Ford Invents a School." announced *The New York Times Magazine* in the lead article of its April 13, 1930 edition. "He applies to the training of boys the methods he would use in attempting to solve an engineering problem. His school, like his Model T car of joyous memory, is apparently designed with the sole purpose of taking a person to his destination."

When accepted, each boy was given a scholarship of between $435 and $504 a year (not a bad salary in Depression times), based on his age, class and ability. Out of this he was responsible for his lodging, clothing, medical and entertainment expenses and was expected to start and maintain a bank account for use after graduation. Before receiving the scholarship, each student was required to submit a budget detailing how he intended to spend the money.

Students earned their scholarship—which was paid monthly—by spending at least half of each day involved in on-the-job training. Duties were carefully divided between the agricultural operations and the mill and laboratory, a well-equipped machine shop located on the Carding Mill Pond dam where repairs to automobiles, furniture, boilers, plumbing and electrical apparatus were carried out.

Each student was also responsible for his own laundry, mending and ironing, and was expected to take his turn at housecleaning and kitchen work as well as waiting on table. Housemaster Lou Varrichione Sr.[4] divided the boys into squads of five members, and appointed a leader for each. Squad leaders took turns as proctor, inspecting the cleaning, designating a boy each day to serve as fireman for the furnace in cold weather, and seeing to it that the younger boys were in bed by 9 p.m.

Until the Solomon Dutton House was repaired and enlarged in 1931 to allow 50 boys to participate in the program, the school served grades ten through 12 with eighth and ninth graders added later. Its first graduates, Frank Calvert, Hyman Seligman, Leon Gooch, David Sobel and William Graham, received their diplomas from innkeeper Earl J. Boyer on July 2, 1930, and, a month later, took the train to Dearborn, Michigan, to continue their education at the Ford Trade Schools.

"It is a school based almost on biologic laws," wrote *The New York Times Magazine*. "Its fundamental lessons are not learned from books. They are indeed probably duplicated in no other school in the country.

"They are lessons in self-preservation. First of all a boy is taught how to keep himself alive and well—exactly what to eat and especially what not to eat, how to take care of himself, his clothes, his house. And he receives actual practice in the earning and spending of money. He is, in other words, made to be an independent person with an intelligent understanding of how to maintain himself in health and economic security on a backwoods farm or in the mechanized life on Manhattan."[5]

School days were long, but it was by no means all work and no play. Part of each day was set aside for hobbies, which ranged from photography to raising farm animals as 4-H projects. Joseph Ochedowski constructed a small airplane and Billy Bridges built a hand-powered paddle wheel boat.[6]

The school sponsored football, baseball and track teams that competed with other local high schools. Their first mascot was a billy goat, which was later replaced by a pair of owls.

"Henry Ford's school is still in the experimental stage," *The New York Times Magazine* correctly concluded. "Not every boy, it has been found, can be educated in its Spartan confines. The artist, the poet, the individualist and the anarchist do not fit in. But whether, like the Model T car, it will prove the vehicle to carry the millions to better and brighter destinations remains to be seen."[7]

The Times' assessment proved to be correct. The Wayside Inn Boys School wasn't for everyone. Boys left because they didn't like the work, the discipline or the food. Henry Ford's philosophy on proper diet which called for lots of grains, fruits, vegetables and dairy products and very little meat wasn't shared by many of the students.

All its graduates weren't instant successes. But many did go on to successful professional careers, and others fought valiantly in World War II. Bill Cummings, who became a pilot during World War II, returned to the Inn in 1945 sporting five oak leaf clusters, a Presidential Citation, the Purple Heart and two medals for outstanding flying. William Cash, a graduate of the Class of 1941 whose ambition had always been to be a newspaper reporter, got his first job as a stringer for a small newspaper in Greenwich Village, New York, and later became a reporter for the *Boston Globe*.

In the summer of 1930, Ford realized that he needed a school in which young graduates of the Redstone could continue to learn. He rebuilt the nearby Southwest District School, which had first opened in 1849 and later burned down. The Southwest opened in September of 1930, and accommodated grades five through eight. Southwest graduates continued their education at the Sudbury High School, located in what is now the Alan F. Flynn office building in Sudbury Center. As was the case with the Redstone, Friday afternoons were reserved for dancing lessons at the Inn under the direction of Professor Albert Haynes.

Old fashioned dancing was one of Ford's favorite pastimes,[8] and it became popular with the students as well, many of whom still remember Friday afternoons and evenings with fondness. Professor Haynes, nicknamed "Hollywood" by the older students because of his natty dress and his California background, taught the intricate steps of the Badger Gavotte, the Portland Fancy and the Varsovienne, in addition to waltzes, polkas and contra dancing.*

The Wayside Inn Schools were only one of many such projects that Ford sponsored all over the world. According to the September 1938 issue of *The Forum Magazine*, 2,000 children attended one of his many schools that year, and more than 6,000 had graduated from his programs.

Some of the projects included an institute to teach mechanized farming in England; six rural schools and a village high school for black children near his Ways, Georgia, winter home; schools for rubber workers and their children in the jungles of Brazil; and rural schools in half a dozen Michigan villages near his Dearborn home. In all these places he delighted pupils with a kind of education that was part progressive, part old fashioned and essentially as unconventional as Ford himself.

"As a matter of fact," he told *The Forum*, "it isn't really necessary to teach children. All you need to do is let them learn. We adults would find life much pleasanter if we went about it as a child does—always wanting to learn, always sharing what we've learned, never satisified with what we know, always wondering what we don't know."

The Southwest and Boys schools closed their doors soon after Ford's death in 1947 and the Redstone graduated its last class in June of 1951. Among the students was Earl Meader, whose mother Eleanor Stone Meader was one of the school's original students 24 years before.

---

*In the 1980's, the Sudbury Companies of Militia and Minute still keep this tradition alive with dancing lessons and parties at the Inn.

XVIII

A $1 Highway, A Chapel And A Mill

Having finished the Inn and bought all the surrounding land, we then began to put the whole neighborhood into somewhat of its former condition," Henry Ford wrote in the July 1926 *Garden and Home Builder.* "We picked up two old sawmills of the time, one of them in Rhode Island. These we are reassembling. On the property there was already a grist mill with a breast water wheel, which was grinding only feed.* This we are putting back into the exact condition it was in during the Revolution—with an overshot wheel—so that it will grind wheat, rye and corn. We are working on an old blacksmith shop and shall have it ready with the forge, tools and benches of the time."

Although he was reluctant to announce this in so many words, Henry Ford was building a miniature Utopia similar to others on a larger scale created by rich men during that same period in American history. Very few survived the test of time, even when supported by a seemingly inexhaustible supply of money.

After he had restored the Inn buildings and protected them by buying up surrounding property, Ford undertook the task of creating a self-sufficient community with the ancient hostelry as its centerpiece. It would grow to include three schools, a working farm, grist and saw mills, and a chapel. Ford's aim was to create a living historical museum which would show how people lived in the seventeenth and eighteenth centuries.

Work had started on the new mill as early as the spring of 1924, with crews of men enlarging the brook between the dam and the new spillway, while groaning oxen drew stone boats laden with native boulders for the building's two-foot-thick walls. The new building was some ninety yards from the site of the old mill, on the opposite side of the valley.

*This was the old Calvin Howe nail mill, an L-shaped building which was located much nearer the dam and the Wayside Inn Road than the present mill.

Four massive Buhr millstones weighing more than a ton each, were ordered from La Ferte sous Jouarre in France, and Ford's agents began hunting far and wide for authentic eighteenth century milling machinery, which was installed under the direction of hydraulic engineer John Blake Campbell of Philadelphia, who also designed and supervised the installation of the giant overshot waterwheel.[1]

On Thanksgiving morning in 1929, Erwin R. Smith of Hopkinton, the third generation of a family of millers in that town, turned the iron wheel to open the floodgates and set the big millstones whirring. Soon the mill was busy grinding corn, wheat and rye for use at the Inn and at the Boys School.[2]

That same winter the Parmenter-Garfield General Store in Sudbury Center, which Ford had purchased the previous year, was raised from its foundation, placed on runners and moved by oxen to a site on the Post Road beside Hager's Mill Pond. On Friday, June 20, 1930, it served its first customers as the Wayside Inn Roadside Market, with Mrs. Henry Ford on hand for the occasion.[3]*

Meanwhile, Ford continued to acquire other houses and property. In 1929 he bought and restored the old Plympton house which was originally owned by Adam How, who had sold it to the Wheeler family. Ford acquired it from an old man named Myrick Carr, a Wheeler descendant, who was failing in his wits. Ford built a small house so that Carr could live out his years quietly, when the Plympton-Carr house was moved to the Greenfield Village Museum in Dearborn.[4]

On September 16, 1930, the house and farm on the ridge south of the Inn, once owned by Ezekiel How Jr., became part of the Ford holdings and immediately joined the Inn's dairy operation.

By July 17, 1930 when the Middlesex County Farmers Picnic was once again hosted by the Inn, the dairy, located at the Parmenter Garrison and Ezekiel How Jr. farms, boasted 31 head of Devon cattle, including five recently imported from England. Seventy-six Cheviot sheep were pastured near the Grist Mill, and 42 goats had a pasture of their own on Dutton Road. The Inn's poultry range near the dairy barn housed a flock of

---

*A few years before his death Ford sold the store to Milt Swanson with a proviso in the deed that it always remain a country store. It remains so to this day. The story of the Wayside Country Store is worthy of a book in its own right.

1,259 white leghorn chickens and 77 turkey poults. A piggery sheltering 24 Berkshire hogs was located a discreet distance away on Hager road near the apple, peach and quince orchards. Fields to the rear of the Inn and on Peakham Road were planted in corn, squash, potatoes and various vegetables much as they are today. [5]

Later, after Ford had acquired the John D. Pearmain property, including most of the west slopes of Nobscot Mountain at the end of Brimstone Lane, he expanded his orchard operation. Fruits and vegetables were stored in a naturally cooled and ventilated underground storage cellar across the street from the Inn, which also contained the cider press.

Ford's land acquisitions and new projects on the Inn property caused a great deal of speculation and, in some cases, consternation among his Sudbury neighbors. When he purchased the 200-acre Gately estate near Mirror Lake on the Sudbury-Stow boundary in 1928, rumors sprang up that he was planning an airplane manufacturing plant complete with hangars and airstrip. Most of this land was later turned over to the U.S. government and is now part of the Sudbury Military Reservation. [6]

Changes and additions were underway at the Inn as well. Stonemasons began work on a fieldstone foundation for an enlarged north wing that contained a new dining room on the ground floor and a spacious ballroom upstairs. Ford directed that automobile springs (Ford, naturally) be installed beneath the hardwood dance floor to give it the "bounce" that was lacking in the pine floor of the old 1800 ballroom. Later, in 1938, the coach house was moved from its old location near the Longfellow Garden wall to the south side of the Boston Post Road, where it now stands.

There were other projects that would have stumped men of lesser means, but Ford tackled them with relish. In 1926, engineers determined that vibrations from the automobile traffic on the Post Road were damaging the foundations of the Inn so Ford ordered that the road be moved. The Wayside Inn bypass, a mile and one half stretch of highway that left the Post Road a quarter mile east of the Inn and rejoined it at a point near Hager's Pond, would cost him $280,000. He sold it to the Commonwealth of Massachusetts for $1. [7]

Not all the projects were successful. "Ford's Folly," a 400-foot-long concrete dam on the side of Nobscot Mountain, designed to impound a small stream and provide water for the Inn and its farm buildings, was a failure. The dam's foundation was incorrectly laid and hydraulic pressure would cause sand boils beneath its foundation whenever it was more than half full. It made a fine swimming hole for the neighborhood boys, but never served the purpose for which it was intended. [8]

There were problems at the Grist Mill too. In 1932 heavy rains swelled the millpond to overflowing and water washed out 15 feet of the embankment protecting the millrace.

Six years later, another crisis paved the way for the construction of the Martha-Mary Chapel. Ground was broken in late August of 1939, almost a year to the day after the 1938 hurricane knocked down a magnificent stand of white pine on the knoll behind the Redstone School as if the big trees were so many matchsticks.

Ford directed that the chapel be built wholly from the wood and stone on the estate and by the hands of those who lived, worked and attended school there. By the time the six-foot wrought iron weathervane was placed atop its 78 1/2-foot steeple in time to celebrate Mr. Ford's 77th birthday on July 30, 1940, more than 200 people had had a hand in its construction. More than 100 of them were students at one of the Inn's three schools. [9]

The chapel was the sixth built by Mr. and Mrs. Ford in memory of their mothers, Mary Ford and Martha Bryant. Two are located at Dearborn, in Greenfield Village and at Camp Legion. The others are in Macon, Michigan; Willow Run, Michigan; and Richmond Hill, Georgia. The Chapel's cut-glass chandelier dates back to 1780 and the original maroon carpeting was woven in Greenfield Village. The building's simple lines are modeled after the Bradford meeting house with the addition of a Christopher Wren steeple. [10]

It was Ford's wish that the Chapel belong to the children of the schools. It was there that they would meet for a short non-denominational service each morning before school and hold their graduation exercises each June.

Ann Bradshaw and Barbara Eaton were only two of the many Wayside Inn School students who were later married in the Chapel. On November 20, 1941 when Muriel DeMille, a long-time hostess at the Inn, exchanged vows with Stuart B. Hoppin of Framingham, Ford broke away from labor negotiations with Philip Murray, President of the CIO, to make a special overnight trip from Dearborn in his private railroad car, Fair Lane, in order to arrive in time for the ceremony.

Whether they tilled his land, cared for his stock, worked in the kitchen or taught in his schools, Henry Ford had a special concern for all his Wayside Inn employees. When he learned during a March, 1941, visit that Emma Maki, cook at the Inn since 1925, was having trouble walking because of a badly deteriorated hip joint, he arranged for her to be admitted to the Henry Ford Hospital in Detroit to have the condition corrected. Hostess Priscilla Staples, who accompanied Emma to Detroit, tells the story in the Inn Diary which she kept for many years.

> Emma has been our cook for 16 years. For the past two or three years, Emma has been ailing. We knew it by the way she walked. Every now and then she would have a fall....But would Emma complain? Never. "Work, work, Mees Staples, I love work." This is what she said over and over today as she rested in a beautiful room at the Henry Ford Hospital in Detroit.
>
> The trip from Sudbury to Detroit was made overnight aboard a fast train. (We) were comfortable indeed as we watched the Massachusetts hills roll by from the windows of a drawing room. Night came on. The porter made up the berth while Emma watched. "They treat me like princess," she said.
>
> The Michigan Central station at Detroit was cold and drab as Emma limped through it from train to automobile... The city was veiled in early-morning mist and dampness. Old brick houses and dilapidated warehouses lined the streets. "No white like home. Why no paint on houses?" Emma puzzled.
>
> Emma was born in Austria and came to America when 12 years old. Has been in the cooking service since she was 15. "Sixty-five year, maybe more," she told the doctor when he asked her age. "And what did your father die of?" continued the handsome young man in white. "Nothing," said the patient. "But he work awful hard. All his life he work hard. Just like me. I love work."
>
> When we last saw Emma she was sitting up straight in the bed. Leaning slightly forward, she said in her sweet musical voice. "I tink Heaven no better than this. God my great Doctor. Meester Ford next."

On Monday, May 12, 1941, Emma returned to her room in the Gate House across the street from the Inn and received a royal welcome from her co-workers and friends. The Inn Diary reports:

> Emma is home, in her room at the Gate House and a fine looking Emma is she. She walks without hesitation. Her step is strong and steady. Over and over she says: "I'm all well, dalin'." She points to her mouth, "new teeth," she says, then points to her eyes, "new glass." She came this afternoon and stayed dressed up. She kept on her white lace collar and gold chain and walked over to the Inn for supper. We made her sit upstairs instead of in the kitchen. The night ·watchman shook hands. All were glad to see Emma. She will be back in the kitchen tomorrow, making apple pies, happy in her work and thinking of her long trip and fine treatment at the Henry Ford Hospital. "Nurses all angels," she says. "I never forget what that man and woman (Mr. and Mrs. Ford) do for me. Never forget." [11]

Neither did a lot of other people. On the morning of April 10, 1947, as the Chapel bell's somber tolling spread the sad news, school children, Inn employees and townspeople filled the pews to mourn the passing of the friendly, spare man whose ingenuity and far-sightedness had changed not only their lives, but the way of life of a nation.

Henry Ford was dead, and life at the Wayside Inn would never be quite the same. He had come along in the nick of time a quarter century earlier, just as Henry Wadsworth Longfellow had before him. Thanks to the combined genius of the poet and the motor magnate, what once had been a fallen-down country tavern became a famous hostelry that attracted guests from all over America and the civilized world.

EXCERPTS FROM THE WAYSIDE INN DIARIES

1929-1950

The Inn Diaries are an untapped source of information about the Ford era, a rich mine of information. They are full of incidents which capture the flavor of the period in a unique and charming style. It is to be hoped that at some not too distant future date, a book will be written about this era in which the Diaries will play a more prominent role than space permits here.

The Inn of Henry Ford's time was a world of its own, complete with a large farm and all its activities, three schools, a grist mill, a country store, a chapel and numerous other ancillary functions. Each of these topics is also worthy of a book in itself or at least a short story. We are dealing with the Inn *per se* and cannot attempt to do justice to these subsidiary activities.

(Adapted from a photograph by Wallace Nutting)

XIX

"Hollyhocks Tall and Stately....Celery and Radishes Were Served...."

The Inn Diaries, which were started at Henry Ford's request and continue unbroken until 1950, are a unique and colorful picture of their times. They are an open window on the history of two fascinating eras—the pre-war Boston society of quiet charm and placid pace, and the less-predictable wartime and postwar years of the 1940's.

They mirror not only the life of the Inn itself in an age when Boston society came to South Sudbury for lunch, tea and dinner and brought visitors from all over America and many foreign countries, but also record important events in the life of the nation and the wider world.

The stage upon which the diaries are set is national and international in scope as well as local. The cast of characters is extensive. It includes Priscilla Staples, memorable hostess for nearly three decades; Mr. Lee, the English gardener whose advice on planting was continually sought by visitors; Emma, the cook of twenty years; and Professor Albert Haynes, talented teacher of old-fashioned dances.

Playing key roles are Henry Ford, his family and friends such as Thomas Edison, Harvey Firestone, and Calvin Coolidge; movie stars James Stewart, Greer Garson and Jane Withers; and sports celebrities like Babe Ruth and Francis Ouimet. Boys from the Wayside Inn schools, such as Stephen Gooch and Bill Cash, rub shoulders with Sir Wilfred Grenfell, hero doctor of Labrador, and John Rockefeller, Jr. Touching on the life of the inn from afar are King George VI, Adolf Hitler, Madame Chiang Kai-shek, Franklin Delano Roosevelt, and Winston Churchill.

The diaries are a tapestry of events with a background of the changing seasons, the rhythm of a working farm, boys' laboratory experiments, a steady stream of visitors from abroad who are interested in life in colonial New England, weddings and anniversaries, romance and tragedy.

The calendar of the months in the 1930's is placid and predictable. In January, the "Fraters" visit for a three-day retreat

(Ford never let anyone who was a minister pay for room and board.) In February, there are blizzards, and the boys from the school are engaged in plowing and cutting ice from Josephine Pond to store for warmer months. Sometime between late January and early March, the first snowdrops appear outside the kitchen and are hailed with delight; in March the first lambs are born in the Lamson barn and, later on, the first goats.

In April, Paul Revere's ride and Colonel Ezekiel How's march to Concord are remembered with pride. Lilacs bloom in May in time for great annual crowds on Mother's Day. Parents and students celebrate graduations in the Old Kitchen, and the Bowkers bring especially beautiful roses throughout the month of June. In July, the Ford grandchildren visit on the way to Seal Harbor, and Ford continues the tradition of the Farmers Picnic with as many as 3,000 guests spending the day on the grounds.

Record numbers of people visit in bus tours and individually in August, as many as 500 to 1,000 in a single day. The fall foliage is lyrically described in September and October. Football weekends and college students occupy November along with Thanksgiving preparations. The Christmas pageant, performed outdoors near the Country Store by students and staff, is highlighted in December, along with the traditional Yuletide visit of the Dieffenbach sisters.

Above and beyond these repeated annual events, there are some entries in the daily log which reveal the life of the Inn in each of the decades so well that we have chosen a few which speak for themselves:

1929

March 5—Mrs. Ford is very thoughtful and painstaking in her choice of blossoms...flowers throughout the house...Tulips, hyacinths, snapdragons, jonquils...She is a lover of gardens and flowers.

March 13—Trade School boys are tapping trees for syrup along the roadway.

March 15—Signs of spring...baby lambs...flock of blackbirds...snowdrops.

March 30—Childe Hassam, painter, who scratched his name on the parlor window in 1882, returned to visit.

April 26—The Trade School Dramatic Club gave a play in the ballroom with music by Miss DeMille. Music followed for dancing the Virginia Reel and the waltz.

April 29— Mr. Koussevitzky, conductor of the Boston Symphony Orchestra, visited.

April 30—Professor Dana, grandson of Longfellow, entertained children from the Redstone School at Craigie House.

May 7—Barn swallows are building a nest of mud. The children of the Redstone schoolhouse go out almost daily for a bird and flower walk.

May 15—Sheep shearing is going on. Celery and radishes were served to guests before dinner.

May 26—There was a baseball game between the Boys School and Wayside Inn employees.

June 1—An American magazine editor wrote in the guest book: "This is a great place to renew one's faith in the world."

June 19—Nearly 400 persons were here today. Canterbury bells, snapdragons, phlox, and tall, blue delphiniums are at their best.

July 5—Mrs. Edmond Smith visited. As Mary Dewing, she took weekly Italian lessons from Luigi Monti...

July 22—The Country Store was transferred to Mr. Ford. It was owned and operated by William Parmenter for 49 years. He was born at the Inn when his father worked as a chore boy for Squire Howe.

August 16—Large crowds here today. Often two hostesses were in different rooms, each talking to audiences of 40 or 50 people at a time.

September 9—Baron and Baroness de Luze visited from France with two daughters...There were guests from Johannesburg, South Africa, Turkey, China, Syria, and India.

September 25—"Ford Team Wins at Southborough"—Wayside Inn horses and oxen won blue ribbons at the Southborough Fair.

October 3—Mr. John Slack of Brockton visited. His father drove the old stage coach, now in the barn, between Marlborough and Worcester when it stopped in Northborough and Shrewsbury.

October 4—The dancing classes run by Miss Elliott are a great success. "I can't wait for the next Friday evening and the next lesson," one young man was heard to say as he left.

October 5—Prime Minister Ramsay MacDonald of Great Britain visited.

October 10—Autumn is at its peak...Here is a mass of bright yellow and over there a deep red coloring and many shades of brown, orange and pink in between. It is as if all nature were decking out in its gayest attire and leaving us with a memory of this gay, cheerful spirit to abide with us during the cold, colorless days of the winter season.

October 15—Mrs. James Storrow of Boston brought Dame Katherine Fruse to lunch. She organized the Womens' Royal Naval Service during the war and was one of the first women to win the title Dame of the British Empire.

October 21—Trade School boys join in the celebration of Light's Golden Jubilee. A crowd listened to the broadcast from Dearborn honoring Edison and watched a program staged by the boys.

October 26—Saturdays are busy during football season. Guests on their way to or from games in Cambridge stop at the Inn and there is much discussion of forward passes and goal lines around the fireplaces. Fur coats and heavy blankets are piled in the Washington bedroom. No institution as modern as a checkroom exists in this famous inn.

November 21—First snow. A visiting South African boy exclaimed: "See all the pretty white feathers."

November 27—Mr. and Mrs. Ford arrived to spend Thanksgiving....Ford had muffins from meal ground at the mill.

December 12—We heard a tinkle of bells, looked out and saw prancing horses bringing logs to the inn on a pung.

December 25—258 guests for dinner today.

1930

January 10—Last evening Miss Elliott started a dancing class for the Trade School boys and about 30 young ladies from Marlborough came down to be partners...the Varsovienne was attempted and everyone seemed to step into it with remarkable ease and grace.

January 13—There was quite a stir among radio enthusiasts here at noontime when the wives of Amos and Andy came in for luncheon.

January 16—A Mr. and Mrs. Potter from Newtonville came for dinner to celebrate their 29th wedding anniversary...On their wedding day they came out on the four-horse coach Cricket which used to run between the Hotel Touraine and the Inn.

January 26—The beginning of the Universalist Ministers 28th Annual Retreat...they come with an earnest purpose as churchmen, blended with a frank intent to play together and be boys.

February 5—Today...the Sudbury Town Hall was discovered to be in flames. There was an attempt to save the building, but lack of an adequate water supply made it a hopeless task....We at the inn feel it is a kind of "handwriting on the wall."...Smoking has been prohibited in the inn.

February 27—A wreath was placed at Mount Auburn Cemetery. Mr. Lee made this from inn plants. Princess pine, spruce, hemlock, boxwood, laurel, periwinkle, and bayberries. [This annual custom marked Longfellow's birthday.]

March 17—St. Patrick's Day brought forth three baby lambs, the first this season...and up on Dutton Road in the Lamson barn are a dozen or more newly-born kids.

April 4—The Inn gives much to its guests and takes much in return. It gives a respect and reverence for our Puritan ancestors. The guests bring new thoughts from afar which keep the Inn alive and interesting....

May 6—A short, dark gentleman arrived and inquired if he might have lunch. He said very modestly that his name was John Rockefeller Jr. We had been expecting him but did not think he would arrive in such an unpretentious way. He came primarily to learn something of the management of the Inn that he might incorporate some of its workings into his own recently-acquired Raleigh Tavern in Williamsburg, Virginia.

June 2—June again and we think it is the most beautiful time of all the year at the Wayside Inn. Warm, sunny days with a deep blue sky overhead and the closely-clipped lawn under our feet like a green velvet carpet.

June 13—Closing exercises of Redstone School in large ballroom. Each certificate was personally signed by Mr. Ford. According to Mr. Lovett from Dearborn: "It gave Mr. Ford more pleasure to sign these certificates than to sign a contract for 50,000 new Ford automobiles."

July 12—Work on rebuilding the old Southwest District School was begun this week...it will house the grammar grades and enable the children who have attended Redstone to further their education at the Wayside Inn.

July 14—Hollyhocks in our garden this year rise up tall and stately over all the other blossoms and give the effect of a tall pink hedge against the landscape.

September 4—Miss Marion Boyer [Innkeeper Earl Boyer's

daughter] will enter the training school for nurses at the Henry Ford Hospital in Detroit, Michigan.

September 6—In this day and age when most everything is commercialized we are very proud to tell people that the Wayside Inn is closed on Sundays.

September 12—Twice a year the Inn looks forward to a visit from the Ford grandchildren...Today they arrived with their grandmother...Thrilling events are crammed into a few short hours...a ride on the old stage coach, drinking from the pump, a ride on the fire engine.

September 16—The Worcestershire England soccer team, numbering 20, dined here as the guests of Mr. Ford...Today the Ezekiel How Jr. house on Wayside Road up past the red barn becomes the property of the Wayside Inn.

September 20—Fifteen fine gentlemen from Japan, visiting this country as students of American industries, were guests of Mr. Ford for luncheon...These men were of small stature but their minds, like great cameras, made mental pictures of places and experiences whenever these would prove useful to the progress of their homeland.

October 1—A guest to the Inn, a man whose name means much to the world of golf. Francis Ouimet. He has recently been playing the unconquerable Bobby Jones.

October 4—Today was Mr. and Mrs. Coolidge's 25th anniversary of their marriage and we all felt very proud that we had as our guests at the Wayside Inn the ex-president of the United States and his wife...Calvin Coolidge and John Quincy Adams are both descendants of Edmund Rice.

October 30—A perfect night, beautiful moon and everyone in the spirit of fun. There were some very clever costumes. Mr. and Mrs. Boyer were dressed in harem costumes. Miss DeMille and Miss Allen as two black cats.

December 11—G. K. Chesterton, English essayist and his wife, were shown about the Inn and had tea.

December 21—Tonight was the Christmas pageant. Although we had not much heart to go through with it, for our beloved Marion Boyer was run down by a reckless driver in Detroit and is on the danger list.

December 24—We were to have a Christmas Party of the Inn family tonight but owing to chicken pox in the Boys School Mr. Boyer decided not to have it. Marion Boyer holding her own...

1931

January 14—Mayor James Michael Curley of Boston visited the Wayside Inn.

February 14—Mabel Welch, oldest of the hostesses at the Wayside Inn died today.

May 14—The 20 millionth Ford car visited the Inn today.

May 29—Jane Cowl visited and reported that she has several pieces of furniture in her home that were purchased when the old Inn was sold.

July 5—Seven members of the graduating class of the Boys School are off to Detroit to work in the Ford plant.

September 2—Another guest today was Priscilla Staples whose popularity can be gauged by the fact that even though she's been away for a year, people still ask for her.

September 4—A guest told us today that her great great-uncle, Edwin Mead, visited the Inn a great many years ago...wrote an editorial about it in the Boston papers...Mr. Lemon saw Mr. Mead's article, came out to Sudbury and bought the old Inn.

September 7, Labor Day—1,349 guests at the Inn. Nine hundred and eighteen at Redstone school. From 24 states, Sweden, Scotland, Canada and the Canal Zone...

September 16—Guy Lombardo and the Royal Canadians visited.

September 29—Visit from a Hindu priestess, Gayatri Devi from Bengal.

October 5—Early frosts have laid light fingers upon the foliage...across the road we see sheep grazing on slopes and in the distance a background of gorgeously-tinted trees.

October 19–21—Will be remembered as a day of sadness for it marked the passing of one of the greatest men in the history of the world, Thomas Alva Edison...Inquiries to see Edison's bed all day long from visitors...all over the country, lights were dimmed for one minute at 10 o'clock as a last tribute to Edison.

November 12—Even these days, the ugly ducklings of the family of days, are not devoid of color. If one looks closely one can find in the landscape the rich and mellow beauty of an oriental rug whose colors have been subdued by wear and age.

November 16—The Country Store drew Christmas shoppers ...linens, mats, hand-woven shawls, pottery, dolls, caravans of small soap animals.

1932

January 16—Soon it will be Easter and planting time and then summer again. To see Mr. Lee, our gardener, poring over seed catalogs makes one realize that the back of winter is broken.

January 24—The retreat of the Universalist Ministers...A regular feature of these gatherings, since their inception in 1903, has been the twilight hour. At 4 o'clock, the men gather in the old kitchen and hold a service of song and prayer.

February 22—Two hundred and sixty-six guests were served tea, dinner or lunch during the day...This, in consideration of the depression and hard times we hear so much about is most encouraging.

March 9—The chief topic of conversation is the kidnapping of Colonel and Mrs. Lindbergh's baby. We feel we knew the Lindbergh family as a result of Mrs. Evangeline Lindbergh's visit a few years ago...

March 10—Traffic on Dutton Road was held up this morning by the sheep being transferred from the Lamson barn to the one across from the Inn...Automobile horns and the shouts of men.

August 12—Princess Eugenie Oubousson of Russia came for a short visit.

October 22—While going through the Inn today, Mrs. S.W. Tenney, a resident of Holliston, told us that her mother took Spanish lessons from Isaac Edrehi, the Spanish Jew of the Tales.

November 14—Mr. and Mrs. Ford visited the Redstone School yesterday morning. The boys were quite thrilled to shake hands with the man they'd only dreamed of meeting.

1933

January 9—The laboratory has been a busy center for the past few months. Besides keeping our fleet of cars and tractors in repair, the men have set up a new boiler in the basement of the laboratory which is to provide heat and hot water to the building.

February 1—The oxen have been idle for the past two weeks. They worked hard during the last cold spell while the ground was frozen and injured their feet.

February 2—The snowdrop bed in front of the Ford apartment is once again in blossom.

March 18—At this time each year, Mr. Lee commences to prepare his plants and bulbs for planting in the Inn gardens. The greenhouse will be the center of his activities for the next few weeks.

April 29—During the past month listed in the register were: Hungary, Canada, Egypt, Scotland, England, Belgium, Puerto Rico, France, Poland, Australia, Austria, China....

June 20—Seventy-five members and wives of the Class of 1883 of Harvard gathered this noon to celebrate their 50th or golden anniversary.

July 10—A very interesting person was at the Inn today. Mr. George A. Fay of Wakefield proudly told us that he at one time drove the old Marlborough-Worcester Coach that is in the barn across the street and that his father drove it for 17 years before he died.

July 15—Vegetable stand at the General Store is doing a fairly good business now that we have our own vegetables regularly.

July 23—Another famous name, Ruth St. Denis, considered one of America's foremost dancers, visited the Inn and had dinner.

August 9—A group of 36 teachers from Iowa made a stop at the Inn today touring on the Drake University tour for history and geography.

August 31—The canning kitchen in the basement of the Inn has already preserved over 1,000 jars of jams, jellies, pickles, string beans, tomatoes etc. and 602 quart jars of tomato juice.

October 15—Over 700 people visited the Inn today. The largest number to come here in more than two years.

The Inn hostesses took turns keeping these diaries as part of their daily duties. Three who performed this task in the five years described above were Priscilla Staples, who started working at the Inn in 1925, Muriel DeMille and Stephen Gooch, a graduate of the Boys School.

These individuals had to be tireless because, in addition to long days at the front desk in the old bar room, guiding tours for politicians, educators and theatrical celebrities, they dealt with children of all ages, inquisitive crowds from many states, and visiting royalty. They were old-fashioned "hostesses" with rigorous discipline as well as flawless courtesy in their dealings with guests.

1934

January 11—The students of the Boys School are kept busy this time of year traversing the orchards and the estate destroying the bothersome gypsy moth.

January 18—A few of the boys worked today on the Josephine Pond pushing cakes of ice up the chute to the ice house. The average thickness of the ice today was 12 inches.

February 6—Since opportunities to use sleighs are so few and far between these days, Mr. Walker is taking advantage of the snow and is using a sleigh in place of a team to do his work about the farm.

February 9—Today proved to be the coldest day on record in the city of Boston. The temperature in Sudbury went as low as 38 degrees below zero.

February 20—The snowstorm which started last night and continued through today was the worst this section of the country has had for years. Many of the employees on the estate were unable to come to work. Fifteen inches of snow fell, obstructing all highways. Not even busses made their regular runs.

March 4—The first real signs of spring—countless squirrels scurrying along the stone walls—a flock of pheasants in the meadow partaking of the corn which Mr. Coulter scatters for them.

May 22—A yearly delight is the Wayside Inn asparagus. This was served today for the first time this season.

July 23—Miss Muriel DeMille is familiar to all who have visited the Inn during the past eight years. Her story has special appeal to the children who visit us.

August 1—Captain Cooke, who is in charge of our renowned ship *Constitution*, dined with us again tonight...He mentioned that he uses the very sensibly established rules of the Inn to enforce his own rules on smoking on his famous ship.

August 21—Our outstanding visitor today was Mr. William K. Vanderbilt of New York who arrived in Boston this morning on his yacht.

August 29—Fred Waring was a guest for breakfast this morning.

November 21—Mrs. Jesse Welsh Rose and children, Stephen Foster and Dorothy Jane, were here today. Mrs. Rose is the granddaughter of Stephen Foster, the author of *Swanee River, My Old Kentucky Home* and other songs which will be ever popular.

1935

January 29—Mr. Young invited the clergy of the Fraters meeting to the Dutton Lodge for lunch. They enjoyed seeing the boys again and had a nice visit with them.

February 10—The snow carnival was held on Ezekiel How hill today. This is an annual event, an outdoor day for the boys at the school.

March 22—Mr. Lee returned to work today and is busy planting in the old fashioned garden...Mr. Duggan was shoveling away a huge snowbank at the back of the Inn at the same time Mr. Lee was planting.

April 11—Congratulations to Mr. and Mrs. Ford on their 47th wedding anniversary.

April 18—Funeral services were conducted for Mr. Lee this afternoon at his home in Marlborough. We will always remember him as a good workman and a comrade to his fellow employees.

April 22—William Cardinal O'Connell, Archbishop of Boston, was a guest for tea this afternoon.

May 5—Governor James M. Curley gave a dinner party at the Inn today for 20 people.

May 10—Seventy-six members of the New England Baptist Hospital Alumni Association had dinner tonight...There was dancing after dinner directed by Mr. Haynes with music by Miss Muriel DeMille and Miss Florence Fisher.

September 17—Miss Perkins, President of Wellesley College, came to dinner tonight with friends.

November 20—Dr. Miriam Van Waters, who is head of the Sherborn Reformatory for Women, came here again today with guests for dinner.

1936

January 21—The world was saddened by the death last night of Great Britain's beloved King George...With his passing, the Prince of Wales will ascend to the throne. He is immensely popular and destined to be greatly beloved.

Note should be made also of the death of Rudyard Kipling, Britain's great poet and author, who died at the age of 70. Kipling will be buried in the Poets Corner at Westminster Abbey....The usual sewing classes were held for the children of the Redstone and Southwest Schools.

February 1—The waitresses have been enjoying the heat from the radiator which has been installed in the pantry. The pantry being on the north side of the house and having five large windows has been very cold and hard to heat.

February 23—When his parents were being told about the number of acres surrounding the Inn, a seven-year-old boy from Wisconsin looked up quickly and said: "Who pays the taxes?"

April 4—Trina Scariadina, author of "The First to Go Back," was a visitor today. The book tells of the author's experiences as an exile of the Russian Revolution. She told us briefly that her father and mother had been killed and she had been imprisoned.

May 30—Among our 200 dinner guests was Mr. Sumner Wells, Assistant Secretary of State and former Ambassador to Cuba.

June 16—Commencement week and graduations...We felt that a great many sacrifices had been made to give these students a college education...Therefore, this visit to the Wayside Inn was a kind of celebration, a great event, something that occurs only once.

June 17—Mr. J.P. Marquand ordered tea this afternoon....It seems that he has been here several times before.

June 26—Conversations in French, Swedish, Spanish and Italian came floating to our ears as 22 countries were represented in the group who came for dinner this evening.

August 14—An elderly gentleman today contributed information about the flax hetchel (it has long, large spikes) that when a child was particularly naughty in the old days, his mother would say "That child needs hetcheling."

August 28—All day long we've entertained members of the American Bar Association and their wives from a convention in session in Boston.

October 6—Nearly 200 prairie farmers came this afternoon as guests of Mr. Ford.

November 18—President and Mrs. Conant of Harvard University were here today.

December 27—Mr. and Mrs. Bowker brought us an armful of gifts, one for each waitress and one for each hostess.

1937

January 12—A Mrs. Holcomb told us of her thrill at finding a copy of the *Tales of a Wayside Inn* at a YMCA library in Hankow, China...established for American sailors.

January 22—Outside the kitchen window we saw little green snowdrops with large white buds on them poking their heads up...This is due to our unusually mild winter.

April 19—Members of the D'Oyle Carte Opera Company of London signed in our guest book. They are presenting Gilbert and Sullivan operas at the Colonial Theatre in Boston.

May 1—A new family visited the Inn today...The daughter is a lover of horses...When visiting the royal stables in London, she was presented with horseshoes from the saddle horses of Princess Elizabeth and Princess Margaret Rose.

June 12—The Bowkers came this afternoon and brought two large boxes of roses...We have never seen such a variety of colors and size of rose blossoms. They are rose experts and have won many prizes.

July 16—The Tauck Tours are the best conducted that we have ever seen of the Inn.

September 29—The Inn has lost a very good friend, Mr. Edward A. Filene. He died in Paris last Sunday. Mr. Filene knew the Inn well in the days of Mr. Lemon's proprietorship when he was a frequent visitor and came as secretary to the meetings of the Paint and Clay Club.

November 20—At dinner time, fur coats, raincoats, bright scarves, overshoes, caps and gloves were seen draped near the fireplaces drying out. They belonged to guests who had sat in the Harvard Stadium all afternoon watching the Harvard-Yale game. The first snowstorm of the season arrived early this morning.

1938

January 2—The day dawned bright and clear after the snowstorm of yesterday. The boys lost no time in getting the new snow plow out. They kept it going all day. The plow was purchased last year but had done nothing until today to earn its board and keep.

January 23—Dr. Tomlinson has left the retreat. Dr. Sykes and Dr. Hammatt said in no uncertain terms that they expected this to be their last time. Dr. Tomlinson, one of the oldest members himself, said: "I told the boys I don't want to hear that guff."

January 26—Dr. John Van Schaick sat in front of the bar room fire peeling an apple. "I like to sit here alone and enjoy the ticking of the old clock."

February 28—The Inn has some new arrivals. Twin lambs were born in the sheep barn some time last night, white and fluffy with long legs and stiff little ears.

April 2—The word "Tip" as we use it now—to mean a gratuity—is made up of the initial letters of the three words "To Insure Promptness." Signs with these words were attached to small boxes in the old days.

May 12—We recently had the pleasure of entertaining Mr. F. O. Stanley, a portly, white-haired gentleman and manufacturer of the Stanley Steamer automobile. He reminded us that he made automobiles long before Mr. Ford put his horseless carriage on the road.

June 16—Dr. Tomlinson died today. Exactly one year ago today, he was with us as our commencement speaker.

June 25—A guest was Mr. Shah, a descendant of a real Persian Shah...He showed Miss Fisher a gorgeous ring 500 years old.

July 11—Instead of a bellowing coach horn there was the sound of shrilling sirens. A long, shiny motor car drew up at the front door. On either side were uniformed men on motorcycles. Prince Bertil of Sweden stepped out. He spoke in English and understood it perfectly.

July 14—A guest commented today: "In most old houses, the hostesses are not well-informed. Here you seem to have a very good background for your story and know what you're talking about."

July 19—Miss DeMille explained the process of preparing wool for the spinning wheel in detail to a family. The little brother spoke up: "Aw, shucks, what's the use of trying to learn that stuff. It'll all be out of style by the time we're grown up."

August 26—We entertained Miss Moody of Shrewsbury, Mass. who still owns a shawl once worn by Jerusha How.

September 29—The chief topic of conversation is the storm [the 1938 hurricane] and how much damage it caused...An overnight guest who stopped here about two weeks ago wrote a letter enclosing three cents for a stamp and postcard asking us to report by return mail if the Inn had remained intact.

October 28—This evening a Lincoln Zephyr motor car glided to the front door. Mr. and Mrs. Ford stepped from it into the front door of their ancient hostelry.

November 11—For the first time, November 11 is a national holiday. At the end of the day nearly 600 people had eaten their holiday dinner at the Wayside Inn.

November 19—Sir Wilfred Grenfell visited again.

December 22—*Marlborough Enterprise*: "Nativity pageant presented by boys of Wayside School...Hundreds come from surrounding towns and motor parties stop on highway to witness scene..."

December 27—Emma, our cook, came out in the early afternoon with some bread crumbs and corn bread and scattered them under the birds' Christmas tree...The birds flocked down around Emma. They know her. They were not afraid of this Christmas innovation, and to reward those who planned it they chirped and sang and fluttered until the late afternoon.

1939

January 27—Miss Staples received a card today from Mr. Samuel Chamberlain telling her that his little book on the Wayside Inn has been named one of the 50 books of the year.

May 5—Our Bible box has a heavy lock and key. A guest explained that Bibles were always kept under lock and key in the old days until all the eligible young ladies of the family had been married...To prevent any prospective bridegroom from learning the age of his sweetheart.

May 29—The tables were turned the other day when a guest, instead of remarking on the ingenuity and inventiveness of our ancestors, said: "Aren't we dumb?"

June 5—An African princess lunched here today. She registered as Nina Sogo and is the first woman of her South African tribe ever to attend a world missionary conference.

June 24—Conrad Nagel, famed movie actor, and his daughter were luncheon guests today.

July 1—Mrs. Jane Bennett, teacher in the Southwest School, has joined the hostess staff. In the afternoon, she will keep the Redstone School open to visitors.

September 3—To this quiet peaceful inn there came this morning the shocking news that war had been declared between Great Britain and Germany and later in the morning that France joined with England. Right away we felt the tenseness of the situation among our guests.

XX

"An Oasis of Peace"

The decade which began in 1940 was a striking contrast to the one that preceded it. The pace quickened and the Inn reflected events in the larger world. Soon after Great Britain's declaration of war on Germany, the Inn began to receive visits from a trickle of evacuee children, and radio speeches by Prime Minister Winston Churchill held the attention of guests and hostesses. Two years later, Japan's attack on Pearl Harbor was noted, bringing America into the war. In the years that followed the Inn was visited by sailors who had been rescued from lifeboats of torpedoed ships, civilians who had survived days on rafts lost at sea, and airmen who had been shot down over the Rhine. Stories of heroism and hardship dominate the pages of the diaries.

Gasoline was rationed and visitors were not so numerous. People found ingenious new-old ways to travel—on horseback, in carriages, on bicycles. Graduates of the Wayside Inn Boys School, now in uniform, came to visit and wrote from military bases in this country and overseas. The Inn and its staff became "an oasis of peace" in a world of war. People who had visited as guests or worked at the Inn as students or conductors of bus tours, were now in war service. Some of them were killed or missing. The war was a sharp reality as the hostesses recorded the daily life of the hostelry in an era which tested the discipline of civilians as well as the courage of men in uniform.

In eloquent contrast to the events of World War II are the continuing seasonal happenings in the Inn's own life: old-fashioned dancing every Friday; pheasants in the winter's snow; carol singing at Christmas; pussy willows and jonquils in the early spring; and lilacs in bloom for Mother's Day. In the words of one hostess, the Inn helped through the war years to "conserve the things that can't be bombed, but could be lost...."

1939
(Continued)

September 17—A real war refugee came today. She was a pretty young college graduate and until a week ago was employed in the Paris office of the Holland-American Line. When the news of War came, our guest was able to get passage back to America on the *S.S. Stattendam* which reached New York yesterday. It was the *Stattendam* that picked up members of the crew of a British freighter captured by the Germans.

September 23—Today Mr. Lawrence Dane, better known as "The Roving Reporter," dropped in after a summer spent reporting for the *Boston Herald* on the raising of the sunken submarine *Squalis.*

October 19—Today's distinguished visitor is young, only 14, and has already distinguished herself in the cinema. She is Jane Withers. A motorcycle escort and a bodyguard accompanied her. In our guest book, Jane wrote: "I love this place. Jane Withers, Hollywood."

November 29—Abbie is filling great pewter bowls with all kinds of fruit...On the mantle shelves and window sills, pine boughs and turnips, yellow corn and carrots have been arranged. A picture in itself...We have sent favors to the Gookins, the old couple from Cambridge, now too feeble to come at all.

December 19—The ex-Chancellor of Germany, Heinrich Bruening, was a guest in the house this evening. He revealed the fact that there is a very rapid turnover of money in Germany at the present time.

December 24—Christmas Eve at the Wayside Inn. All is calm, all is still. We wish everybody in the world could see the Inn this Christmas night when men are at war....

1941
January 27—A few of the Fraters walked to the new chapel after breakfast and came back enthused about the simple service that takes place every school day morning at the beautiful new edifice at the corner of Dutton Road....Dr. Van Schaick conducted the communion service which for the first time was held in our chapel.

February 9—Prime Minister Winston Churchill spoke over the radio from London. It was a great speech. He asked for help, not for an army, but for the support and confidence of the

American people in supplying war materials to England. "Give us the tools and we will finish the job."

March 1—Mr. Boyer is a Frenchman...Speaking with a slight accent he said: "My 81-year-old mother is starving; my bank employees are starving. What am I to do but return to France? He expects to leave within three weeks. The family will stay in America.

March 28—As if to wake us from a peaceful slumber, the war sometimes comes to our very threshold. This week Mr. Patrick M. Buckley, a young sailor from Bristol, England, was here. He reached America as a gunner aboard an oil tanker, but not without a terrifying experience. The oil tanker was torpedoed and Mr. Buckley rescued from a life boat.

June 22—Two English sailors paid a visit to the Inn today and they were proud to be from His Majesty's Ship *Rodney*. The *Rodney* is now in Boston undergoing repairs after sinking the large German battleship *Bismark*.

July 1—Governors from more than half the 48 states were luncheon guests today. The day was a scorcher and particularly warm when the governors arrived...The speaker of the day was Mayor Fiorello LaGuardia of New York.

August 28—A guest at the Inn was Mr. John W. Thompson of Westfield, New Jersey, descended from Samuel How. His third great-grandfather was Samuel's son Ebenezer.

September 6—Distinguished visitors this evening were Colonel Theodore Roosevelt, Jr., his wife and son Quentin. He and his son are stationed at Fort Devens.

September 21—The deep shadows of the war are coming at more frequent intervals. The Baronne de Villiers Terrage handed us their card today...Her husband, the Baron, is in a German prison camp. She took a pencil, drew a line on the card, crossing out the word "Baron." In that line we felt hardship, suffering, yearning and despair.

October 1—Overnight guests, coming from a large city, were highly amused when they telephoned the Sudbury depot to send a telegram. The operator reported that: "The man was out delivering a telegram and would not be back for about 15 minutes."

October 15—Raymond Massey, the actor, was here today. Mr. Massey is tall and stooped. Deep lines in his face and a cleft chin like the Lincoln whom he portrayed in both stage and screen productions of *Abe Lincoln in Illinois*.

November 20—Thanksgiving dinners were served to hundreds of people and among them were many of our old friends. Mr. and Mrs. Bryant, friends of the Inn in Mr. Lemon's time and still coming, remarked: "When we come here for Thanksgiving, we feel as if we were coming to great-grandmother's."

December 7—A remark that was overheard today as two women guests were leaving: "Tea here is like tea in little old inns in England."

December 8—Everyone in the house was stirred today when news came that war had been declared between the United States and Japan. For several minutes at noon time the radio was brought into the bar room and the Inn family and guests gathered around it to hear the President of the United States proclaim the existence of war. The playing of the Star Spangled Banner followed. Everyone present rose to his feet.

December 13—The war is talked about every day. Germany and Italy have declared war on the United States. The great tragedy at Pearl Harbor last Sunday is discussed by practically all of the guests. Mrs. Katwinckle, wife of a busy Boston doctor, expressed what we want to say in a very few words: "The Inn is like an oasis of peace."

December 25—The shadow of war hung over the Christmas festivities....We knew that many of our guests felt the great sadness brought on in time of war.

1942

January 1—An overnight guest was Captain S. Tagan...He is with the Free French Army in Africa. He is purchasing supplies in this country.

January 5—An attractive youngster of five years was a luncheon guest...He announced: "I'm an Englishman, here for the war."

February 9—By Congressional enactment at 2 a.m. this morning the nation went on "War Time." Clocks were pushed an hour ahead.

February 16—The Inn is fulfilling a very great War need...We must safeguard the emotional stability of the nation and conserve the things that can't be bombed, but could be lost.

April 29—Hostess explaining things in the Old Kitchen. "Men 100 years ago, used to present household utensils as birthday and Valentine gifts." Pretty young woman: "They still do!"

May 4—We listened with admiration to the story of a guest here today...She lost her whole family in the Coventry Blitz which wiped out her whole street, the house completely destroyed, daughter and son-in-law gone...[in that city] a mass funeral for 400.

May 15—Today we experienced a dropping off of guests due to gasoline rationing. Owners of automobiles are not allowed more than three gallons of gasoline a week for pleasure driving which has put thousands of motorists off the road.

May 24—Tonight we welcomed our old friend, Mr. Lawrence Dane, writer and explorer. He pedalled from Boston on ''Rosy,'' a bicycle as much travelled as her owner. Mr. Dane told us of his latest experiences as an agent in Lisbon, Portugal, where he helped all sorts of refugees—men, women and children of all nationalities.

June 1—Gray Line sightseeing busses will not run after today. Gray Line will operate in the city of Boston in old-time carriages and stage coaches.

August 1—An interesting guest today was a woman who had been a missionary in Japan. She taught school there and translated several of the *Tales* into Japanese.

August 17—Army captains Kennard and Pritchard, who have been studying guerilla warfare under a British Colonel at Middlesex School in Concord on the grounds of the Revolutionary battle, were guests today. Capt. Pritchard told us of a postcript Capt. Kennard added to a letter to his wife. ''A colonel of British commandos instructing American soldiers within sight of Concord Bridge.''

August 20—Today the news headlines indicated a change for the better...Our Marines have invaded the shores of France for the first time in this Second World War....

October 22—Mrs. Allen, who dines here frequently, told us a story of coming here 25 years ago when they had no car and travelled by train. On a beautiful evening they arrived at the station just in time to see the train pull out...There was nothing they could do but walk...A car stopped and asked if they wanted a lift. In the course of the journey Mr. Allen, noticing with what flair the driver managed the car, asked if he were in the automobile business. He answered laconically: ''No—baseball.'' The next day, Mr. and Mrs. Allen recognized their good Samaritan from a picture in the newspaper. It was Babe Ruth.

November 8—With the usual Sunday sprinkling of U.S. Army and Navy uniforms, six Navy nurses in trim blue suits and white caps and Dutch officers, our dining room presented a very military picture.

November 24—*Yankee Magazine* published a picture of the Wayside Inn Kitchen this month. In the same issue appears a letter to the editor: "The first time I saw a copy of *Yankee* was in Henry Ford's Wayside Inn...I have since become a subscriber since *Yankee Magazine* and the Wayside Inn are both trying to keep alive the spirit and industry so close to the New England soil."

December 28—Two Royal Air Force men visited today. One of these studied the Calvin Coolidge bucket and when he recognized the signature of the Duke of Windsor, excitedly called to his friend: "I say! Here's Eddie! Eddie!"

1943

January 10—All persons driving automobiles for pleasure have been requested to keep off the roads...The Bowkers ventured from Worcester last evening, taking about two hours to come by bus...There have been very few guests.

February 8—Floyd Noyes, a graduate of the Boys School in 1942, is stationed at the Naval Air Base at Quonset Point, Rhode Island....Miss Fisher carries on quite a voluminous correspondence with our boys.

April 4—Among today's guests was Mary Martin of stage and screen. She was with Mr. and Mrs. Howard Dietz; he is the advertising manager of Metro-Goldwyn-Mayer.

April 26—A brush fire which started this morning spread to a point alarmingly near the Inn...Boys in the Wayside Inn School helped and all the men on the farm stopped whatever they were doing to fight the fire....Leaving time came around 8 o'clock in the evening...Two tired young firefighters came to see the Wayside Inn: "Gee, I'm glad we saved this," they said, as they apologized for their clothes which were torn and dirty. They are two buck privates from Chicago.

May 15—A glimpse of Hitler in the Munich Station was described today by one of our guests, a retired school teacher from Houston, Texas. She visited Germany in 1939 and was leaving the Munich Station just as the Führer and his aides arrived. Everywhere, people were shouting "Heil Hitler."

May 22—One person for whom we feel a bit sorry is Phil Merriman. He is our Tauck Tour conducter who is now working at the Pratt-Whitney Aircraft Company in Hartford. Once in every six weeks he has a Sunday off....Tonight, Phil came again and his appearence was alarming, the difference between outdoor and indoor work. When making his tour trips, Phil was robust and healthy, but now his face is thin and pale...Tells us Sunday here is a good tonic.

May 26—The Inn was saddened and shocked today by the news of Mr. Edsel Ford's death.

May 29—A return to another era was witnessed here this afternoon when a horse and a two-seated carriage was seen in the parking space. Mr. Welch came over from Framingham to meet friends for tea...Every day guests come again by carriage, horseback or on bicycles.

September 25—A most thrilling story came to our attention today....Mrs. Ethel G. Bell was a guest. She was one of 19 who spent 20 days on a raft after her ship returning from Africa was torpedoed and sunk in two minutes. Mrs. Bell and her two children, nine and 12 years old clung to a plank until a raft came near enough for them to climb aboard it...Nineteen days and nights they tossed about. Rations were small....Mrs. Bell conducted a short prayer service morning and night....The raft was finally sighted by a convoy.

October 29—A gentleman today was impressed by the old hand-made implements he found in the kitchen and as he left, remarked: "when you think of what people went through to get us what we have today, it seems a shame we can't make better use of what they achieved."

November 14—Another notable visitor this afternoon was Greer Garson who attracted much attention in the dining room as the principal character in "Mrs. Miniver."

December 17—Wayside Inn was alarmed today when flames burst forth from the Calvin Howe House, dormitory of the Boys School. Fire engines arrived from Sudbury, Marlborough and Framingham. The boys who lost their sleeping quarters were temporarily lodged in Dutton House.

December 20—Christmas cards are arriving from Wayside Inn School boys now in the armed forces...From Arkansas, Seattle, San Francisco and parts unknown.

December 25—Sitting before the spinet this afternoon was a captain of the Marines. Captain Culp was his name, just home from the Pacific. The music drew several guests into the parlor and soon a harmony of voices was heard singing "It Came

Upon a Midnight Clear."...A lady looked proudly at the young man, then whispered to the hostess: "He led the carol singing on Guadalcanal last Christmas."

1944

January 8—This year marks the 15th anniversary of the Wayside Inn diary.

January 11—Miss Jean Speiser of *Life Magazine* appeared with pencil and notebook to do an article about the Inn.

March 18—About 25 hikers took a train from Boston to Sudbury this afternoon and walked to the Wayside Inn from the Sudbury station. They were members of the Appalachian Mountain Club.

April 3—"If you'd been in the war as long as I have, you would appreciate a place like this," remarked a good-looking lieutenant. Then he turned to his wife and asked: "Shall we skip Portland?" The wife answered yes and arrangements were made to stay for three or four days.

April 20—Twelve wounded war veterans filed into the bar room one by one. Most of these boys were from homes in Massachusetts and are now recuperating at the new hospital in Framingham after Guadalcanal and Italy.

April 26—Word has come from Stanley Farr, a graduate of the Boys School in the Aleutians...He finds life there pretty dull. The one bright spot was his description of finding pictures of the Inn in a recent *Life Magazine* article: "I enjoyed the pictures because they brought back some very pleasant memories."

June 6—While word of the Invasion has been expected for some time, the news came as a surprise early this morning. When the chapel bell rang at 9 o'clock everyone who could be spared from their daily work joined the children at the services. Invasion news was brought in by the guests at subsequent intervals during the day. It was a day when the historic significance of events touched the hearts and souls of all who entered here.

July 6—A friendly letter from a British flyer, a one-time guest, was received today: "Have you ever considered how lucky you are to live where you do or do you just take it for granted? The beauty of the Wayside Inn is that it can afford to give the world the go-by. I shall have to close as I am flying tonight and it is usually quite a scuffle."

July 14—The death of Colonel Theodore Roosevelt has sent us searching for his signature. He is registered this way: "Theodore Roosevelt, Col. 26th Infantry, September 6, 1941. At that time he was stationed at Fort Devens and dropped in for dinner. He died during the invasion of Normandy.

July 30—"I have just eaten the best Sunday morning breakfast in America!" exclaimed Mr. Robert F. Duncan, house guest, as he emerged from the dining room early this morning.

August 13—Two hundred guests were seated in the Martha-Mary Chapel to hear children of the Wayside Inn Schools go on the air as a part of a "Greenfield Chorus" radio program presented by Mr. and Mrs. Ford to a national radio audience.

August 18—What part can an old inn play in a great war? One answer to this question came today when a lonely mother arrived, recalling her sailor son, now overseas. "He came here when he was a little boy," she said, "and he always loved the place." She spoke as if he had gone away forever and perhaps he has—His last letter was dated May 14—Mother's Day. The Inn is a refuge and shelter for the lonely in spirit and the brave of heart.

October 1—A letter from somewhere in New Guinea: "I just wanted to drop you a line and tell you how often I look back on the wonderful times I had at the Wayside Inn...The friends who accompanied me are all over the world...Ensign Trent is on a destroyer in the Pacific, Ensign Tobias is in Fiji and Ensign Wheeler is in an amphibious attack squadron...One thing that makes places like this bearable is that we are able to hang on to such lovely memories."

December 23—Mr. and Mrs. Bowker arrived from Worcester tonight, their arms were filled with beautifully wrapped packages, one for everyone. They didn't forget a cook in the kitchen or a watchman. These dear people filled the Inn with the real Christmas spirit.

1945

February 19—In the summer of 1941, Fitzpatrick Travelogues made a colored sound picture of the Inn. He asked Miss DeMille and Miss Staples to walk towards the front door as he snapped his picture...Today a letter came from England from a member of the R.A.F. who came to visit the Inn a year ago: "The other evening the air bomber and I popped into a cinema in Nottingham...Wasn't I surprised when I saw the Wayside Inn in Technicolor and Miss Staples walking in the old doorway."

March 1—A Wayside Inn truck driver and his assistant saw 14 deer running over a hill silhouetted against the white snow.

April 13—A beautiful spring day with lilac blossoms in bud and the feathery haze of tiny leaves...But the guests were conspicuous by their absence. People walked quietly through the rooms and conversed very little. A long, slow funeral train made its way north towards Washington bearing a flag-draped coffin with our late President Roosevelt. The Inn remained quiet between the hours of four and six this afternoon out of respect to President Roosevelt. No meals were served and quietness prevailed.

May 8—Peace in Europe was declared at 9 a.m. this morning....We were able to listen to the actual announcement by President Truman and a short speech from Prime Minister Churchill...A momentous occasion.

May 21—We had a most pleasant surprise tonight at dancing class when Bill Cummings appeared unexpectedly. It was good to see him after three years overseas. He is in the Air Corps and has five oak leaf clusters, a presidential citation, the purple heart and two medals for outstanding flying.

July 27—"Fifty years have gone by faster than the smell of that gravy!" said the editor of a Boston paper. "But I must hurry home to tell the world what I think of the British election and the defeat of Chuchill."

August 14—Suspense filled every nook and corner of the old Inn today as guests and the Inn family awaited news of the Japanese surrender. It seemed as if the long-awaited official news would never come until a few minutes after 7 o'clock in the evening the telephone rang and brought the good news. Yes, the war was over! Hostesses ran for the pantry to tell waitresses while waitresses ran to the kitchen to tell cooks. Guests clapped their hands.

September 14—Dame May Whitty, now playing in Boston with Eva LeGallienne and Victor Jory was a most interested spectator of the children's classes this afternoon. She had luncheon with a group of friends on the front porch where her rich, melodious voice could be heard in conversation.

October 16—We had an interesting talk with a Mr. Harris today, a machinist's mate first class who was with the amphibious forces at Okinawa and Iwo Jima...He had three ships sunk under him and was severely wounded by an exploding Japanese plane. When we referred to his Hollywood address he told us that before the war he had been a stunt man in the movies and felt that was pretty good preparation for some phases of Navy life.

December 20—Encompassed by an all-day snowstorm as if preparing for a long winter's nap, the Inn family sat around the bar room hearth while Tony Angelico told of his experiences of the past five years. These included flapping pancakes for army buddies in Africa as he used to do over the kitchen range at the Inn.

V-J Day in August, 1945, brought joy and the return of many old friends. Graduates of the Boys School and other servicemen came back to the dancing classes on Friday nights and told the students of their war experiences. From then on the Inn was more conscious that it belonged to an international world and was no longer just a quiet New England refuge. Henry Ford celebrated his 83rd birthday in July of 1946, and his death in 1947 marked the end of his stewardship. The closing of the Southwest School was announced in January of 1947, and the Wayside Inn Boys School was closed the following May.

The 1948 World Series in Boston between the Braves and the Cleveland Indians was another landmark, and by 1950, uniforms were back in the Inn as the Korean War began.

1946

January 4—Another former Wayside Inn boy attended dancing class tonight, Peter Kosak, lately discharged from the Army....He spent many long, weary months in hospitals in Europe and Fort Devens because of a wound in his leg. It was wonderful to see him dancing a quadrille quite like his old self.

January 22—A distinguished luncheon guest, Sir Adrian Boult, wrote in our special register, "A delightful day."

February 8—"Hank" Muser, the star halfback of the West Point football team during 1941-43, was a dinner guest tonight. The boys in the dancing class applauded enthusiastically when Mr. Haynes introduced him.

February 22—On this Washington's birthday 1946 let us honor Joseph Venditti who belongs in the list of our country's heroes. Joe graduated from the Boys School in 1942 and was executed by the Japanese almost a year ago.

March 7—The first real signs of approaching spring are here. A robin comes to the feeder every day for his lunch...Pussy willows have been brought in for table decoration...Children bring their jump ropes with them.

April 8—Mr. and Mrs. Lampman and their two daughters are spending a few days with us. They came to see the survivors of the Bataan Death March parade in Boston.

May 19—The most important event of the day was the dinner and business meeting held for the purpose of organizing an alumni association of the Wayside Inn Boys School. About 40 came...William Cash of '41 was the instigator.

May 20—The old hawthorne in front of the Inn, a victim of age and two hurricanes, has taken a new lease on life and is covered with little pink blossoms.

May 30—It was a lovely day for America's first peacetime Memorial Day since 1941. The majority of our guests were family groups. One of them, Mr. Borst, told us that 30 years ago he came here on his honeymoon. Mr. Lemon met them at the station with a horse and buggy.

July 26—Tonight we greeted Mrs. Enrico Caruso who came in for dinner.

July 30—Today Mr. Ford is 83 years old and in Dearborn his friends and neighbors have planned to make it a gala occasion. Here at the Wayside Inn another happy birthday was sung in the pantry for [waitress] Alice Congdon.

August 26—This is the time of year when the number of questions asked reaches a maximum. Today we answered one that was a bit out of the ordinary. A guest was looking at the signboard which reads ''Longfellow's Wayside Inn'' and asked: ''This used to be called Ford's Wayside Inn. Have you changed the name?''

October 14—Today the Inn is taking on an expectant look. Mr. and Mrs. Ford are expected to pay us a visit and we want them to know how welcome they are...The countryside donned its best autumn dress this morning, one of brilliant red and yellow. Mr. and Mrs. Ford arrived after an absence of nearly two years.

October 22—Two distinguished visitors were recognized today as they ordered luncheon under assumed names. They were

Ronald Colman and Richard Barthelemess accompanied by their wives.

December 16—Mr. Coulter was busy today putting electric candles in all the windows. When night came, guests began driving by on the way to the pageant at the Chapel...Red ribbons were tied on all the wreaths as Mr. Davieau brought them in. The brass knocker on the front door supported a large one and smaller wreaths were hung at each window encircling the lighted candle within.

1947

January 5—Karl Compton, President of MIT, was one of our dinner guests this evening...Mr. Compton is a member of the board of the Ford Foundation and has been to the Inn several times.

January 25—The Inn welcomed Mrs. Marshall Field from Chicago and her young son, a student at St. Mark's School....Mrs. Field looked chic as was to be expected in a brown suit with Navy blue accessories.

January 29—Some sad news for us and for the people of Sudbury—the closing of the Southwest School. It has served the town for 15 years and Mrs. Bennett has taught there since the opening of the school...Her pupils have been outstanding and they are going to miss the lady whom they fondly call "Ma Bennett."

February 22—A tall, stately woman appeared in the doorway, advanced to the desk and said: "I'm Mrs. Franklin Delano Roosevelt and I have a reservation for dinner." Mrs. Roosevelt looked charming in her black crepe wool dress, black coat with silver fox neckpiece and modest black hat.

April 5—One of our guests said that during the war when manual labor was scarce and next to impossible to get... a small boy came to help in her garden...She asked how much he expected to receive for an hour's work. The reply came quickly: "Sixty cents if you don't boss me, Ma'am and 75 if you do."

April 8-10—The death of Mr. Ford has saddened us all. There are no adequate words to express sincerely enough our sense of this loss. This morning at a simple and reverent service held at the chapel that seemed so closely associated with him, some of the old hymns that Mr. Ford liked especially were sung. Excerpts from Mr. Ford's autobiography, *My Life and Work,* were read by one of the boys. His friendly handshake will never be forgotten....

May 28—Over the radio this morning, the public was notified of an event momentous to us, the closing of the Wayside Inn Boys School. Everyone will miss the boys. A brighter side to the picture was the opening of the Grist Mill on Monday. Mr. Perry has been grinding furiously to make up for lost time.

August 5—On some summer days, as many as 1,000 people dropped in. Today we had over 500 including the wives of men attending a convention of lawn bowling clubs in Boston.

October 5—One of our girls was married this afternoon in the chapel. She was Ann Bradshaw, South Sudbury, whose father owns the general store and is known the countryside over. Ann attended both our Mary Lamb and Southwest Schools. Ann later served the Inn as a hostess.

November 16—A unique event took place today when the first retreiver trials held in New England were run down near the Sudbury River.

November 18—Dr. John Van Schaick, one of the oldest and most beloved of the Fraters, was here last night...It is pathetic to see our friend groping for a chair or bending low to read a book. He is nearly blind.

1948

February 2—The snowbanks around the Inn are getting higher with each snowfall...A paradise for our pheasants...as it enables them to reach the berries still hanging from some bushes along the side of the road.

February 15—Barbara Eaton, our summertime hostess, appeared around noontime looking very beautiful in a blue ski jacket and a fringe of blonde hair framing her pink cheeks...Mr. Aaron, a photographer, made an appointment to take Barbara's picture dressed as a Puritan maiden, with white apron and cap...Barbara is a tall, handsome girl, always well-dressed and well-groomed. We are happy to have her featured as a model.

February 27—This afternoon the Inn welcomed Mrs. Stuart Hoppin, the former Muriel DeMille, for many years a hostess here.

May 16—The birds don't seem discouraged by cold and rain, but have arrived in their gay spring plumage. Two brilliant scarlet tanagers were seen today.

May 31—A visitor from far away was Dr. Hume Wai who registered from Satar District, India. We learned that Ghandi's son was a patient of his and that Ghandi himself had been to see Dr. Wai several times.

August 16—Guests are commenting on the Red Sox versus the Cleveland Indians. The Inn is crowded with guests.... Everyone seems to be baseball conscious these days. A house guest from Cleveland had a friendly argument with the hostesses as to whether the Red Sox or the Indians would win the pennant this year.

August 25—The passing of "The Babe," as Babe Ruth was called, was felt in every community throughout the United States. In his early days of fame, he was seen frequently here in Sudbury for he owned a lovely old farmhouse on Dutton Road.

October 7—The World Series is attracting hundreds of people to Boston and in consequence all the hotels are full and our rooms are taken night after night.

1949

January 3—Mr. Bradshaw, town clerk of Sudbury, called to get the names of brides and grooms married at the chapel for his 1948 record. Our book kept for this purpose since July contains the dates of 23 weddings bringing the total up to 139.

March 1—Professor Schell always has an interesting speaker for the Waysiders....Tonight a young man in his early 30's, modest and unassuming, took his place among others of the group. Who was he? It was hard to believe when we were told that this young man is the president of the Polaroid Company and one of the outstanding scientists of our time. Dr. Land is his name.

March 27—Mary Martin the actress, and her husband Richard Halliday, arrived here this morning for a weekend rest after the performance of South Pacific last night.

April 8—The pupils from the Mary Lamb School enjoyed their dancing class in the ball room this afternoon...The good afternoon waltz was enjoyed by all...Later Mr. Haynes and Mrs. Bennett did an exhibition Gallop while the children watched.

April 16—The spring season is upon us and we are glad to see maple buds, jonquils and forsythia in bloom in the old-fashioned garden...This being the Easter weekend...Miss Fisher has been busy painting baskets which will be filled with gay flowers and placed throughout the Inn.

May 25—This was a busy day for Barbara Eaton...Although she has been connected with the Inn for a long time, graduating from both the Mary Lamb and the Southwest Schools, this was the first time she was on her own. She took two school groups through the house and told the complete story from first to last.

June 2—In the dining room today were Mrs. Charles Lindbergh and her mother Mrs. Morrow...It seemed to give Mrs. Lindbergh great pleasure to sit at the same table on our dining porch where she and Charles had sat several years ago.

June 3—A distinguished guest today was Judy Garland, screen actress who is in Boston for a rest and treatments at Peter Bent Brigham Hospital.

August 15—No relief from the drought is yet in sight. Thunderstorms have been too few and far between to do much good and several wells in the neighborhood have gone dry. Mr. Clarke had to stop watering the garden and the flowers will suffer in consequence.

September 18—The cool and sparkling days of late September flow like golden wine into the bowl of autumn...If anyone asked me what happiness is I'd say it is a September day in New England.

October 27—Mr. Loring Coleman, Sudbury artist, has been seen around the Inn lately...Mr. Coleman is painting a picture of the Inn which will be used in the January issue of the *Ford Times Magazine*.

1950

March 19—Emma Maki, who has worked so faithfully in the kitchen for 18 years...is opening a small restaurant in the town of Maynard...Everyone will miss her but we wish her the best of luck in her new undertaking.

April 4—A pleasant lady this afternoon told us of being here in April of 1917. She remembered walking into the parlor and seeing Sarah Bernhardt there talking to Edward A. Filene.

May 5—A guest giving her name as Miss MacDonald turned out to be the glamorous Jeanette of concert, stage and movie fame. She is giving a concert in Worcester Saturday night.

May 14—Today is Mother's Day and it brought over 500 dinner guests to the Inn. The lilacs are in full bloom.

July 18—Khaki uniforms are beginning to filter in among our guests and it is hard to believe we are at war again.

July 24—A man from Pittsburgh stopped at the desk and

asked if he might get a record of the ticking of the parlor clock. We often have requests to take pictures, but this is the first time anyone requested permission to take sound recordings.

August 15—An item of interest to the town of Sudbury is the report of Miss Lottie M. Smith of the Mass. Audubon Society who has identified 36 birds in the new wildlife sanctuary ...property formerly owned by the Wayside Inn.

August 16—A memorable day. The Inn appeared on television for the first time in all its long history.

August 31—Someone has said that true graciousness is the art of making a person feel important and comfortable at the same time. That is the duty of every Wayside Inn hostess.

September 29—We heard early this morning of the passing away of Mrs. Ford who was our most loyal friend and the diary's most devoted reader.

Clara Ford's death marked the end of an era. Her grandsons, who had visited the Inn as boys on their way to Seal Harbor, Maine, for their summer vacations were busy trying to rescue the Ford Motor Company from financial ruin caused by mismanagement following Edsel Ford's death in 1943. They had little time or interest for the old times and the old things that their grandparents loved.

A Wayside Inn Corporation was formed with William Clay Ford, Donald K. David, President of the Ford Foundation, Frank Campsall and Dr. Don Shelly, Curator of the Edison Institute at Greenfield Village at Dearborn among the trustees. Over the years, as expenses mounted, the farms and woodlots that Henry Ford had painstakingly acquired were sold off one by one, until only the 300 acres immediately surrounding the Inn, Chapel and Grist Mill remained.

Tour busses and school groups still made pilgrimages to the ancient hostelry as the decade of the 50's rolled toward its midway point, and the hostesses still gave their daily tours, but the Inn ceased to be the living museum it once was.

XXI

The Inn's On Fire!

Curt Harding and Jeanne Fredey were two of the most popular members of the Sudbury High School Class of '53 and their wedding at Newton's Grace Episcopal Church on the evening of December 21, 1955 reflects that popularity. Two of Curt's basketball teammates are in the wedding party. Guy Palmer is best man and David Hawes is one of the ushers. The guest list is a Who's Who of old Sudbury families, and is so extensive that Jean Fredey, the father of the bride, is compelled to book the spacious north ballroom at the Wayside Inn for the wedding reception. Among the guests dining and dancing before the roaring fire in the great north fireplace are Eleanor and Jim Greenawalt.

Greenawalt has recently been promoted to the rank of captain in the Sudbury Fire Department and lives just down the street from the fire station. His wife, the former Eleanor Goulding, is very much at home at the Inn. She was one of the children chosen to attend the Southwest School started by Henry Ford in 1931, and learned to dance in the same low-ceilinged ballroom.

Outside in the parking lot, cars start hard as the last guests head homeward at 11:30 p.m. The cold snap that has held the Northeast in its grip for the better part of a week seems likely to continue. The temperature is already zero and falling. Since it is a Tuesday night there are no overnight guests at the Inn.

Night watchman William Mann of Marlborough comes on duty at midnight, makes his first set of rounds and then goes to work cleaning up the north ballroom. The job is still not completed by 2 a.m. when his second round is due to start. On the lower floor, near one of the pantries, he smells something unusual. He opens the door to the boiler room and is greeted by a puff of smoke.

Mann slams the door, returns to the front desk in the old bar room and phones Assistant Director George Griffin who is asleep in the coach house across the street. It takes several rings before Griffin is awake. He tells Mann to notify Inn-keeper John Saint, hangs up and dials the fire department.

Meanwhile others are aware that something is amiss. A trailer truck driver on the Route 20 bypass smells smoke and sees flames. He flags down a Marlborough cruiser and passes on the information, but by the time the message is relayed to Sudbury, the alarm has already been given. At about the same time, a resident of Dutton Road is awakened by a bright light shining in her bedroom window. She looks out to see the entire north wing of the Inn in flames.

Leo Quinn, the town's only permanent firefighter besides Fire Chief Albert St. Germaine, glances at the clock as he picks up the telephone on his bedside table in the Loring Parsonage next door to the fire station. It says 2:20 a.m. He puts out the call over the monitors of the town's 20 call firemen and cranks up Engine Three, a 1942 International which carries 500 gallons of water. It is the nearest thing to a piece of Class A fire apparatus that Sudbury owns.

The call box awakens St. Germaine out of a sound sleep at his home on Peakham Road, about a ten-minute drive from the Inn. He turns on the radio in his cruiser and immediately gets a call from Police Sergeant Ernest Ryan, who has heard the alarm and is already at the scene. "It's bad," says Ryan. "I'd send for as much mutual aid as you can get." St. Germaine radios a second alarm to Framingham, Marlborough, South-borough, Wayland, Weston and Concord.

Quinn races Engine Three down the service road to the rear of the Inn and pulls up as close to the building as he dares. Flames are already shooting out of the serving room windows on the second floor of the North Wing. Mickey Hriniak, a call fireman with only one arm, helps Quinn pull booster lines off the truck, but the fire is too hot and the water does no good.

It is 2:35 a.m. by the time St. Germaine arrives on the scene. The second floor of the north wing is totally engulfed in flames and the fire is working back down to the kitchens below. As the chief radios in a third alarm for more mutual aid, Captain Greenawalt, who left the building only hours before, arrives with Engine Two, a 1938 Ford pumper that was donated to the town by the Wayside Inn trustees only the year before.

Greenawalt and St. Germaine begin chopping a hole in the ice of Josephine Pond, a small impoundment behind the Inn that services the ice house. The ice is 16 inches thick and it takes nearly ten minutes before they reach water. By this time a Marlborough pumper arrives. Both engines start drawing water from the pond and supplying water to the other trucks as they arrive.

By 2:45 a.m. there are eleven pieces of apparatus on the scene, four from Sudbury, two each from Framingham, Marlborough and Wayland and a ladder truck from Concord. Several try to draw water from the mill brook beside the Inn but end up sucking air. The nearest fire hydrant is more than a mile to the east at Ecke's Motel.

By 3 a.m. nearly 100 firefighters are pouring thousands of gallons of water on the inferno from 20 hose lines, but the fire is still making headway. Flames have spread to the west wing, containing the 1800 ballroom and have started to work their way horizontally toward the older rooms in the front of the building, which are filled with priceless antiques.

Two engines from Framingham concentrate on cutting the fire off in the East Wing and succeed in stopping the flames at the Old Kitchen. The display pewter on the tables is melted by the intense heat and the wainscoting and the ceiling planks are scorched, but a coating of ice preserves most of the furniture.

Elsewhere things aren't going quite as well. The 16-below-zero temperatures slush up the water in the pumps of the two big engines beside the pond, and gasoline heaters have to be rushed in to get them going again. A gauge freezes on one of the Wayland pumpers, increasing pressure in an inch-and-a-half hand line to more than 1,000 pounds, which sends two firefighters sprawling. Robert Groton of Wayland is transported to Leonard Morse Hospital in Natick with a broken leg.

Trucks start to run low on fuel and Algy Alexander and the Interstate Gas and Oil Company open their stations and relay gas and oil to the site to keep them going. By the time the fire is finally extinguished, 200 gallons of fuel will have been consumed.

There is a touch of humor as well. Freddie Craig, the ranger at the Nobscot Scout Reservation and a Sudbury call firefighter, reaches into the icy water of Josephine Pond to clear an intake strainer and comes up with a handful of one very-surprised horned pout.

Meanwhile the word has spread throughout the town. The Sudbury Civil Defense, Red Cross and Grange set up a canteen at the town hall, and start relaying coffee and sandwiches to the Inn, where Mrs. Alfred Gardner and Mrs. Thomas Cahill distribute them to the firefighters. Paul Ecke, the owner of Ecke's Motel, brings a huge Thermos of Irish Coffee.

By 3:30 a.m. the fire has been controlled in the East Wing but flames have broken through the gambrel roof on the main house and the fire is venting itself out. Police Chief John McGovern is on the spot with his cameras just as firefighters force the front door, only to be greeted by a flash of flame and smoke. His dramatic picture is picked up by the Associated Press Wire Service and is carried in newspapers all over the world.

Several volunteers rush into the Longfellow Parlor to see what they can save, but Jerusha Howe's piano and the "sombre clock" that Longfellow immortalized are frozen to the floor and covered with a thick coating of ice. Small items such as the Molineaux etchings are saved. The How coat of arms is covered with a thick layer of carbon, but survives. Two priceless Paul Revere prints are a total loss and the How family Bible and its box are badly scorched. Water pouring down the front stairs quickly freezes into a giant cascade.

Outside, the firefighters are barely recognizable, their helmets and heavy jackets and boots coated with layers of ice. Wilfred Spiller's picture also makes the wire services and is run in many New England papers.

By 4 a.m., the North and West wings are totally demolished and firefighters concentrate their efforts on the front of the building. St. Germaine declares the building a "total loss," and later sets damages at $200,000 not counting the many priceless antiques. By the time the blaze is brought under control, a million gallons of water, more than four times the capacity of the town's storage tank on Goodmans Hill, has been pumped onto the remains of the Inn. Beneath the ice of Josephine Pond there is only mud.

By dawn the word has spread far and wide. The Inn fire is front page news in all the Boston and Worcester papers and has made the wire services. The hill behind the Inn barn is dotted with people silently and sadly watching. Ira Amesbury, a local poet, sums up their feelings in a few short lines.

A tranquil scene
Soon broken;
The snow grayed by night,
Turned red—
Old Wayside was dying;
Torn by hungry fire,
Its memories
Scattered to the sky
And frozen ground.

In waking morn
The trees despaired,
Looked about;
Old Wayside, black and cold—
Was dead.

How The Wayside Inn Grew

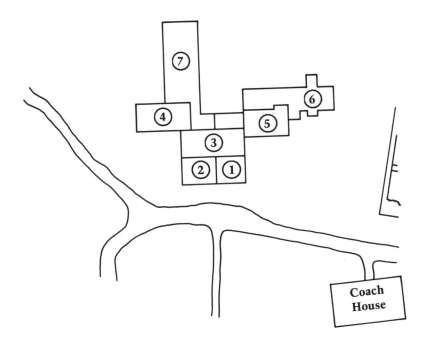

1. Original Building, David How, 1702
2. First Addition, David How, 1716
3. Second Addition, Ezekiel How, 1746
4. Third Addition, Ezekiel How, 1790
5. Old Kitchen, Adam Howe, 1815
6. Fifth Addition, Edward R. Lemon, 1898
7. North Wing, Henry Ford, 1926

XXII

"Nothing That Is Good Ever Dies"

Priscilla Staples, Bertram Little and Russell Kettell picked their way through a tangle of charred and broken chairs, paintings, hooked rugs, pewter and kitchen utensils in what two days before had been the bustling front hallway of the Wayside Inn. Normally the building would have been filled with the sounds of laughter and music as guests waited their turn for dinner or enjoyed a drink in front of the fireplace in the old bar room.

But the fire of December 22, 1955 had changed all that. The old building was silent now, the only sounds the occasional dripping of melting snow through a gaping hole in the gambrel roof. Outside the Sudbury police had erected ropes to keep the curious at bay, and volunteer guards working two-hour shifts kept a sharp eye out for possible looters.

Miss Staples, the Inn's Assistant Manager, Little, the President of the Society for the Preservation of New England Antiquities, and Kettell, the President of the Concord Antiquarian Society, were on official business. Their job was to see what of the Inn's contents could be salvaged and take steps to protect it from further damage. Privately they all shared the same terrible thought with many other townspeople: would the Inn ever open its doors again?

At the back stairs that once led up to the Lafayette bedroom and the 1800 ballroom, Miss Staples received a pleasant surprise. There, in a tiny closet, Inn records going back to the 1700's and beyond, and two of Ole Bull's precious violins had escaped all but minor damage from smoke and water. "It was as if God's hand had kept the fire away," she later told the *Worcester Evening Gazette*, as workers transferred the records to the vaults of the Framingham Trust Company for safekeeping.

In the Longfellow Parlor, Jerusha Howe's piano and the "sombre clock" of Longfellow's poem remained frozen to the floor. The glass covering the How coat of arms hanging over the mantlepiece was covered with black carbon, but the arms

259

themselves, protected by a layer of ice, were undamaged. Upstairs in Jerusha Howe's bedroom over the Old Kitchen, the low four-poster bed stood undamaged, its thick, tufted white spread glazed with ice and stiff as a board. The hooked rugs were frozen so solid that they appeared to be part of the floor.

Even as Staples, Little and Kettell made plans for the removal of salvageable antiques to shelter in the coach house, other friends of the Inn were organizing to see that the ancient hostelry would be rebuilt. Less than six hours after the last piece of fire apparatus returned to quarters, the Sudbury Board of Selectmen met and voted unanimously to offer the Ford Foundation "any cooperation and community effort deemed necessary," to rebuild the Inn.

The following day, groups all over town were meeting. Twenty neighbors whose land abutted Wayside Inn property met at the home of Robert Caldwell on Peakham Road, which only a few years before was Ford's Southwest Schoolhouse. Don Atkins called an emergency meeting of the Sudbury-Wayland Kiwanis Club, and the Reverend Ernest Bodenweber of the Memorial Congregational Church hosted a meeting of the Sudbury clergy. Out of these meetings came the formation of the Citizen's Committee for the Preservation of the Wayside Inn, with Boston banker Edmund Sears as chairman and Calvin Smith, attorney John C. Powers, and insurance man Leslie Hall as prime movers.

The committee lost no time in getting to work. Ford Vice President for Public Relations Charles F. Moore had announced that a task force of experts from the Ford Foundation and the Ford Motor Company would make a fact-finding trip to Sudbury in early January. It was important that the Ford representatives know how much the Inn meant to its Sudbury neighbors. A massive letter-writing campaign was the only answer.

More than 40,000 brochures explaining the Inn's plight and including a quote from Henry Ford, "Nothing that is good ever dies," were printed and sent to public officials, private citizens and civic groups all over the country. The Sudbury High School Student Council sent a check to cover part of the $1,000 postage bill, and members of the committee dug into their pockets to come up with the rest. The junior and senior classes at Sudbury High School volunteered to stamp and address letters, and Student Council President Sheila Moynihan galvanized the Junior High into action as well.

Albert R. Blanchard, credit manager for the Hood Rubber Company, took a suitcase full of brochures on a cross-country business trip, dropping them off where they would do the most good.

Their efforts paid off in spades. By the time Moore and his delegation arrived in Sudbury on January 4, more than 10,000 letters had arrived at either Sudbury or Dearborn and more were on their way. They included appeals from former President Harry S Truman, Senator John F. Kennedy, former Speaker of the House Joe Martin and Supreme Court Justice Felix Frankfurter.

Townspeople hoping for a quick decision from the Ford people were disappointed. Moore stated that the meetings with the Citizens Committee were beneficial, but it would be at least two weeks to a month before any decision would be made.

"We don't want to just erect another building," he told the *Boston Traveler*. "Our decision will be based on cost, the ability to obtain materials and whether the experts feel there is enough left of the building upon which to start. My personal impression is that enough of the original building and materials remain to justify a restoration job."

Unbeknownst to the Sudbury Citizen's Committee, Moore had more than his personal observations to go on. The day after the fire, Dr. Donald A. Shelly, Director of the Henry Ford Museum at Greenfield Village in Dearborn, had sent Roy Baker, the Chief Custodian for the Society for the Preservation of New England Antiquities, to see if the Inn was worth restoring. Baker not only said that it was, but told Shelly he'd be very interested in supervising the job.

Meanwhile local residents were hedging their bets. Representative James DeNormandie of Lincoln introduced a resolution in the Massachusetts House of Representatives calling for the restoration of the Wayside Inn. It was approved on January 6.

The rest of January dragged on without word from Dearborn, and nerves in Sudbury were fraying. On February 12, the *Boston Herald* carried the Page One headline: "Sudbury Ready to Restore Wayside Inn if Fords Don't." The Citizens Committee stood ready to call on thousands of offers of assistance from all over the world if the Fords failed to come through.

Six days later, their wait was over. On February 18, William Clay Ford, President of the Wayside Inn Board of Trustees, delivered the good news: "I am delighted to report that the

Ford Foundation, through its president Mr. H. Rowan Gaither, Jr., has informed me that the Foundation will undertake financial responsibility for the restoration of the Wayside Inn."

On February 23, Gaither made it official with the announcement that the Foundation would supply $500,000 for the restoration work. Just two months and two days after the fire— 64 days that seemed more like an eternity—the *Sudbury Citizen* carried the news in a banner headline across its front page: "Wayside Inn to Live Again."

Henry Ford's words were prophetic. "Nothing that is good ever dies."

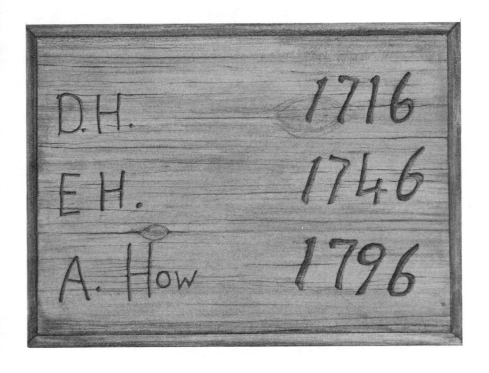

XXIII

A Phoenix Rises From The Ashes

Roy Woodbury Baker of Antrim, New Hampshire, was used to getting phone calls about old houses. He was, after all, the Chief Custodian for the Society for the Preservation of New England Antiquities, with 58 homes under his care. People called for advice all the time.

But this call on the morning of December 23, 1955 was different. It was long distance from Dr. Donald A. Shelly, the director of the Henry Ford Museum in Dearborn, Michigan. Had Baker heard about the fire at the Wayside Inn the day before? Baker had. Could he go down to Sudbury and determine if there was enough of the original building still intact for a meaningful restoration?[1]

Baker hung up the phone, stuck his pipe in his coat pocket and headed out the door. Three hours later, he was poking through the still-steaming remains of the Wayside Inn. The more he looked, the more excited he became. Yes, he told Shelly the following day, the Inn could be restored and he would be more than happy to be involved with the restoration.

"I found a house that was comfortable, but not pretentious," he later told the *Christian Science Monitor.* "A house that was hospitable, but not grand."[2]

Over the next three years, Baker would come to know this house better than any living person. The fire had peeled away the layers to reveal clues that would be meaningful only to an expert in ancient architecture.

Building Inspector Albert St. Germaine issued a building permit for the restoration on January 8, 1957, but Baker was at work long before that. Poking through the rubble of the old part of the house and poring over old papers and records that Priscilla Staples had salvaged from the fire, he searched for evidence that would tell him what the original house had looked like and when it was built.

And he found it. Uncovering a corner post, he discovered mortise holes in the plate (beam) on the north side of the old bar room. These originally held wall studs, indicating that this had once been an outside wall. Examining the western wall, he searched for evidence of a fireplace. Since the floor had been replaced several times, he turned his attention to the second floor girt and found the clue he was looking for. There, a small area had been cut out to accommodate a hearthstone. Probing it with his pocket knife, he discovered bits of clay that had been placed there 250 years before as bedding for the hearth.

The giant chestnut girt held other clues as well. Further down, two more small mortises indicated that this virgin timber had supported a long-gone staircase, which had wound around an extinct chimney built inside the western wall. Directly across the hall, Baker discovered another girt with a cutout identical to the first, indicating that David How had doubled the size of the fireplace when he made his first two-room addition around 1716. David raised the ceiling of his new first floor room seven inches, which accounts for the step down into the Drivers and Drovers room and the low ceiling in the upstairs hallway and Longfellow bedroom of today's Inn.

Turning his attention to the second floor ceiling posts, Baker found the mortises that anchored the original gabled roof. Enough key beams had been spared by the fire to determine exactly where the first roof extended, and the angle of the mortises allowed him to recreate the pitch of the rafters. [3]

Bit by bit, Roy Baker put the pieces of the puzzle together in his mind. The old bar room and the Edison room (now Drivers and Drovers) above it constituted "House No. 1," which was built early in the eighteenth century and featured an entrance hall and fireplace on its west end with a circular stairway leading around the chimney to the second floor.

The only evidence that didn't fit a building date in the early 1700's were the windows. These were of a style common in the late 1600's, but were probably built by Samuel How, who was a glazier, well before the building was erected, or even salvaged from another older structure.

In the southwest corner of the Longfellow bedroom, Baker discovered a pair of original posts that extended all the way from the first floor to the attic. Mortise holes in the girt above the fireplace on the north wall provided all the proof he needed that House No. 2 was a four-room building.

He also discovered that all the structural timbers of the first and second floors of the west gable end, which included the Longfellow parlor and bedroom, the How sitting room and Hobgoblin Hall, were old at the time of the fire. This was not the case with the east gable (the old bar room, Drivers and Drovers room, Lafayette room and Washington dining room), where all but two corner posts and the second and third floor level girts had been replaced during the Henry Ford ownership. [4]

He determined that the third addition in the early construction of the Inn probably came about 1740 when Ezekiel How added a third story, replaced the gable roof with the now-familiar gambrel with no dormer windows, replaced the huge central chimney with two others and added four more rooms to the rear of the building.

Court records revealed another secret. Going over the transcripts of a civil case between Edward R. Lemon, who made extensive renovations to the Inn in the 1890's, and builder Charles F. Jones, Baker discovered that Jones had moved a wall at the head of the rear stairs to create an upstairs corridor and turn what had been Ezekiel's "Hobgoblin Hall," a small ball room, into a bedroom. [5]

Because of severe fire damage, Baker had little physical evidence to determine when the West wing, containing the 1800 ballroom and the tap room, was built, but here the Inn records proved invaluable. Ezekiel How's will mentions a "new kitchen" on the ground floor with a "long chamber" overhead which were probably built shortly before the beginning of the nineteenth century.

On January 2, 1957 the first loads of hand-hewn oak and pine timbers began arriving from New Hampshire mills, and Baker's workmen started the painstaking chore of dismantling the building piece by piece. Each beam and timber, no matter how badly damaged, was tested for strength, labelled as to location, and piled carefully in the rear of the building. By the time he had finished, every beam that was sound had found its way back to its original location. Damaged timbers were spliced into new wood. [6]

The Longfellow parlor and the Howe sitting room proved to be the least damaged. Elsewhere, only the summer beams, an occasional girt and a few corner braces and studs proved to be reuseable. All the panels in the front door were saved and used in the reconstruction, but the door stiles encircling the panels had to be replaced. A part of the door frame was also saved and re-used.

While his workmen cleared away the rubble and salvaged what they could, Baker conferred with Dr. Shelly, and together they determined that the building should be restored to the way it looked in Longfellow's time. The Ford Foundation granted an additional $250,000 for the work.

Meanwhile, Ralph E. Carpenter Jr., a trustee of both the Wayside Inn and the National Trust for Historic Preservation, was supervising the restoration and refinishing of the Inn's furnishings, 80 percent of which proved to be sound and reusable. The "sombre clock's" lacquered case and the hutch table in the old bar room were sent to Ruben and Silverstein, a Boston cabinetmaking firm, for refinishing. At the same time, the Attwill Furniture company of Lynn started work on 75 other pieces of antique furniture saved from the fire. Ole Bull's two violins were sent to John A. Gould and Sons in Boston, a firm that first opened its doors in 1889. [7]

By mid-summer the exterior work on the old part of the building was complete, and the Old Kitchen was restored and open to the public. Bus tours had continued to stop at the Inn during the previous year and 2,000 cars driving by for a look at Baker's progress wasn't unusual on a sunny Sunday.

Both Baker and Miss Staples had to deal with their share of sidewalk superintendents, most of them older people who wondered where the four dormer windows at the front of the building had gone. Baker told the *Wayland Town Crier* of one such exchange with an elderly resident who announced indignantly: "The dormers are gone."

"I asked him how old he was," Baker recalled. "He said: 'I'm 78.' I told him 'Those dormers were built when you were 18.' So he went out and said to his wife, 'Those dormers weren't old. I was 18 when they were built.'"

"Yes, the four dormer windows have disappeared from the fourth floor," Miss Staples explained to the *Boston Herald* in early September. "Mr. Lemon put them there for light and air when he used the top story for sleeping rooms. His porch by the front door won't go back either. You can see the simple pediment above the door instead."

Baker was also adding touches that were not readily visible to the casual observer. He constructed a replica of the roof framing of Houses 1 and 2 under the gambrel roof in the attic, so that visitors interested in ancient building techniques could see the difference between the old style of principal rafters and purlins supporting vertical roof boards, a throwback to England's tiled and thatched roofs, which was used on House No. 1, and the later principal and common rafters supporting horizontal boarding as used by David How in House No. 2.

All the mortise and tenon joints in the house were secured with wooden pegs, and old beams that were too damaged to function on their own were spliced with new. Baker took particular pride in the fact that the original summer beams were replaced in all the rooms, and in the discovery that gray was the original color of the Edison (Drivers and Drovers) room's wooden trim. [8]

Baker's attention to detail was meticulous. Lathing to hold the old-style cow-hair plaster was made by splitting thin planking with a hatchet and spreading it apart to create cracks to hold the plaster before nailing it to the studs.

"This is 1800 plastering," Baker told the *Christian Science Monitor.* "Today's is put on with a smooth coat. We throw the levels and straight edges away and finish it up so it looks like this, [rough and uneven]."

In modern construction, plastering is done first and the wood trim is the final touch, but in early American construction it is done the other way around. Wainscoting, window frames and baseboards are finished off and then the plaster follows. [9]

All the rooms except one were finished in rough plaster in keeping with the style of the 1860's when Longfellow visited the Inn. The one exception is the Lafayette room where the Scottish bluebell wallpaper was carefully reproduced. Ernest LoNano, a New York expert on 18th century fabrics, designed the draperies and furniture covers. [10]

The National Trust for Historic Preservation officially took over management of the Inn from the Ford Foundation on July 15, 1957 with Mrs. Francis B. Crowninshield of Boston as president. The following January they made plans for reopening. On February 24, 1958, the *Christian Science Monitor* spread the glad tidings. Its Page 2 headline read: "'New' Wayside Inn to Pop Rice at June Brides." On June 7, 1958, two and one half years after the ravages of fire threatened to close it forever, the Wayside Inn would open its doors to travelers once more.

Governor Foster Furcolo headed a large delegation of dignitaries to the reopening ceremonies, which featured a parade of stagecoaches and antique cars from South Sudbury to the Inn. More than 2,000 people picnicked on the grounds and gathered to watch Richard Holland, President of the National Trust for Historic Preservation, cut a 15-foot-long orchid lei sent by the schoolchildren of Oahu, Hawaii. [11]

As the hostesses took groups of people through the house that he had brought back almost from the ashes, Roy Woodbury Baker of Antrim, New Hampshire, stood in the same corner of the old bar room where he had stood that winter afternoon of December 23, 1955 and admired his handiwork.

"It may not be familiar to people who visited here in the last 50 years," he told an inquiring writer. "But Longfellow would feel right at home."

XXIV

"Food And Lodging For Man, Woman And Beast"

Thomas Boylston Adams was beginning to wonder just what he had let himself in for as he sat at his desk in the executive offices of the Sheraton Hotel on High Street in Boston that winter morning in 1959. Less than a year before, he had acceded to the request of close friend Walter Whitehill of the National Trust for Historic Preservation and become a trustee of the Wayside Inn. Now it was clear why Whitehill had asked him to join the board.

The newly restored Inn had reopened the previous June, three years after the 1955 fire. Following an initial surge of interest, traffic had fallen off badly and the overstaffed hostelry was running at a deficit of more than $20,000 a month. Whitehill had picked up the phone and called Adams. He knew the hotel business; was there anything that could be done?

"I took a tip from Ernie Henderson, who was a very sharp man," Adams recalled later. "He always said that if you're losing money, fire the manager. Another axiom of his was that you couldn't be a good hotel man without being a good accountant."

Consequently, innkeeper William Osborne, who had been hired by the National Trust for Historic Preservation, was asked to leave and Adams was given the task of finding a replacement. One of his first moves was to telephone Arthur Lee, a Sheraton associate who had recently opened Hotel 128 in Dedham. That phone call was to usher in an era of unprecedented hospitality at the Wayside Inn.

"Arthur told me he had an accountant that he thought very highly of," said Adams. "He came in and I liked him at once. His name was Francis Koppeis."

Recently, Francis Koppeis settled down at the table in the old Washington Dining Room and recalled that February day in 1959 when—with just eight months experience in the hotel business—he became landlord of the Wayside Inn.

"When Arthur Lee and I first came out that bleary day, it was something," he said. "I thought we'd never get here. There was snow in the parking lot, but I was enamored of the place. It just grabbed me. Sitting there in the darkness in the evening with snow on the ground, I was enraptured, you might say. I fell in love with the damn place and it's stuck with me.

"I accepted coming up here without knowing the picture. I didn't know any better, and thank goodness I didn't. Today I would have said 'Oh, forget it!' I wouldn't think about it. You do things when you're young you wouldn't think about when you're older."

Assistant Innkeeper Barbara Deveneau, a hostess before the 1955 fire and a long-time employee, remembers that day. "We heard that Bill Osborne was leaving and another man coming in and, of course, nobody could pronounce his name and everybody said he's got to be Greek.

"What are they doing? What will he know or care of the history of the Wayside Inn? We all made up our minds that there was no way that he was going to make it or that we were going to like this man whose name we couldn't even pronounce."

With just eight months experience in hotel management, the Inn proved to be a baptism of fire for Frank Koppeis. His first look at the financial statement revealed that the payroll equalled the sales in the dining room, not a healthy condition for even a nonprofit operation.

"Francis Koppeis was an exceptional man," said Adams. "He knew how to prevent profits from going out the back door and had the extraordinary ability to get on with his customers and with his help. The first year or two he was there, there seemed to be 365 crises a year and he managed them all."

The first major crisis was not long in coming. Ever since the reopening, the Inn had been closed on Mondays and most of the staff worked a six-day week. When Koppeis announced that he planned to open on Mondays, the entire kitchen staff, with the exception of two dishwashers, gave notice. Their last day of work was the Saturday before Mother's Day.

"It was the usual thing when new management comes in," said Koppeis. "Everybody was running scared and all sorts of rumors cropped up. The whole kitchen crew—all the cooks— thought they were going to get a bad deal out of it and they all left. Then the chef came in and told me that he wouldn't be able to hold his head up if all his people walked out and he stayed. So he left too."

And so, with two chefs borrowed from Hotel 128 doing the cooking, and assistant manager Fred Russell peeling potatoes and cleaning shrimp, the new innkeeper spent his busiest day of the year in the kitchen helping out with salads, and a crisis was averted.

In order to promote the dining room, Koppeis obtained lists of people who owned Cadillac, Lincoln or Packard automobiles and offered two dinners for the price of one, cocktails not included.

"The rationale was simple. We didn't want to lose staff. The payroll was the same whether we had 50 people, 100, 150 or 200 in the dining room. The only difference was the low pay of the waitresses who made most of their income on tips. This way the girls and boys had work and got their tips."

Meanwhile, advice and encouragement were coming from other quarters. A nucleus of Sudbury residents who remembered the Inn from the old days became regular customers once again. Herbert Atkinson, who lived in the house on Dutton Road once owned by Babe Ruth and ran Sudbury Laboratories, made suggestions on menu items that were popular at other nearby restaurants, and Abel Cutting, then owner of Sudbury Nurseries, advised turning the Old Kitchen into a small dining room.

"Abe said that people wanted to get into the place and use it," said the Innkeeper. "It shouldn't be a mausoleum; it should be a living thing. There was a fence across the end of the Old Kitchen and we took it down. Then Herb came down one day and said: 'Frank, the trouble with this damn place is that you're more worried about what's on the draperies over here than getting some food on the table for people to eat.'

"What they were telling me was that they wanted a place they could enjoy. This is an inn. This is a public house of entertainment. With that, we made the Old Kitchen, which wasn't in use before, into a dining room. We moved the gift shop back from the old bar to where it is now and used the old bar as a place for people to gather because there wasn't enough room for everyone to have a drink either before dinner or in the early evening.

"It's the idea of food, drink and lodging for man, woman and beast. We found out that nobody else put your horse up. That's why we're the oldest inn. Nowhere—and I checked out Williamsburg, Santa Fe, St. Augustine—is there a place that will put you up and put your horse up. In fact, none of them have older places. They're reproductions.''

The Innkeeper also received the support of a dedicated group of trustees, a tradition that continues today. Following the restoration in 1957–58, the Ford Foundation turned over trusteeship to the National Trust for Historic Preservation which, in turn, transferred control to the current Wayside Inn Trust in August of 1960.

"The trustees are here to keep the Inn alive," he explained. "The trustees today are mostly from the Boston area and they're keenly interested in preserving this bit of history here. Several are trustees of other historic houses.

"I find it refreshing that people are interested and that they don't look for any glory or profit. You don't know who they are. They pay for their meals and they pay if they spend the night. Once a year they have to meet officially to satisfy the legal requirements of a nonprofit corporation.''

While the Inn pays no taxes, it does reimburse the town for police, fire and other services and makes its facilities available for many civic functions at little or no charge. The Sudbury Minute and Militia Companies meet at the Inn eight times a year and hold their annual fair in the field across the street the last Saturday of September. The Innkeeper was one of the founding fathers of the Sudbury Companies and still marches to Concord with them each April 19.

In the spring of 1968, the companies got a chance to repay the Innkeeper for his hospitality. In early March, a terrific downpour filled the millpond and water started pouring over the top of the dam, endangering both the Grist Mill and the Inn itself. Koppeis called Minute Companies Colonel John Cheney who relayed the distress call to Alarm Company Captain Bill Vollheim. Within an hour, more than 100 minutemen and other volunteers were on the scene, filling sandbags and reinforcing the dam. Their efforts were successful and the Inn and the Mill were saved.

"That's why the townspeople have a good feeling for the Inn," he said. "It is important that we be a part of the town. If the town has a disagreement with us or an unhappy feeling, that is not good. We like their jealous attitude. When I was putting in a new $60,000 septic system over here, Ed Thompson (The Town's Executive Secretary) called up and said: 'Frank, what the devil you doing over in the field there?' I said we're putting up a motel. We're putting up 50 rooms!''

The relationship between the town and the Inn has always been a good one in the Koppeis era, just as it was in David and Ezekiel How's time. When the trustees considered installing a sprinkler system in the early '60s which would cut the Inn's fire insurance bill by 82 percent, the Sudbury Water District offered to allow the Inn to pay the $40,000 it would cost to lay a mile and a tenth of pipe from Ecke's Motel in ten interest-free installments of $4,000 each. Rather like cooperative sales of lumber to the town for bridges in the eighteenth century.

The Wayside Inn has continued to shelter and feed the great and near-great. Television shows and commercials have been filmed on the grounds, and the guest book near the front door bristles with the names of celebrities from the worlds of politics, entertainment and sports.

One name that you will not find there is that of Saudi Arabia's King Saud. This incident is one of the Innkeeper's favorite stories. "The king was in Boston for an operation and wanted to book the entire place for a couple of weeks to convalesce privately," he said. "We turned him down because the Inn is not for one person or one particular company. It made for some newsworthy comment in the papers: 'Wayside Inn Turns King Away!!' ''

In 1974, a mail coach pulled up to the doors of the Inn for the first time in nearly a century, climaxing a two-year restoration of the Inn's Abbott and Downing stagecoach which Henry Ford had purchased soon after acquiring the Inn.

"That was something," the Innkeeper recalled with a smile. "Bill Cossart (former Colonel of the Sudbury Companies of Militia and Minute) came up and said, 'Hey, Frank. Can we use the stagecoach to dedicate Frank Feely Park?' '' Koppeis agreed, but warned Cossart that the coach was not in good condition and might break down. Cossart took a look at the coach and said that the Inn really ought to have it repaired.

So the Innkeeper cut a deal. In return for the use of the coach, Cossart was to supervise its restoration. A couple of phone calls revealed that Edward and Barbara Rowse of Louden, New Hampshire, restored old Abbott and Downing Coach bodies for a hobby and that a neighbor, Harry Fellows, was an expert in the restoration and repair of the heavy leather thorough braces that served as springs.

Sudbury Contractor Mike DiModica transported the coach to Louden at no charge on a flatbed heavy equipment hauler. When it was ready to come back some two years and $5,000 later, Cossart had a bright idea. Why not pull the coach down with horses and get a head start on the Bicentennial?

Francis Koppeis had a better one. Why not have a mail run? "We got Tommy McDonough, the Postmaster, to approach his superiors about a mail run and we got the OK because one William Bolger, who later became Postmaster General, was head of the New England area," he explained. "He not only approved, but he had a special cachet made."

The U.S. Post Office Department contracted with the Inn for a star route from Louden, New Hampshire to Sudbury with stops at selected post offices along the way. Retired Sudbury Postmaster Forrest Bradshaw rode the coach as the official representative of the Post Office Department. Compensation for the trip was $1.

"Forrest had a delightful time," said the Innkeeper. "His wife, Kay, drove along before and after, making contact. When she was stopped by a New Hampshire state trooper for speeding, she told him, 'Look here, sonny boy. I'm taking care of that stagecoach up there. My husband's on there with the mail and I've got to get going. And besides, my son (Jack Bradshaw) is the President of the (New Hampshire) Senate.'"

There have been other crises along the way, but the Innkeeper downplays them. "The fire of 1965 was probably the biggest," he says. "The fire codes were not in place at that time. The exhaust ducts for the kitchen, which included the French frier and the broiler, went up into the ceiling and made five 90-degree angles.

"The broiler caught fire and heated up that grease in those ducts and that's what set off the alarm at the fire station. (Fire Chief Al) St. Germaine called a second alarm right off the bat and seven companies came in."

Engines answering the second alarm also attracted many Sudbury residents to the scene including artist Loring Coleman and his wife, Tinka, who arrived before police lines were set up and helped remove valuable Inn records from the old bar room and Longfellow parlor.

"Before breakfast we heard these tremendous sirens because

they called in Concord and all the outlying districts," said Coleman. "We said to ourselves that that could only be one thing. It's got to be the Wayside Inn.

"We got in our car, drove right through and parked by the Grist Mill and walked back to the Inn. There was nobody around but the firemen. Most of the action was toward the kitchen and we just walked in the front door. We saw water coming down the stairs and somebody said, 'My God we've got to get the furniture out of here.' We grabbed tables, chairs and the spinet and rushed them out on the front lawn where they'd be safe. It looked like a flea market out there."

"It was a blessing, actually," added the Innkeeper. "When we put the Inn back together, St. Germaine made us follow the safety codes and the most important thing, which was not done after the '55 fire was the installation of sprinklers. It was obvious we had to have fire protection here. Roy Baker knew a lot about restoring old buildings, but he had no idea about fire protection."

The Grist Mill and Martha-Mary Chapel are also the Innkeeper's responsibility. The Mill, which has more yearly visitors than the Inn, is administered by a Miller who keeps the building open for tours from April through November, and grinds corn and wheat for use at the Inn and for sale in the Inn gift shop. In years past it ground wheat for Pepperidge Farms and King Arthur Flour.

The Chapel is another matter. "I never thought about weddings at all," said the Innkeeper. "They grew from 55 to 60 in 1959 to 481 a couple of years ago. We're not out to see how many we can get, we just try to accommodate as many as we can do properly." The Inn does not advertise the availability of the Chapel for weddings. It gets more requests than it can handle simply through word of mouth publicity. On special occasions, the Innkeeper dons an eighteenth-century wig and cuts the wedding cake with a Revolutionary sword.

The Wayside Inn has 10 guest rooms, a restaurant and the same facilities as most hotels, albeit on a smaller scale, yet one feels at home within its walls whether there for just a meal or an overnight stay. The Innkeeper explains it in one word: hospitality.

"A hotel is a commercial establishment," he said. "It's like the bank. 'Yes sir. How much would you like to deposit? Yes, sir. Are you spending one night or two?' We do the same thing, but in a different way. We provide an innkeeper's hospitality.

"A hotel has to have an innkeeper's license to run, but with 4,000 rooms how many people can you ask 'Gee, how long are you going to be with us?' You don't have the opportunity for a one-on-one relationship with people which people dearly treasure and love.

"This is the result. You look at the little questionnaires we ask the people to fill out before they leave and this is the point. They like the hospitality. They like the quaintness. They like the lack of glass and concrete, steel and that sort of thing."

Daniel Coolidge, the President of the Wayside Inn Trustees, agrees and gives the credit to Koppeis. "Frank Koppeis is the essence of what an innkeeper should be," he said. "His enthusiasm for people—guests and staff—is contagious."

Thomas Boylston Adams emphatically concurs. "Francis Koppeis takes a great interest in people," he said. "His was one of those cases where an unusual slot was filled by an unusual man."

The trustees have always appreciated the fact that the Innkeeper is a self-starter, a confidence that Koppeis appreciates. "They have been very liberal," he said of his Board. "They look to me to keep hospitality alive."

Coleman, like many of the Innkeeper's close friends, calls him "Kopey" and remembers his early years at the Inn. "When Kopey first took over the Inn, I just heard what a great thing it was to have a guy you could talk to who had a sense of humor," he said. "It was like a breath of fresh air. I didn't get to know him well until I met him on our walks with the Sudbury Minutemen. He would always supply the coffee and the donuts."

The days of having to run promotions to get people through the doors for dinner are long gone. Today advance reservations for dinner are almost always necessary and booking for Thanksgiving, New Year's Eve, Easter or Mother's Day is a matter of luck unless you are a regular patron on one of those holidays. The Inn is traditionally closed on Christmas.

"We have a reservation date for each holiday," the Innkeeper explains. "November 1 for New Year's Eve, February 1 for Easter, March 1 for Mother's Day and September 1 for Thanksgiving. The only one we have a serious problem with is Thanksgiving. People start calling at 7 a.m. on September 1 and we're filled in 26 minutes."

Dealing with people comes naturally to Francis Koppeis.

Born in St. Louis of European parents, he left school to work in his father's bakery during the depression. He was a mess sergeant in the army during World War II before graduating from Officer Candidate School and eventually becoming a pilot. In the early '50s, he spent eight years working for Wonder Bread in Washington, D.C. before coming to Massachusetts.

"Hospitality was a part of my family background," he said. "When we'd visit my grandmother's dairy farm, we'd take some bakery products out to them. And when we came back they'd always give us some milk or cream, a turkey or a goose if it was around Christmas. It was a practice. You go to someone's house, you take a little gift. It's a traditional hospitality, I think, amongst many people, not just among Europeans. So when I took over here, I told the folks we want people to feel welcome.

"At home we always had goose for Christmas. People visiting the Inn began to ask, 'When are you going to start serving goose?' Now from November 30 to the middle of January, we have goose on the menu. People like goose and the apple stuffing the chef makes for it."

Some items on the Inn menu such as the chicken pie, duckling and baked Indian pudding go back to the days when Henry Ford ran the Inn. Others are of more recent vintage.

"We accommodate," the Innkeeper admits. "Lobster wasn't something you'd find at an early inn, but people come to New England and they want lobster....Now we've added more fish. Swordfish, Cape scallops. These are entrees an inland inn wouldn't have.

"We've got old drinks. The Coow-Woow and the Stonewall. A buddy of mine named Byustis Cusnell looked them up. Coow-Woow in the early days was made of rum and ginger. Today we use ginger-flavored brandy for the Coow-Woow and gin and applejack for the Stonewall, which is light. Colonial flip we haven't done much with. It needs a hot fire and a loggerhead poker. On cold days we'll whip it up. On Christmas Eve we'll have eggnog for the staff from the Innkeeper."

Whether he is dealing with a guest from across the street or across the ocean, the Innkeeper's ultimate goal is to make that person feel at home.

"Hospitality, so I tell people, according to the old innkeeping laws is to look after a man, his horse and his cattle," he explained. "It means looking after your well-being while you're a guest and caring for your property as well. You look after people. You offer them coffee or tea. We always hold the coffee until everybody's checked in.

"I think the most satisfying thing to me over the years has been the people who appreciate the Inn and who get a feeling that we do make them welcome here. I guess it's a verification of accommodating people."

Testimonials to the hospitality of Francis Koppeis and the Wayside Inn are not limited to Americans. Many people visit from Europe where old inns and taverns are a way of life. One such visitor in the early '70s was Sir Gordon Russell, whose family ran the 400-year-old Lygon Arms Inn in Broadway, Worcestershire for more than fifty years. He wrote of his visit to Katharine Scott Ridley, one of the writers' mothers:

> Dear Katharine:
>   ....Quite by chance I have come upon an old inn here in New England, Longfellow's Wayside Inn, which is quite enchanting. It is not a museum as I thought it might be, but a place to stay. It reminds me a lot of the Lygon although it is built of wood as most buildings are here, not of stone as in the Cotswolds, and is smaller and more homelike.
>
>   The landlord is a splendid fellow—courteous and attentive in an unpretentious Yankee way. I wish your dear father [Colonel Frank A. Scott, a frequent visitor to the Lygon before World War II] could have visited Sudbury. In all events, I believe you and the children would enjoy this place as much as I have.
>
>   As Ever, Gordon

Whether his guests are knights of the realm or hitchhikers looking for a chance to warm up and dry off in front of the fire in the old bar room, Francis Koppeis has always been there to greet them and make them feel at home. His constant presence in the dining room or near the front desk is one of the things that guests remember about their visit to the Inn.

"I worked here under other managers and I know that very seldom would you see them around," said Mrs. Deveneau. "But Frank's always here and it means so much to the people. If he's among the missing, even on his day off, people say: 'Where's Frank? He's not sick is he?' He's just got a feel for the place. I think it's because he exudes hospitality and that's what the Inn is all about.

"I said once that it was fate or something that brought him here. I just think that Zeke How and David and all the rest are looking down and saying: 'Boy, He's a How from the word go.' "

This chapter is based on interviews with Thomas B. Adams, Loring Coleman, Daniel Coolidge, Barbara Deveneau, and Francis Koppeis. Permission to include the letter from Sir Gordon Russell was kindly granted by the family of Colonel Frank A. Scott.

The Evolution of the Wayside Inn Signboard. David How's first sign (upper left) probably had a prancing horse on one side and his initials and "1716" on the back. The sign that Samuel Adams Drake describes in 1874 (upper right) had been altered with "1686" following David How's initials. Edward R. Lemon changed the shape of the sign from horizontal to vertical (lower left) and added his name at the bottom along with those of all the landlords. Henry Ford (lower right) deleted Lemon's name from his sign but kept the rest of the names and dates intact.

XXV

Signs of the Times—Horses of a Different Color

Isaiah Thomas cursed to himself as he pulled the snow away from the broken runner of his covered pung that frigid January morning in 1808. He and his three passengers had hoped to be in Boston by nightfall, but now there seemed little chance of that. Even if one of Adam Howe's boys could fix the sled in that extreme cold, most of the day would be wasted.

Thomas was the publisher of the *Massachusetts Spy*. His newspaper had championed the cause of liberty at several locations since before the Revolution. He finally settled in Worcester and travelled this road frequently, gathering news and supplies. Howe's place was a convenient stopping point.

"January 4, 1808. Very cold," he wrote in his journal. "Set off with Miss R. Armstrong, Frazier and Levi in a covered sleigh for Boston. Broke the sleigh at Sudbury. Very bad travelling. Snow light. Broke the Sleigh a few rods from Howe's at the black horse in Sudbury. Could not get it repaired nor get another large sleigh. Send to Sudbury Causeway for the Stage to come and take us to Boston tomorrow. Tarried at Howe's from II o'clock this forenoon. Slept there this night which was exceedingly cold...." [1]

Lydia Maria Francis's thoughts were on romance as she rode along beside David Lee Child on one of those magic summer days that only happen in New England in early June. Later she would take up her pen in the abolitionist cause, but today she was simply a young lady in love with the man beside her, and all the glory that nature had spread over the countryside, as they rode from Boston to Sudbury that June day in 1828.

"...the young birches, dressed in white, with lively green trimmings, were moving to the breath of the breeze as light and airy as a troop of dancing girls..." she wrote. "What wonder that I remember so well that time when nature and I were young together in the mating season which brings human souls into spontaneous sympathy with all life and love? We rode on till we came to an inn with the sign of a black horse swinging in the wind. It was an old establishment known to all the surrounding region as 'Adam Howe's Tavern....'' [2]

The wind was bending the spring-green grasses of the river marshes as Henry David Thoreau and Ellery Channing set off on the morning of May 22, 1853 to climb Nobscot Mountain. Thoreau describes the scene in his *Journal*:

> This is the third windy day following two days of rain...a washing day...such as we always have at this season methinks. The grass has sprung up as by magic since the rains. The birds are heard through pleasant dashing wind that enlivens everything....Left our horse at the Howe Tavern. The oldest date on the sign is 'D.H. 1716.' An old woman, who had been a servant in the family, said she was ninety-one and that this was the first house built on the spot. Went on to Nobscot.'' [3]

These are only three of the many conflicting references to the Wayside Inn sign that have come to light as we have researched and written this book. The Red Horse signboard and how it may have changed and evolved over the centuries is a story in itself.

What shape was the signboard—horizontal or vertical? What color was the horse at various times? Was the horse walking in a spirited manner, *prancing*, or was he *rearing* as he does now? What initials of what landlords were on the sign? Were these initials on the front or the back of the sign or both?

The exact answers to these questions could tell us much about the history of the Inn. Unfortunately, the answers are not exact. Any sign which is at the mercy of wind and weather, season after season, changes constantly. Its size, shape, and color may be altered not by conscious decision, but simply by the availability of a piece of wood or a pot of leftover red ochre paint.

We have endeavored to sift through the bits and pieces of fact and tradition and put the jigsaw puzzle into some order. We leave it up to you, the reader, to draw your own conclusions.

According to nineteenth-century writers Samuel Adams Drake (1874) and Samuel Arthur Bent (1897), Ezekiel How is supposed to have put up the sign of the red horse in 1746 or close to that date when he took over the operation of the Inn from his father, David. Other later writers attest to the same theory. It has become, like so much about the Inn, a strong tradition.

The red horse is supposed to have gone up to distinguish the Howe Tavern in Sudbury from its counterpart—the Black Horse Tavern—in Marlborough, which was also run by descendants of John How since 1661, and as a fitting counterpoint to the White Horse Tavern in Boston, which was the starting point for the stage coach route.

If one accepts the Warwickshire background discussed in Chapter XII, this first horse may have resembled the Red Horse of Tysoe or at least have been inspired by it. This Red Saxon horse is walking or prancing on the hillside, not rearing. It is a *horizontal* figure of a horse.

But we have no actual proof that a signboard with a red horse was put up either before or after the Revolution. It could have been put up earlier or much later. The tavern went on being referred to as "Mr. How's place," "How's place," and later as "Adam Howe's place," making it all but impossible to pinpoint any precise date when it automatically became the Red Horse Tavern.

In fact, the two documented references to the sign during Adam Howe's time—Isaiah Thomas in 1808 and Lydia Maria Francis twenty years later in 1828—both state that the horse was black. Neither mentions the initials and dates of the innkeepers on either side of the sign.

Thomas was an accurate observer of events, used to dealing with type and printing presses. Because his business was spread out in Boston, Worcester and Albany, he frequently travelled the Boston Post Road, which led past the Inn. His *Massachusetts Spy* had espoused the cause of civil liberties since 1770, and he may well have visited the Inn during Ezekiel How's time. It is unlikely that he would have mistakenly mentioned a black horse instead of a red one. If Ezekiel did, in fact, put up a red horse, it may well have weathered black by time in a dozen years or more, or Adam Howe simply may have wanted to distinguish his tenure from that of his father and changed the color of the horse.

Lydia Maria (Francis) Child's account of her visit to Adam Howe's in 1828 goes on to describe the tavern and grounds in detail, as well as her dinner with Adam, his wife Jerusha, and the other children. Even though her account was written from memory some years later, there is no reason to doubt that she saw a black horse swinging in the wind.

Regardless of the color of the horse, the shape of the signboard in the 1700's and early 1800's was probably horizontal, with the horse on one side and the landlords' initials on the other. A sketch done by Albert Fitch Bellows, which is frequently reproduced in brochures as "the inn of earlier days," portrays covered wagons, a stage coach and horses in front of the gambreled-roofed building. Hanging from the branch of a huge tree beside the inn is a horizontal sign with the figure of a walking horse.

Bellows was a New England landscape painter, born in Milford, Massachusetts in 1829. [4] He could have seen the Inn in Adam's heyday and remembered enough to paint the scene from memory or he could have drawn the scene in person as a boy or as a young man. The sketch has become well-known and is probably the earliest visual indication of what the first sign looked like. The sign sketched by Bellows was almost certainly the same sign that Thoreau saw in his 1853 visit during Lyman Howe's time. Thoreau was also an impeccably accurate observer and cannot be doubted. From his account we know that in 1853, eight years before Lyman Howe's death, the sign had David How's initials, the right date (1716) for the first landlord, and two other sets of initials all on one side.

We think that this sign showed a horse on the opposite side. Thoreau does not mention it, but he may have glimpsed only one side of the wooden signboard or he may not have been sufficiently struck by the horse to mention its color or shape.*

Sometime between Thoreau's visit in 1853, and 1874 when Samuel Adams Drake published his *Historic Fields and Mansions of Middlesex* someone changed the date after David How's initials from the correct "1716" to "1686." Just who did the deed and why is still a mystery.

Drake includes a picture of one side of the horizontal sign with "D.H. 1686," "E.H. 1746" and "A.How 1796" and states: "The Red Horse in Sudbury was built about 1686." Had David

---

*The fact that Thoreau and Channing left their horse at How's before going on to Nobscot indicates that they approached from the west, probably coming from Concord through North Sudbury and down what is now Dutton Road. In that case they probably never saw the horse on the opposite side which would have faced east. Thomas Boylston Adams tells of riding to the Inn from Lincoln in the 1930's and taking the exact same route.

How been the landlord then, he would have been all of 12 years old.

"The name of the house was the Red Horse and at the other end of the route, belonging to the same family, in rivalry of good cheer, was the White Horse in old Boston Town," Drake wrote. "The horse has always been a favorite symbol with publicans. However tedious the way may have been, however shambling or void of spirit your hackney of the road, the steed on the hostel sign always pranced proudly, was of high mettle and of as gallant carriage as was ever blazoned on Saxon's* shield." [5]

When Henry Wadsworth Longfellow visited the Inn in October, 1862 with his publisher, James T. Fields, to gather background material for his "Sudbury Tales," which were to become the *Tales of a Wayside Inn*, he did not mention the sign in his note of thanks to Miss Eaton. But he wrote in his diary for that day: "...A rambling, tumble-down old building, two hundred years old, and till now in the family of the Howes, who have kept it as an inn for one hundred and seventy five years...."

The fact that Longfellow says "one hundred and seventy five years" suggests that he saw a different sign from the one observed by Thoreau in 1853. If he had seen '1716' as 'the oldest date' on this sign, he would have said something closer to "one hundred and fifty years." This diary entry also suggests that the poet saw a signboard with the date '1686' replacing '1716' after David How's initials. Longfellow is only a year off from 1686 when he says, in 1862, that the Inn has been in the hands of the same family for "one hundred and seventy five years."

If Longfellow *did* see such a sign, that would pinpoint the change to the nine years between 1853 and 1862. But there is a good possibility that Longellow did not *see* a sign at all,† but

---

*One wonders why Drake used the word "Saxon." It was the Saxon farmers who first scoured the red earth of Tysoe to create the horse for the Red Horse Easter Ritual. Could Drake have known? The Red Horses of Tysoe are all horizontal, prancing horses.

†At the time of Longfellow's visit, which was about 19 months after Lyman Howe's death, the signboard may not have been visible. One source tells us that J. Calvin Howe purchased the signboard at the auction in 1861 and later gave it to his brother who "chopped it up." This story was related to Earl Boyer, Henry Ford's first innkeeper, by Mr. and Mrs. Seymour, tenants at the Inn between 1889 and 1897. Whether it was bought at the auction or not, it may not have been chopped up, but survived as "boards in a horse barn" as a later account relates, and been found by Mr. Lemon after 1897.

simply heard about it from one of his friends who frequented the Inn in Lyman's time—Monti, Parsons or Treadwell. His Cambridge friends would have remembered that:

> Half effaced by rain and shine
> The red horse prances on his sign.

Note that the poet uses the word "prances" which would indicated a horse *walking* in a spirited manner, not *rearing* as in the signboards of Edward R. Lemon's time and later. The sign that Longfellow saw or heard of was certainly one similar to the first horizontal sign, upon which the horse prances or walks on one side and the landlords' initials are painted or carved on the side opposite.

The next witnesses in this mystery are three old newspaper writers, who contended with each other in the pages of *The Boston Journal* in the late 1860's and early 1870's, under the pen names 'Zed,' 'Occasional,' and 'Medicus.' These old cronies were friendly rivals and enjoyed correcting each other's mistakes. And mistakes there were—hearsay taken for proof and few items checked—but the fact remains that they were writing close to the time they were talking about and are a unique source. In August, 1868, one of the Inn sheds was struck by lightning and burned. The Inn itself was spared. Zed gave an account.

> ...it is possible that the christening by the name of the Red Horse did not take place till the 'stand' had been running...an error in a newspaper now before me says that the 'Red Horse' was built in 1686. This ...error may have arisen from a record on the old swinging sign board which was taken down a few years ago, but is still in existence. On one side was a picture of a red horse, on the other, the following:
>
> > D.H. 1686
> > E.H. 1745
> > A. How 1796
>
> The 'D.H.' stands for David Howe, for I have a copy of the Family Tree of this family and in it David is recorded as keeping the inn when 'there were but two houses between it and Worcester.' 'E.H.' I take to have been Ezekiel, but I am not sure of the date; it looks like 1745, but it could be '17'

something else. The 'A. How' was, without doubt, Antipas.*
The Inn descended to Lyman Howe, in direct descent. He
died a bachelor a few years ago and the estate went to a Mrs.
Puffer of Sudbury, then 95 years old, and the 'Red Horse' sign
came down. But its hall is still used for dancing parties.

ZED

Despite his own errors, Zed's description is clear enough to
leave no doubt that he had seen this sign. He also observes that
the sign is "still in existence" and there seems no reason to
doubt him.

Four years later, 'Occasional' wrote another account as part
of his "Ramblings in the Country" about the 'Old Howe
Tavern or Wayside Inn in Sudbury.'

August 5, 1872.

...The numerous barns and sheds with the exception of the
one that was burned by lightning four years ago...to the
present month, still remain occupied by the good-natured
husbandman who leases the farm, but are rapidly falling to
decay. And...the signpost in the veritable position described.
The sign was removed several years ago and sold at auction
along with other effects. It is now preserved as a relic by one
of the family descendants. A red horse is represented as being
in a prancing position...while underneath [could Occasional
have seen the sign lying flat on the floor of a barn or shed with
the horse facing up and the intials on the "underneath"
side?] are designated the respective years that the hotel has
changed proprietors....

If, in fact, the initials *were* underneath the horse on the *same*
side and not on the *other* side of the sign, this reference may
give us a clue as to when the shape of the sign changed from
horizontal to vertical. Accounts thus far have spoken of a horse
visible on one side and initials on the other as Zed does, or refer
to the initials or horse only, as do Thoreau and Longfellow.
Drake's sketch of the sign between 1860 and 1874 is horizontal.
Depending upon one's interpretation of the sentence, Occasional is the first person to refer to initials *underneath* the
horse which suggests a vertical sign.

*We have to assume that 'Antipas' was a nickname for Adam, used by
contemporaries. It is unlikely that Zed could be mistaken about a man who
died only twenty eight years before this article was written and whom he
remembered seeing as a boy.

Occasional and Zed were old enough to remember both Adam Howe and his sons Lyman and Adam Jr., the "bachelor brothers" mentioned in Thomas Parsons's poem "The Old House at Sudbury." The theory that Lyman himself, or possibly young Adam who had a reputation as a practical joker, changed the color of the horse from black to red and altered the date from "1716" to "1686" cannot be discounted.*

"Young" Adam certainly had the means and the talent. In 1923, Mr. David Howe of Taunton, a direct descendant of David How the innkeeper, wrote Henry Ford about an old writing desk at the Inn. "It was built by Adam Howe, brother of Lyman Howe..." he said. "...who liked to amuse himself by working in wood and for that purpose he had a shop which was about three hundred feet North East of the Inn near where the barn stood that was burned lately...there was a work bench on each side of the door and some shelves on the back side of the room...there was a wooden vise fastened to one of the benches...I have been in that shop when I was a boy and went to school...my father was well acquainted with both Lyman and Adam Howe and he knew that Adam Howe built the writing desk...it is painted red and is not very handsome but it is valuable for its age and associations...."[6]

It is certainly suggestive that in Lyman's time, a family member had a wood working shop and a supply of mixed red paint on the premises. Adam, who lost his first love to illness before they were married, spent most of his adult life at the Inn with his older brother and probably whiled away the time he

---

*The simplest explanation for the presence of the date 1686 on the sign, both in 1868 when Zed was writing about it and in 1872 when Occasional took up the tale, (and possibly as early as Longfellow's visit) is that it was Lyman himself who, at some point between 1853 and 1861, changed the date which was seen by Thoreau to 1686. It seems unlikely that Lyman Howe, who was interested in books and education, would have deliberately authorized an erroneous sign. But he may have persuaded himself or allowed himself to be persuaded that his great grandfather was living on the site at the age of 12. It is also conceivable that some well-meaning person who was burrowing in the Sudbury Town Records or the Colony tavern licenses for the seventeenth century, came upon Mr. Thomas Walker's license for the year 1686. (Mr. Walker was a long-time Sudbury innkeeper and his license does, in fact, appear in February, 1686). Also, Walker married one of Samuel How's daughters and Lyman may have convinced himself that this entitled Walker to be considered a "How innkeeper." There are all sorts of reasons why Lyman might have felt it quite legitimate to change the date and there is no reason to assume that tall tales around the fireside were any less prevalent then than they are now.

was not farming as best he could. The wooden desk he made in his shop was a fairly complicated piece of furniture with "large drawers," "small drawers," and "pigeon holes."[7] Anyone with the talent to design and build it could easily have built and painted any number of wooden signs.

Another candidate for the sign painter's role is Orin Dadmun, who lived at the inn as a tenant from soon after Lyman's death in 1861 until 1878. He may have become aware of the Indian deed of July 11, 1684, that officially conveyed the New Grant lands, which included the Wayside Inn property, to the town of Sudbury. Dadmun perhaps surmised that Lot #50 came into the hands of the How family immediately, and that the house was built and the tavern operating within two years. Therefore he may have thought himself warranted in changing the signboard date of 1716 to 1686.

It is also possible that Dadmun came across a copy of the deed by which Peter King sold the Inn property, Lot #50, to Samuel How in 1676. He could have mistaken this date, old and faded, for '1686' and "so, in good faith, placed '1686' on the signboard. He would have believed, from tradition, that David How was the first person to live on the site after it had been conveyed to his father, and would have also assumed that David built the homestead and opened the tavern immediately...."[8]*

Whether Dadmun re-painted an old sign and put '1686' on it instead of the '1716' which he found there, or whether he made a new sign with new dates, and perhaps a different shape, we do not know. But Occasional's account, written in the year 1872, makes it quite possible for Dadmun to have put up the sign sometime in the previous twelve years and then taken it down in time for Occasional to have seen it lying in a barn.

If indeed he *did* redesign the sign, Dadmun probably didn't keep it hanging for long. This "good-natured husbandman," as Occasional describes him, had no Aunt Margey or other housekeeper to serve travellers, and within a short time he would have grown weary of requests for food and a night's

---

*Frank Noyes is responsible for both these theories based on old deeds. No one has yet accounted for the date '1686' in any solid fashion. Mr. Noyes's theories are as plausible as any others and fit the situation at the Inn after Lyman's death—the long tenancy of Orin Dadmun, who was known to be interested in the Inn's history, and the presence of a new sign with new and misleading dates sometime after Thoreau's visit in 1853.

lodging at a place no longer an inn. So he took it down and retired it more permanently. The sign must have been out of sight by 1874 when Samuel Adams Drake's account of a visit to the Inn includes this statement:

.On the other side of the broad space left for the road are the capacious barns and outhouses belonging to the establishment, and standing there like a blazed tree in a clearing, but bereft of its ancient symbol, is also the old sign post.

Wallace Downes adds another piece to the puzzle in an article that appeared in the *New England Magazine and Bay State Monthly* in 1887 after a visit to the Inn where he was given a tour by Mrs. Lafayette Dadmun. [9]

But alas! for the old time inn with it jollity and good cheer. How rapidly it is becoming a thing of the past!....Thus thinking, I, one day in autumn, made a journey to the old Wayside Inn at Sudbury....About an hour's ride on the Mass Central Railroad brought us to the ancient town of Sudbury on the outskirts of which we meet the old Boston and Worcester Turnpike—over which, but a generation ago, the stage coach lumbered twice a week, conveying travellers and the mail....The building, as a tavern, withstood the fitful blasts and storms of nearly two centuries...the hospitality of such a place was, of course, proverbial....

At the termination of its career, the old sign bore on one side the painting of the prancing red horse, and on the other the initials of the past tavern-keepers (except Lyman) with the dates of the beginning of the possession of each, Viz.:

D.H. 1686
E.H. 1746
A. Howe, 1796

Since Mr. Downes later mentions such details of the interior and exterior of the building as the "great oaks" and "brass knocker" at the entrance, but does *not* mention any hanging sign in view, it is logical to assume that the sign was not up at the time of this visit. His use of the phrase "at the termination of its career" suggests that Downes saw the sign he described sometime between 1853 and 1861 when it *was* hanging in front of the Inn. The alternative is that he could have poked about in the outbuildings and seen what was left of the sign lying disused in a corner in 1887.

During the tenancy of Mr. and Mrs. Horace Seymour from 1889 to 1897, there was no sign visible. Newspaper accounts of this period, although they often describe what was left of the Inn in lyrical terms, make no mention of a sign. In fact, in some cases, they emphatically draw attention to its absence.

> 1892. September 4. *New York Tribune*....an enormous elm tree, from which, in the old days, the sign of the red horse hung to tempt travellers....
>
> 1893. Unidentified New York paper. ...a large elm tree, from whose lowest limbs, in the old days, the sign of the 'Red Horse' hung....
>
> 1895 December *Boston Traveler*. Arriving at the inn, the party looked in vain for the sign of the Red Horse Tavern, which, under the regime of Landlord How, father and son, previous to and during the Revolution, was firmly set in the trunk of the towering elm fronting the entrance...

When Edward Rivers Lemon acquired the property in 1897, the lead article in the *Boston Herald* for January 29th of that year, described his plans for the restoration of the old hostelry and included a photograph of the front entrance. No sign appeared in the picture and none was mentioned in the article. Presumably there was none.

But Lemon, the first of the landlords to play up Longfellow's connection with the Inn for commercial purposes, made a signboard one of his first priorities, anticipating a large crowd the summer after his purchase. When Samuel Arthur Bent addressed several hundred members of the Society of Colonial Wars at the Inn in June, barely six months after Lemon's takeover, he implied that the sign was swinging once more.

> Pilgrims from this land and from all lands...until their number was swollen to thousands in these later years...and one wiser and more prescient than the rest wrote: 'The time will come when the sign of the Red Horse will swing before the Wayside Inn again and pilgrims from far and near...shall gather....' And lo! the prophetic words fall true and again the doors of the Wayside Inn fly open to the expected guests; the descendants of the men of earlier days recall around these tables the good old Colony times...Mr. Governor and fellow members, let me be your toast master today. Representing indirectly four generations of worthy hosts, let me wish renewed prosperity, long, aye, a still longer life to the Red Horse Tavern of ancient Sudbury! [10]

The November 20, 1897 edition of *The New York Times* leaves no doubt about the presence of a new sign: "The signboard swinging in the front looks so ancient that it is a disappointment to learn that it is but a modern reproduction of the old Red Horse sign...."

Lemon made no secret of the fact that he put up a "reproduction." Later publications in the early part of the twentieth century tell us that he found an old sign in a horse stall, had someone copy it, and put it up. Our only proof of when this happened is that a sign was *not* visible in January of 1897 and *was* visible to Bent's crowd in June of that same year.

Whether or not Lemon copied a sign he found in one of the barns, or designed a new one of his own, using bits and pieces of tradition and legend, it was vertical in shape and is the forerunner of the signboard that hangs in front of the Inn today.

A vertical sign appears in a photograph illustrating an article in the July, 1914 issue of *House Beautiful* by Joseph S. Seabury, entitled "The Wayside Inn, Its Construction and Its Story." Seabury states:

> The sign of the "Red Horse" was presumably made and hung out by Colonel Ezekiel How in 1746. We are told that it disappeared soon after the death of Squire Lyman Howe and was recently discovered in a hay loft. Today it swings in its old place.

Our first good look at the lettering on the sign doesn't come until May 27, 1922 in an article in the *Christian Science Monitor* headlined "A Sixth Regime of Ampler Hospitality is Planned for the Historic Wayside Inn." One of the illustrations shows a vertical sign with the initials of David, Ezekiel, Adam, and Lyman Howe below which is hung a wooden rocker with the name of Edward R. Lemon. At the top of the sign is the mysterious date '1683' which remains there to this day.

How Lemon arrived at the '1683' and the 'sixth regime' is a puzzle that continues to trigger hot debate and remains a tantalizing mystery. Perhaps he was thinking of a record of Colonel Thomas How's innkeeping at the Black Horse at Marlborough in 1683. (John How died in 1680; his wife, Mary, and son, Thomas, re-opened the tavern soon after 1681 and continued in the business with annual license renewals.)

Lemon, who had been a collector of antiques and appreciated history, would doubtless have known that some settlers had built homes on the New Grant land long before the official deed from the Indians was recorded in 1684 and guessed that a tavern might possibly have been on the site a year earlier to shelter those who were building homesteads.*

Another far-fetched, but no less likely explanation for the '1683,' is that Lemon decided that Longfellow, as the man responsible for the Inn's notoriety and new name, properly belonged on the sign. He gave instructions to a sign painter, who happened to be in need of work, to place '1863' on the top of the sign for the year that the *Tales* were published, and his name, with the date that he purchased the Inn, at the bottom with the four Howe landlords in between. He would have enjoyed associating himself prominently with the famous poet. To make more room, he asked that the red horse be rearing instead of prancing, as Longfellow described it in his poem.†

The sign painter, left alone to his work, may have become confused, or may have thought that the oldest date should be at the top of the sign, and so transposed the digits '8' and '6' in the first date, turning '1863' into '1683'.

Regardless of what information or whim he based it on, Lemon's vertical sign and rearing horse is the one that remains with us today. When Henry Ford bought the Inn he struck Lemon's name and date from the bottom of the sign but kept the rest, continuing a tradition which probably started with the early innkeepers who adapted the shape and color of their signboard to suit their whims. There were undoubtedly many more signboard changes than have been recorded.‡

*The General Court awarded the New Grant land to the Town of Sudbury in 1649. However, the Indian deed that confirmed this transaction was not recorded until much later, in the year 1684. Also, as Mr. Noyes points out: "The article on the Wayside Inn, published in the September, 1899 issue of the *Ladies Home Journal*, while Edward R. Lemon was owner of the Inn, said that the deed to him was 'the first deed of the estate in over two hundred years,' together with the fact that A.S. Hudson had written, as early as 1889, 'the only previous deed was the Indian deed signed in 1684,' indicates that there was current in Sudbury, at that time, a tradition that this Indian deed was what first vested in the early owners of the New Grant land the title to their respective individual holdings."

†Lemon greatly admired Longfellow, which gives added substance to this idea. He designed and built the Longfellow Garden with a copy of the famous Westminster Abbey bust, as noted in Chapter 15.

‡Despite Lemon's new vertical format, there exists an article in the *Boston Sunday Globe Magazine* for August 5, 1923, by Charles Lawrence, which hints that the old horizontal sign with the horse on one side and the initials on the other was still around in Lemon's time. Lawrence, a writer and illustrator, was a Sudbury resident and a good friend of Cora Lemon, which makes the following account at least as accurate if not more so than those of other contemporary writers:

As Henry Ford's quest to recover authentic antiques to furnish the Inn became widely known, the auto magnate's agents were besieged with letters and calls from people with "authentic" Howe memorabilia and antiques, including at least two signboards, both of which were brought back to the Inn. Antique dealer E.A. Huebener of Dorchester sold one of these signs to Ford for one cent. A picture of the sign and Ford's cancelled check for a penny still hang in the Ford sitting room today. The second, which is hanging over the fireplace in the tap room, was donated to Ford by William Diehl of Wellesley, who found it in a sleigh he had rented to a group of students for a trip to Sudbury.

Ironically, neither of these horses is red. Both are black and no definite date of painting can be assigned to them. They may well have been just a part of the Ford "production" and have absolutely nothing to do with the inn signboard. So where does all this leave us? With clues, questions and no hard and fast solutions. The sign that hangs from its wrought iron brackets outside the door of today's Wayside Inn is certainly not the same one that hung from the branches of the gigantic elm beside the Boston Post Road in David, Ezekiel and Adam Howe's time.

Nor should it be. The signboard is a microcosm of the Inn itself. The personalities of five generations of Howes, of Henry Wadsworth Longfellow, of Edward Rivers Lemon, of Henry Ford and of the thousands of people who have crossed its threshold have all made their mark on the Wayside Inn. It is vastly different now than it was when David How and his

---

The place was originally known as the Red Horse tavern as that prancing animal was painted upon its signboard. When Mr. Lemon began to renovate the place he found a very old board in the barn but so split, slivered and battered by wind and sleet as to be out of the question for use. (Some sources have Lemon find this signboard in the barn, others in the hayloft, still others in a shed. One may conclude that it was found in some auxiliary building on the premises.) The present sign is, however, its successor and shows on one edge the marks of fire. (This may have been due to the fire from lightning which burned a shed in August, 1868, as reported by Zed.) But upon the back of the oldest sign as well as its successor are the letters:
    D.H. 1686 E.H. 1746 A. How 1796
A pretty good record of continuous family holding.

Lawrence's drawings for the 1923 article are dated '1916' indicating that he was familiar with the Inn before Edward R. Lemon's death. His description of the "very old board" which Lemon found in a barn is probably correct, as is what was written on the back and how Lemon reproduced it.

father laid its sills nearly 300 years ago, and will be different still another century hence.

Whether we stay for a night, have a meal, or just look around, these old walls touch the lives of each of us. We are in company with Samuel Sewall, William Molineaux, Isaiah Thomas, Lydia Maria Child, Luigi Monti, Thomas Edison, Eleanor Roosevelt and all the other pilgrims who have passed this way. The hospitality of the Wayside Inn has reached out to touch us all.

> As ancient is this hostelry
> As any in the land may be,
> Built in the old Colonial day,
> When men lived in a grander way,
> With ampler hospitality

Endnotes

Abbreviations used throughout the endnotes after the primary reference are as follows:

HG: Howe Genealogies, Judge Daniel Wait Howe (Boston: New England Historic Genealogical Society, 1929).

MAC: Massachusetts Archives Collection, Columbia Point, 220 Morrissey Blvd., Boston, Mass.

MCG: Middlesex Court of General Sessions Records, East Cambridge, Mass.

MRDPC: Middlesex Registry of Deeds and Probate Court Records, East Cambridge, Mass. Deeds and Estates.

MSCF: Middlesex Superior Court, County Court, Folio Collection, Columbia Point, Boston, Mass.

SC: Thomas Stearns Collection, 1640–1840, Goodnow Library, Sudbury, Mass., and New England Historical Society, 1154 Boylston Street, Boston, Mass.

TRP: Sudbury Town Records, 1639–1695, ed. Sumner Chilton Powell, Sudbury, Mass., 1963.

TR: Sudbury Town Records 1695–1855, Goodnow Library, Sudbury, Mass.

WR: Warwick County Records, Records of baptisms, marriages and deaths, 1576–1932, Warwick County Records Office, Priory Place, Cape Road, Warwick, England.

WIA: Wayside Inn Archives, Wayside Inn, Sudbury, Mass.

Chapter I

1. *Sudbury Town Records, 1639–1695*, transcribed and edited by Sumner Chilton Powell (Sudbury, Mass., June 1965), p. 26. Hereafter cited as *TRP*.

2. *Ibid.*, p. 4.

3. *Ibid.*, p. 26.

4. *Ibid.*, pp. 37–38.

5. *Ibid.*, pp. 40–41.

6. *Ibid.*, p. 50.

7. *Ibid.*, p. 118.

8. Sumner C. Powell, *Puritan Village, The Formation of a New England Town* (Middletown, Connecticut: Wesleyan University Press, 1963), pp. 80–91.

9. *TRP*, p. 119.
10. *Ibid.*, pp. 99–100.
11. *Ibid.*, p. 119.
12. *Ibid.*, p. 120.
13. *Ibid.*
14. *Ibid.*, pp. 127–29.
15. *Ibid.*, p. 128.
16. Powell, p. 124.
17. *TRP*, p. 129.
18. *Ibid.*, p. 7.
19. Powell, p. 124.
20. *Ibid.*
21. *Ibid.*
22. *Ibid.*
23. TRP, p. 132.
24. *Ibid.*, p. 133.
25. *Ibid.*, p. 135.
26. Powell, p. 129.
27. *Ibid.*
28. *Ibid.*, p. 127.
29. *Ibid.*, p. 130.
30. *TRP*, p. 137.
31. *Ibid.*, p. 139.
32. *Ibid.*, p. 137.
33. *Ibid.*, p. 141.

Chapter II

1. Charles Hudson, *History of the Town of Marlborough* (Boston: T.R. Marvin & Son, 1862), p. 26, and Powell, p. 132.

2. Charles Hudson, p. 29, and Powell, p. 132.

3. *TRP*, p. 141.

4. Judge Daniel Wait Howe, *Howe Genealogies*, Vol. 1 (Boston: New England Historic Genealogical Society, 1929), p. 6. Hereafter cited as *HG*.

5. *Massachusetts Archives Collection*, Vol. 113, p. 524. Hereafter cited as *MAC*.

6. *Worcester Magazine and Historical Journal*, ed. by William Lincoln & C. C. Baldwin (Worcester: Charles Griffin, 1826), Vol. 2, p. 130.

7. Charles Hudson, p. 381.

8. *Worcester Magazine*, p. 130.

9. Charles Hudson, pp. 40–41.

10. *Middlesex Superior Court, County Court, Folio Collection*, Folio 28. Hereafter cited as *MSCF*.

11. *MAC*, Vol. 67, p. 253.

12. Charles Hudson, pp. 44-47

13. *Ibid.*, p. 46.

14. *Frank H. Noyes Collection, 1630-1960*, MSS 47 (Boston: New England Historic Genealogical Society, 1960). Deeds of Peter and Elizabeth Bent to Samuel How, May 11, 1664, Book 7, p. 311. Between 1950 and 1960, Frank H. Noyes, attorney, extensively researched deeds of many members of the How family in the seventeenth and eighteenth centuries. He left his accumulated unpublished research notes to the Society. For those interested in How family history, they are well worth examining.

15. *MSCF*, Folio 31.

16. *MAC*, Vol. 67, p. 277.

17. Charles Hudson, p. 95.

18. *Middlesex Registry of Deeds and Probate Court Records*, East Cambridge, Mass. Hereafter cited as *MRDPC*. Deeds and Estates. Will No. 8495.

19. *MSCF*, Folio 95.

Chapter III

1. A.S. Hudson, *History of Sudbury, Massachusetts, 1638-1889* (Sudbury: 1889), p. 256.

2. *MRDPC*. Estates No. 12097.

3. *TRP*, p. 154.

4. *Thomas Stearns Collection*, Goodnow Library, Sudbury, Mass., Vol. 1, p. 41-b. Hereafter cited as *SC*.

5. *MSCF*, Folio 68.

6. *Middlesex County Court Record Book*, East Cambridge, Mass. Vol. 3, p. 92.

7. *TRP*, pp. 221-23.

8. *Ibid.*, p. 228.

9. *Ibid.*, pp. 228-29.

10. *Ibid.*

11. *TRP*, p. 233.

12. *Ibid.*, p. 246.

13. *Ibid.*

14. *TRP*, pp. 280-81.

15. *Ibid.*, p. 285.

16. *Ibid.*, p. 333.

17. *Ibid.*, p. 335.

18. *Ibid.*, p. 357.

19. *Ibid.*, p. 375.

20. *Ibid.*, p. 378.

21. *Ibid.*, p. 380.

22. *Ibid.*, p. 416.

23. *Ibid.*, pp. 397–99.
24. *Ibid.*, p. 418.
25. *Ibid.*, p. 421.
26. *MAC*, Vol. 30, p. 269.
27. *Ibid.*, p. 361.
28. *MRDPC*, Book 7, p. 314.

Chapter IV

1. *MSCF*, Folio 17.
2. *MAC*, Vol. 4, p. 32.
3. *SC*, Vol. 2, p. 57.
4. *Ibid.*, p. 97.
5. *Ibid.*
6. *Middlesex Court of General Sessions Records, 1692-1722*, East Cambridge, Mass., p. 2. Hereafter cited as *MCG*.
7. *Ibid.*
8. *TRP*, p. 453.
9. *Ibid.*, p. 461.
10. *Ibid.*, p. 434.
11. *Ibid.*, p. 469.
12. *Ibid.*, pp. 439–43.
13. *Ibid.*, p. 465.
14. *Ibid.*, p. 470.
15. *SC*, p. 61c.
16. *MAC*, Vol. 47, p. 106.
17. *Ibid.*, p. 162.
18. *Ibid.*, Vol. 40, p. 442.
19. *Ibid.*, Vol. 47, p. 143.
20. *MCG*, p. 254.
21. *Ibid.*, p. 267.
22. *Ibid.*, p. 279.
23. *MRDPC*, Book 16, p. 280.
24. *MAC*, Ancient Maps and Grants, Vol. 1, p. 224.
25. *HG*, pp. 8–9.
26. *MRDPC*, Book 16, p. 280.
27. *Sudbury Town Records 1695-1722*, Goodnow Library, Sudbury, Mass. Hereafter cited as *TR*.
28. *Frank H. Noyes Collection*, deed dated May 27, 1711.
29. *MRDPC*, Estates. No. 12097.
30. *Ibid.*
31. *HG*, p. 21.

Chapter V

1. *TRP*, pp. 141–43.

2. *SC*, p. 48.
3. *Ibid.*
4. *Ibid.*, p. 61.
5. *MAC*, Ancient Maps and Grants, Vol. I, p. 224. Also Powell, map facing p. 109.
6. *HG*, p. 19.
7. *MAC*, Vol. II, p. 221.
8. *SC*, p. 54 a.
9. *Ibid.*, p. 49.
10. *TRP*, p. 267.
11. A.S. Hudson, p. 286.
12. *MAC*, Vol. 12, pp. 127–28.
13. *SC*, p. 66b.
14. *MAC*, Vol. I, p. 247.
15. *MAC*, Vol. 72, p. 183.
16. *HG*, p. 7.
17. *MRDPC*. Estates. No. 11595.
18. A.S. Hudson, p. 325.
19. *HG*, p. 20.
20. *MAC*, Vol. 38 A, pp. 109–110.
21. A.S. Hudson, pp. 298–99.
22. *MCG, 1622–1722*, pp. 324–28. Also *MSCF*, Folio 62x.
23. *MCG*, pp. 73–85.
24. *Ibid.*, pp. 132–267.
25. *Ibid.*, pp. 287–314.
26. *Ibid.*, pp. 338–39.
27. *Ibid.*, pp. 339 ff.
28. Henry David Thoreau, *Journal*, ed. Bradford Torrey (Boston: Houghton Mifflin, 1906), Vol. 5, p. 179.
29. Samuel Sewall, *Diary 1674–1729*, Collection of Massachusetts Historical Society (Boston: Arno Press, 1972), Vol. 2, p. 100.
30. *Ibid.*, p. 197.
31. *TR*, 1695–1755.
32. *MRDPC*, Deeds. Book 47, pp. 208–10. Also *Frank H. Noyes Collection*.
33. *TR*, 1695–1755.
34. *MRDPC*. Deeds. Book 55, pp. 379–80. Also *Frank H. Noyes Collection*.
35. *MAC*, Vol. 244, p. 382a.
36. *MCG*, 1735–1748, p. 491.
37. *TR*, 1695–1755.
38. *Ibid.*
39. *Ibid.*

40. *MAC*, Vol. 12, pp. 137–38.
41. A.S. Hudson, pp. 309–10.
42. *MCG*, 1748–1761, p. 501.

Chapter VI

1. *MRDPC*, Deeds. Book 49, p. 110.
2. *HG*, pp.40–41.
3. *TR*, 1695–1755 and 1755–1814.
4. *Wayside Inn Archives*. Hereafter cited as *WIA*.
5. *Ibid.*
6. *SC*, p. 82a
7. *TR*, 1755–1814, March 5, 1764.
8. *Ibid.*, January 3, 1774.
9. *Ibid.*, 1774–1779.
10. *Ibid.*, December 20, 1773.
11. *SC*, p. 95a.
12. *TR*, 1755–1814, January 3, 1774.
13. *Ibid.*, January 10, 1774.
14. *Ibid.*, October 3, 1774.
15. *HG*, p. 40.

Chapter VII

1. A.S. Hudson, p. 364.
2. William Barry, *History of Framingham* (Boston: Arthur Forbes, 1874), p. 93.
3. *SC*, p. 97a.
4. *Ibid.*, pp. 97a–98.
5. *Ibid.*, p. 98.
6. *Ibid.*
7. Barry, p. 93.
8. *Ibid.*
9. Allen French, *The Day of Concord and Lexington* (Concord, 1925), p. 219.
10. *Ibid.*, p. 224.
11. A.S. Hudson, p. 365.
12. *Ibid.*, p. 364.

Chapter VIII

1. *WIA*, Military records.
2. *Ibid.*
3. *Ibid.*
4. *U.S. Pension Records*, Washington, D.C. Records of service by Hows during the American Revolution, No. S. 29239, August 30, 1932. Copy of deposition and pension application of Ezekiel How, Jr.

Requested by Gladys Salta, Wayside Inn, Sudbury, Mass., June 25, 1928.

5. *WIA*, Military records.

6. Mrs. Van D. Chenoweth, "The Landlord of the Wayside Inn," *New England Magazine*, Vol. 10, No. 3, 1894, pp. 271-2.

7. *Massachusetts Soldiers and Sailors of the Revolutionary War* (Boston: Wright and Potter, 1907), Vol. 8, p. 334.

8. *TR*, 1755-1814, August 9, 1779.

9. *Ibid.*, December 6, 1779.

10. *Ibid.*, December 2, 1780.

11. Douglas Southall Freeman, *George Washington, a Biography* (New York: Scribners, 1934), Vol. 6, p. 24.

12. *Ibid.*

13. This point is discussed in Chapter XXV.

14. *MRDPC*, Estates. No. 12021. All references to Ezekiel How's will in this and other chapters are taken from this document.

15. *WIA*.

16. *TR*, 1755-1814, January, 1792.

17. *Ibid.*, 1755-1814, May, 1791.

Chapter IX

1. Lydia Maria Child, "The Howe Tavern in Sudbury as it Looked in 1828. A Memory," *The National Standard*, New York, c. 1870.

2. Samuel Arthur Bent, "The Wayside Inn—Its History and Literature," Address to the Society of Colonial Wars, June 17, 1897, p. 18.

3. *Ibid.*, pp. 18-19.

4. *MRDPC*, Estates. No. 12021.

5. *Worcester Magazine*, p. 130.

6. *MRDPC*, Estates. No. 12021.

7. *Boston Street Directory, 1796-1813.* Boston Public Library, Boston, Mass.

8. *WIA*, Letter to "Cousin Littlefield," June 2, 1927.

9. *Dictionary of American History* (New York: Scribners, 1934), Vol. 2, pp. 94-96, and A. Barton Hepburn, *History of Coinage and Currency in the United States* (New York: Kelly, 1967), pp. 41-53.

10. *HG*, p. 86.

11. *TR*, 1755-1814.

12. *Ibid.*, October, 1802.

13. *Ibid.*, October 10, 1804.

14. *Ibid.*, April, 1806.

15. Adeline Lunt, "The Old Red Horse Tavern," *Harpers New Monthly Magazine* (New York, September, 1880), p. 607.

16. J. Bennett Nolan, *Lafayette in America Day by Day* (Baltimore: Johns Hopkins Press, 1934), p. 299.

17. Allan Forbes and Paul F. Cadman, *France and New England:*

Lafayette's Visits to Boston and Other Places in New England (Boston: State Street Trust Company, 1925), Vol. I, pp. 22–50.

18. *Ibid.*, pp. 41–43.

19. *Ibid.*, p. 43.

20. Nolan, p. 292.

21. Forbes, p. 44.

22. Nolan, pp. 92–99.

23. *Ibid.*, pp. 103–04.

24. Dennis R. Laurie, Assistant to the Curator of Newspapers and Serials, American Antiquarian Society, Worcester, Mass., made a thorough search in Worcester and Boston newspapers of the period and was unable to discover any mention of Lafayette in Sudbury on the relevant dates. Newspapers examined include the *Massachusetts Spy, Massachusetts Yeoman, Columbian Centinel, Independent Chronicle* and *Boston Patriot*.

25. *Boston Journal*, August, 1868.

26. MRDCP, Estates. No. 34740.

27. *Boston Journal*, August 19, 1872.

28. Thomas W. Parsons, "The Old House in Sudbury, Twenty Years Afterwards," *Poems* (Boston: Houghton Mifflin, 1893), p. 143.

Chapter X

1. *HG*, p. 86.

2. Child, n.p.

3. Lunt, p. 608.

4. *Ibid.*, p. 609.

5. Chenoweth, p. 270.

6. *WIA*.

7. *Ibid.*

8. *MRDPC*, Estates. No. 34789.

9. *Ibid.*

10. *TR*, 1814–1855, February, 1843.

11. *Ibid.*, March, 1847.

12. *Ibid.*, April, 1847.

13. *MRDPC*, Estates. No. 34789.

Chapter XI

1. Samuel Longfellow, *Life of Henry Wadsworth Longfellow* (Boston: Ticknor & Co., 1886), Vol. I, p. 19.

2. *Ibid.*

3. Lunt, p. 607.

4. *Ibid.*, pp. 611–15.

5. A.S. Hudson, p. 478.

6. *Ibid.*, p. 479.

7. *WIA*.

8. *HG*, p. 86.

9. A.S. Hudson, p. 576.

10. *Ibid*., pp. 876-78.

11. *Ibid*., pp. 518-22.

12. *Ibid*., p. 579.

13. Lunt, p. 608.

14. *Ibid*.

15. *Ibid*., p. 611.

16. *Ibid*., p. 612.

17. *WIA*.

18. Samuel Longfellow, p. 72.

19. A.S. Hudson, p. 596.

20. Child, n.p.

21. *WIA*.

22. Parsons, p. 143.

Chapter XII

1. John Fiske, *Beginnings of New England* (Boston: Houghton Mifflin, 1899), p. 63.

2. Charles Edward Banks, *Topographical Dictionary of 2885 Emigrants to New England, 1620-1650* (Philadelphia, 1937), p. 175.

3. Michael Tepper, *Passengers to America: Consolidation of Ship Passenger Lists From New England Historic and Genealogical Register* (Baltimore: Genealogical Publishing Company, 1900), pp. 50-52.

4. *Ibid*., p. 51.

5. Allen, p. 130.

6. *HG*, p. 1.

7. M.W. Farr, Archivist, County Record Office, Warwick, England. Interviews, April, 1987 and January, 1988.

8. *Victoria History of the County of Warwick*, ed. L.F. Salzman (London: J. Street, 1904-1945), p. 144.

9. Banks, p. 175.

10. *Victoria History*, pp. 144-46.

11. Rev. S.A.H. Hervey, *Ladbroke and Its Owners* (Bury St. Edmunds: 1914), pp. 166-67.

12. *Ibid*.

13. *Ibid*., p. 255.

14. *Warwick County Records*, County Record Office, Warwick, England. Hereafter cited as *WR*. Also International Genealogical Index, No. 00454.

15. *WR*, Baptismal Records for Brinklow, 1550-1625.

16. This John Howe ran the candle factory and is on record as a "chandler" in an old business listing for Brinklow. His son, Sarah Howe's brother, ran the same business after his death.

17. Interviews with Harry Johnson, builder, undertaker and lifetime resident of Brinklow, April, 1987 and January, 1988.

18. Interview with Lucy E. Cryer, October, 1987.

19. *Ibid.*

20. Rev. G.E. Cooke, *An History of the Village and Church [Brinklow]*, 1974, p. 1.

21. *Victoria History*, pp. 42–43.

22. Roger E. Manning, *Village Revolts, Social Protest & Popular Disturbances, 1509–1640* (Oxford: Clarendon Press, 1988), pp. 159–60.

23. *Ibid.*, p. 90.

24. D.E. Williams, *Brinklow's Story* (Brinklow: May, 1967), p. 24.

25. Ann Hughes, *Politics, Society and Civil War in Warwickshire, 1620–1660* (Cambridge: Cambridge University Press, 1987), p. 53.

26. *Ibid.*, p. 121.

27. *Ibid.*, p. 127.

28. *Ibid.*, pp. 70–72.

29. Williams, p. 14.

30. Christopher Hill, *The Century of Revolution, 1603–1714*, 2nd ed. (Berkshire, U.K.: Van Nostrand Reinhold, 1986), p. 20.

31. *Ibid.*, p. 37.

32. *Ibid.*, pp. 37–38.

33. Hughes, pp. 120–21.

34. *Ibid.*, p. 100.

35. *Ibid.*

36. *Ibid.*

37. *Ibid.*, p. 99.

38. *Ibid.*, p. 104.

39. Hill, *God's Englishman* (New York: Penguin Books, 1972), p. 40.

40. Hughes, p. 121.

41. Hill, *Century of Revolution*, p. 19.

42. *Ibid.*

43. Manning, pp. 230–31.

44. *Victoria History*, pp. 162–66.

45. *Ibid.*

46. Manning, p. 235.

47. Hill, *Century of Revolution*, pp. 20–31.

48. Hughes, pp. 120–121.

49. Walker Revised, *Sufferings of the Clergy During the Great Rebellion* (Oxford: Clarendon Press, 1948), pp. 302–03, and Williams, p. 10.

50. Hill, *Century of Revolution*, p. 69.

51. *Ibid.*, p. 38.

52. *WIA*, William Prescott Greenlaw's letter to "Cousin Little-

field," June, 1927.

53. M.W. Farr, correspondence and interviews, April–August, 1988.

54. Tepper, p. 47.

55. W.G. Miller and K.A. Carrdus, *The Red Horse of Tysoe* (Leamington: A.E. Maisey and Son, 1965), p. 36.

56. *Ibid.*

57. *Ibid.*

58. Sarah Markham, *John Loveday of Caversham, 1711-1789, The Life and Tours of an Eighteenth Century Onlooker* (Salisbury: Michael Russell Ltd., 1984), p. 37.

Chapter XIII

1. Samuel Longfellow, *Life of Henry Wadsworth Longfellow* (Boston: Ticknor and Co., 1886), Vol. 2, p. 388.

2. *WIA*, Frank H. Noyes letter to R. C. Purdy. Also *Frank H. Noyes Collection.*

3. *WIA.*

4. Samuel Longfellow, pp. 387–88.

5. Henry Wadsworth Longfellow, *Tales of A Wayside Inn* (New York: David McKay Company, Inc., 1975), p. 4.

6. Samuel Longfellow, pp. 397–98.

7. *Ibid.*, p. 394.

8. *Ibid.*, p. 395.

9. John Van Schaick, Jr., *The Characters in the Tales of a Wayside Inn* (Boston: Universalist Publishing House, 1934), pp. 187–88.

10. *Ibid.*, p. 189.

11. Samuel Longfellow, p. 398.

12. Van Schaick, pp. 159–60.

13. *Ibid.*, p. 85.

Chapter XIV

1. *WIA.*

2. *MRDPC.* Estates. No. 34801.

3. *WIA.*

4. A.S. Hudson, p. 596.

5. *WIA.*

6. *Ibid.*

7. *Ibid.*

8. *HG*, Preface.

9. *Ibid.*

10. Edwin Mead, *New England Magazine, Sept. 1889-Feb. 1890* (Boston: J.S. Cushing & Co.), pp. 318–29.

11. Samuel Adams Drake, *Old Landmarks, Historic Fields and Mansions of Middlesex* (Boston: James P. Osgood & Co., 1874), pp. 420–24.

12. *WIA.*
13. *WIA.*
14. *WIA.*
15. *WIA.*
16. Interview with Mrs. Forrest Bradshaw, January, 1988.
17. Mead, p. 329.
18. *WIA* and interview with Priscilla Staples Rixmann, June, 1988.

Chapter XV

1. *Boston Herald*, July 3, 1897.
2. *Ibid.*
3. Bent, p. 27.
4. *WIA.*
5. Lauriston Bullard, *Historic Summer Haunts* (Boston: Little, Brown & Co., 1912), pp. 130–31.
6. *Ibid.*, pp. 131–32.
7. *WIA.*
8. *Ibid.*
9. *Ibid.*

Chapter XVI

1. "Ford Chauffeur Tells Wayside Inn Tales," *New York Times*, March 28, 1956.
2. Boston News Bureau, July 13, 1924.
3. *Boston Globe, Boston Post* and *Boston Traveler*, February 12, 1924.
4. *Boston Post*, February 10, 1924.
5. *Marlborough Enterprise*, August 14, 1924.
6. *Boston Globe*, August 20, 1924, and *Boston Herald*, August 19, 1924.
7. *Christian Science Monitor*, August 16, 1924.
8. *Wall Street Journal*, "The Wayside Inn: An Investment in Americana," August 13, 1924.
9. *WIA*, Letter to Earl Boyer from Gladys Salta, November, 1927.
10. *WIA*, Letters to Henry Ford, 1924–26.
11. *WIA*, Letters between David Howe and Frank Campsall, March and April, 1924.
12. *Boston Transcript*, February 4, 1924.
13. *Somerville Journal*, August 28, 1925.

Chapter XVII

1. Interview with David Bentley, July, 1988.
2. *WIA*, Reports from E.J. Boyer to Henry Ford, June–November, 1926.
3. *WIA*, Report from E.J. Boyer to Frank Campsall, July 18, 1928.

4. Interview with Louis Varrichione Sr., March, 1986.

5. *New York Times Magazine*, April 13, 1930.

6. *WIA*, Hostess Diaries.

7. *New York Times Magazine*, April 13, 1930.

8. *Boston Traveler*, January 7, 1926.

Chapter XVIII

1. *Sudbury Town Crier*, interview with B.J. Campbell, November 21, 1979, p. 9.

2. *WIA*, Hostess Diaries, 1929.

3. *Ibid.*, June, 1930.

4. *WIA*, Letter from Priscilla Staples to William A. Simonds, January 19, 1937.

5. *Ibid.*, Program, Ninth Annual Middlesex County Extension Service Picnic, July 17, 1930.

6. *Boston Post*, 1928. *Wilbur Raymond Collection*.

7. Interview with Louis Varrichione Sr., March, 1986.

8. Interview with Forrest Bradshaw, February, 1985.

9. *WIA*, Letters from Edison Institute, Dearborn, Michigan, March, 1941, and *Hammond Times*, "Martha and Mary Chapel, Young People's Church," p. 7.

10. *Ibid.*

11. *WIA*, Hostess Diaries, March–May, 1941. Also interviews with Priscilla Staples Rixmann, spring and summer, 1988.

Chapter XXI

1. Sources for this chapter include newspaper accounts in the *Wayside Inn Archives* and *Wilbur Raymond Collection* and interviews with participants and eyewitnesses. Our special thanks to Colonel Ira Amesbury for permission to quote from his moving poem, "Old Wayside."

Chapter XXII

1. Sources for this chapter include *Boston Globe*, *Boston Herald*, *Boston Traveler*, *Christian Science Monitor*, *Detroit Free Press*, *Framingham News*, *Marlborough Enterprise*, *Sudbury Citizen*, *Sudbury Fence Viewer*, and *Worcester Telegram and Gazette* as well as interviews.

Chapter XXIII

1. William E. Dorman, "Colonial Expert Shuns Nails for Wooden Pegs," *Boston Sunday Herald*, January 5, 1958.

2. *Christian Science Monitor*, 1957, n.d.

3. *Boston Sunday Herald*, January 5, 1958.

4. *Frank H. Noyes Collection*. Memorandum from Roy Baker to Priscilla Staples Rixmann, spring, 1958.

5. *WIA*, Transcript of trial, Jones vs. Lemon, January 7, 1898.

6. *Christian Science Monitor*, February 24, 1958.

7. *Worcester Telegram*, November 25, 1956, and *Lynn Item*, May 6, 1958.

8. *Christian Science Monitor*, February 24, 1958.

9. *Ibid.*

10. *Christian Science Monitor*, June 6, 1958.

11. *Gloucester Republican*, June 6, 1958.

Chapter XXV

1. Isaiah Thomas, *Extracts From Diaries and Accounts 1782-1804 and the Year 1808*, ed. Charles L. Nichols (Worcester, Mass.: American Antiquarian Society, 1916), January 4, 1808, p. 11.

2. *WIA*, Child.

3. Thoreau, p. 179.

4. *Dictionary of American Biography* (New York: Scribners, 1957), Vol. 1, p. 167.

5. Drake, p. 421.

6. *WIA*, Letter from David Howe to Henry Ford, February, 1924.

7. *Ibid.*

8. *Frank H. Noyes Collection.*

9. Wallace Downes, *New England Magazine and Bay State Monthly*, 1887, N.D.

10. Bent, p. 27.

Appendix A

How Family Innkeepers 1661–1861

(Principal How landlords are listed in bold-face type)

JOHN HOW
b. Warwickshire c. 1600
m. *Mary* _____*
d. Marlborough 1680

John Jr. b. 1640; m. 1662 Elizabeth Ward he d. 20 April 1676
Samuel How b. 1642; m. 1664 Martha Bent
Sarah b. 1644; m. 1667 Samuel Ward
Mary b. 1646; d. 1647
Isaac b. 1648; m. 1671 Frances Woods
Josiah b. 1650; m. 1671 Mary Haynes
Mary b. 1654; m. 1672 John Wetherbee
Thomas b. 1656; m. 1681 Sarah Hosmer
Daniel b. 1658; d. 1661
Alexander b. 1660; d. 1661
Eleazar b. 1662; m. 1684 Hannah Howe

*Names in italic type are How family members engaged in innkeeping either in Marlborough or in Sudbury, individuals who resided on or near How Tavern property, or men whose military activities are mentioned in the narrative.

SAMUEL HOW
b. 1642
m. 1663 Martha Bent, she d. 1680
m. Sarah Clapp 1685 d. 1713

John b. 1664; m. 1686 Elizabeth Woolson
Mary b. 1665; m. 1685 Thomas Barnes
Samuel b. 1668; m. 1690 Abigail Mixer
Martha b. 1669; m. 1687 *Thomas Walker*
Daniel b. 1672; d. 1680
David b. 1674; m. 1700 Hepzibah Death
Hannah b. 1677; m. John Barnes
Elisha n.b.d.; m. 1718 Hannah Shavally
Daniel b. 1690; m. 1716 Elizabeth Johnson
Nehemiah b. c. 1693; m. Margaret Willard
Moses b. 1695; m. 1718 Eunice Rogers
Ebenezer b. 1697; m. 1724 Lydia Woolcott
Micajah b. 1700; m. Martha _____ n.d.

DAVID HOW
b. 1674
m. Hepzibah Death 1700
d. 1759

Thankful b. 1703; m. 1723 Peter How
Hepzibah b. 1706; m. 1729 Cyprian Keyes
Eliphalet b. 1710; m. Hepzibah Morse, c. 1732
Israel b. 1712; m. 1740 Elizabeth Hubbard
Ruth b. 1715; m. Hezekiah Stone n.d.
David Jr. b. 1717; m. 1743 Abigail Hubbard
Ezekiel b. 1720; m. 1744 Bathsheba Stone

EZEKIEL HOW
b. 1720
m. Bathsheba Stone, she d. _____.
m. 1772 Rebecca Ruggles

Ruth b. 1745; m. 1765 Jesse Gibbs
Ann or "Anna" b. 1747
Hepzibah b. 1749; m. 1765 Hopestill Brown
Bathsheba b. 1752; m. 1770 Daniel Loring
"Molly" b. 1754; m. 1773 Reuben Brown
Ezekiel Jr. b. 1756; m. 1780 Sally Read; she d. 1812; m. 1825
   Asenath Eaton
Olive b. 1758; m. 1776 Uriah Moore
Eliphalet b. 1761; m. 1788 Hannah Henry
Adam (or Adams) b. 1763; m. 1795 Jerusha Balcom
Jane n.b.d.; m. 1788 Phineas Eames

ADAM (ADAMS) HOW
b. 1763
m. 1795 Jerusha Balcom, she d. 1842
d. 1840

Jerusha b. 1797; d. 1842 unm.
Rebecca b. 1799; d. 1803
Lyman b. 1801
Winthrop b. 1804; d. young
Adam b. 1805; m. 1845 Olive Page
Abiel Winthrop b. 1807; m. Eliza Ann Goodnow 1842;
   d. 1845

LYMAN HOWE
b. 1801
d. 1861 unm.

Appendix B

St. Nicholas Parish. A False Trail

Into every historical venture there inevitably go many lost and frustrating hours spent following a clue that proves fruitless. Because we think it may be of interest to some readers, particularly members of the Howe family, we describe one such trail that we followed in Warwickshire which brought to light some new points that pertain to the history of the Sudbury Hows.

Judge Daniel Wait Howe's *Genealogies*, Volume I, which is a full rundown on the origins and descendants of John How of Sudbury and Marlborough, was one of our major sources. In the Preface to his book, Judge Howe made this statement:

> In 1900, at the solicitation of Mr. George R. Howe of Newark, New Jersey, Mr. Richard Savage of Stratford, Secretary of the Shakespeare Birthplace Association, made an investigation of the records of the parishes of Warwickshire, which showed that there were several Hows there at an early date. Among those there in 1580–1588, who were rated for support of the poor, were John How, Thomas How and Lyman How of St. Nicholas Parish. In 1608–09 John How, of the same parish, was tenant of one of the houses owned by the parish, and paid more rent than any other person except one, in the parish. The names of John, Thomas and Lyman are all very common among the descendants of John How of Sudbury and Marlborough.

We were already investigating Hodinhull, Hodnet and Ladbroke as areas in Warwickshire that could be John How's point of origin. St. Nicholas added a new area for research. The reference to Mr. Richard Savage "investigating the parishes of Warwickshire" suggested to us that perhaps Savage discussed other places that could throw light on the problem. Therefore, after failing to find a Mr. George Howe in Newark, we went to the Shakespeare Birthplace Association in England.

In Stratford, two helpful archivists searched for a copy of Mr. Savage's report. None was to be found. They were of the opinion that whatever Mr. Savage wrote was sent to New Jersey and that no copy was kept in Stratford. They told us that Mr. Savage was remembered as an overworked official "who did many private commissions for a fee." He was frequently approached by both British and Americans who were trying to seek their ancestors and consequently he was able to build up a profitable side business which supplemented his secretarial salary.

We were told that in the year 1900, Savage had just finished editing an old document, *Churchwardens Accounts for the Parish of St. Nicholas, Warwick, 1547-1621.* St. Nicholas is one of two major parishes in the city of Warwick, not a separate town or village in itself. The other larger parish is St. Mary's. In lieu of the report which was sent to New Jersey, we examined the *Churchwardens Accounts* with care.

Between the years 1581 and 1621 we discovered, in fact, a number of entries which show receipts from Hows for rents of houses owned by the parish, for seat money for pews in church, and occasionally a receipt for the order to ring the Great Bell (for death). There are also references to Hows serving as church wardens at various times.

Some examples are:

> 1564 Churchwardens for the viijth yere of the rayne of Queen Elizabeth...John How
> 1574 Symon howe, churchwarden...
> 1580 Cheffe Rentes...the house that Symon How holdythe...
> 1581 Item. off Symon How ffor hys wholle yeres rente dewe at Michelmas last past—xiijs iiijd
> 1583 Item. Cheffe Rentes payd to Master Reinolde Brown for an annuelle rent owt off Symon How—vjd...
> 1586 Item. The Great Bell for Annis Howe iij d
> 1613 Allso rec. of John How his half yeres rent of his howse likewise ended at the ladie day last x s

There are many more such entries which show that there were numerous men with the last name How in this half century. It will be noted that the name John How appears several times, Thomas How once, and that there are numerous mentions of 'Symon' Hows. There is no 'Lyman.' Since this is an unusual name on either side of the Atlantic, especially in the sixteenth and seventeenth centuries, this attracted our attention. One can speculate, as we did, that someone mistook the old-style 'S' for an 'L'—the two look very similar in these volumes. The archivists in Stratford agreed that this was a likely explanation.

There are other pertinent entries for the year 1609:

> The accompte of William Willis, John Thomas, John Maudicke, R. Mongo Henderson, Churchwardens of St. Nicholas, recepte of Sertaine Money:
>
> Allso rec. of John Gibbes for his howse likewise ended at Michelmas laste his wholl yeres rente xiiij s
>
> Allso rec. of Thomas Jinkes his wholl yeres rente...xiij s iiijd
>
> Allso rec. of John Howe his wholl yeres Rente of his howse likewise ended at Michelmas laste xiij s iiij d
>
> Allso rec. of Robert Gibbes his wholl yeres rente of his howse likewise ended at Michelmas last xij s

This entry substantiates Judge Howe's idea that John How, someone by that name, "paid more rent than any other person except one" in the year 1609, since he and Thomas Jinkes both paid twelve shillings and threepence each and John Gibbs paid thirteen shillings.

Another important entry in this same book appears a few pages further on, under 'Seate Money' in the year 1621.

"Item. Rec. of John how, glouer [glover] for his seate...vii j d."

We wondered if Josiah Temple had seen this entry, or if someone else had seen it and told him about it before he published his *History of Framingham* in 1887. In this book he mentions, for the first time, that How's profession in England was "glover" (Temple, p. 599). The fact that the John How paying seat money for his church pew in St. Nicholas Parish in 1621 and the man who became a freeman in Massachusetts in 1640 were probably two quite different people is not the point. Although St. Nicholas parish is almost certainly the wrong parish, and this solitary glover is almost equally certainly not related to the Sudbury John How, the entry by itself could conceivably have given rise to the wrong profession being assigned to the Sudbury How.*

---

*Mary Caroline Crawford in her book, *Among Old New England Inns*, states: "In England he [John How] had been a glover, but there being slight demand for glovers in new towns here in the seventeenth century, he turned his attention in 1661 to the trade of tavern keeper." (p. 92) Other authors followed suit and produced varying versions of this erroneous theory.

In the County Record Office in Warwick we examined two other old records. *The Book of John Fisher, Town Clerk and Deputy Recorder of Warwick, 1580–1588* was edited by Thomas Kemp and published in 1900, the same year as Savage's edition of the *Churchwardens Accounts* and the request from Mr. George Howe in America. *The Black Book of Warwick*, also edited by Kemp, is a business listing of "bootchers, taylers, mercers, Poyntmakers, skynners, glovers, etc." for twenty-nine years of Queen Elizabeth's reign.

From the first book we learned that members of the How family were, indeed, "rated for support of the poor in 1580–88."

> ...also a record of assessments for the relief of the poor...and of other matters during the years above mentioned...
>
> In the xxiiij yere of Queen Elizabeth's rane—the names of such persons as are thought able to give towards the relief of the fore named poore taxid by consent...in the said church-...the iiilth day of March.
>
> > John howe j d [one penny]
> > Thomas howe j d [one penny]
> > Symon howe o b [half penny]

This list of those who will support the poor includes the names of 26 substantial citizens, of whom the Hows are three. It is a list from one year only, 1582, but apparently ongoing.*

Howes are also mentioned in *The Black Book of Warwick*. This is a "large and ancient volume," in which are entered minutes of the meetings of the corporation, records of elections of bailiffs and principal burgesses, copies of leases and agreements, election of members of Parliament, accounts of public ceremonials, lawsuits, and other matters relating to municipal life. John Fisher, who kept the book, was Town Clerk and Bailiff in 1564 and the year following and again in 1580 and 1581. He was also a member of Parliament for the borough at various times during this period; the record is for the years 1563–1590. Hows are not numerous enough to be listed in the index, but the name appears sporadically throughout the book.

A typical entry in this long volume is: "1578. The names of commoners chosen to have the accompt of Mr. Okens' rents

---

*The people who are beggars are also listed: "William beggith being x yeres old...Ann Isham...she is but young and hath but one leg and she has a child and they both beg...Henery being xj years and beggith." The words "lame," "idiot," and "Blinde" reoccur.

the first tyme a yere after his death—John howe from Bridgend. Also Thomis howe of the same street...''

These two Howes are among 24 names. In August of the same year ''Thomis and John howe'' are repeated in the same capacity.

The examination of these documents shows that Judge Howe is correct in quoting Savage as saying: 1. A John How paid more rent for a parish house in 1609 than any other person except one and 2. Three men named John, Thomas and Simon How were rated for support of the poor between the years 1580 and 1588, the exact period covered by *The Book of John Fisher.*

Judge Howe, however, through no fault of his own, over-stated the case in saying that Richard Savage ''made an investigation of the parishes of Warwickshire.'' Judge Howe had been told this by Mr. George Howe and possibly he had seen Savage's report, which certainly must have conveyed the impression that a great amount of research had been done. In fact, Savage seems to have investigated *only* St. Nicholas, one parish in the city of Warwick.

Judge Howe was also inadvertently compounding Savage's error by quoting him as saying that *Lyman* Howe was rated for support of the poor, along with John and Thomas.

After examining these documents and records, we drew a few tentative conclusions and had several unanswered questions:

1. Mr. George Howe probably became interested in the mystery of John How's origins as a result of Samuel Arthur Bent's address in 1897, three years before Mr. Howes' inquiry to Stratford. This address, which was carefully prepared, cast doubt on several pre-conceived ideas about Howe origins. Mr. Howe of New Jersey doubtless thought it would be useful to solve the question, once and for all, from England. He would naturally assume that the Shakespeare Birthplace Association was an irreproachable source of historical information.

2. Mr. Savage based his ''report'' to Mr. George Howe primarily on his own edition of the *Churchwardens Accounts.* Since he had just finished this in the year 1900 it would have been the obvious place to look. He was a busy clerk with many commissions and he drew heavily on his nearest source. If he represented himself as having ''investigated the parishes of Warwickshire'' he was vastly exaggerating.

To an American like Mr. Howe, who did not know the geography of the county of Warwick, this ''investigation'' might have seemed plausible. Mr. Savage could have created the impression that he had done an extensive amount of work, whereas he was, in fact, taking all his information from his own book and two others which would have been as ready to hand as they are today—*The Book of John Fisher* and *The Black Book of Warwick*.

3. Who misread the 'S' in Simon for 'L' in Lyman? Was this done intentionally, or at least "accidentally on purpose?" If this was the case, and it must be recognized as a distinct possibility, Richard Savage must have unconsciously been *trying* to find a Lyman, knowing it to be a family name. Instead he found Simon, faintly written and allowed the indistinctness to justify a dubious historical judgment.

4. Is it possible, as we suggested in Chapter XII, that Adam Howe visited Warwickshire sometime between 1780 and 1790? If Adam did go to Warwick, could he have seen the exact same books that Mr. Savage used more than 100 years later? Or could he at least have seen the *Churchwardens Accounts?* We inquired whether this volume would have been available, in raw form, to anyone asking for information in the late 1700s and found that it would have been one of the few sources available to a curious colonist seeking his forebears, in the days before microfilm and other sophisticated modern devices.

5. If Adam did see this book, could it have been he who misread the 'S' for 'L' and later named his oldest son for what he supposed, in good faith, was a distinguished English ancestor?*

Our investigation of St. Nicholas Parish was fascinating, but inconclusive. Baptismal and other church records were examined for the pertinent dates, but failed to reveal a John How baptised anywhere near the beginning of the seventeenth century. Constraints of time prevented a further search of all the old St. Nicholas records, a task which some future chronicler should pursue. Without more precise facts we could not make a case for St. Nicholas as John How's point of origin.

---

*Whether or not Adam believed that his great-great-grandfather came from Warwick itself, from Ladbroke, from Brinklow or from some other village, he would probably have gone to the capital city for information, because even in those days before records were centralized, village church registers would have been hard to decipher and obtaining facts about one's family's roots would have depended upon the knowledge and good will of any particular local vicar.

Appendix C

"The Scroll Reads by the Name of How"

After Lyman Howe's death in 1861, the coat of arms disappeared from view, at least in the Inn. Longfellow saw the "scroll" he wrote about in someone else's house in the fall of 1862. What happened to the coat of arms?

It may have been sold at the auction. Or it may have been sold by Lyman before his death and not been available for auction. It is not mentioned in the inventory of his estate. Warren Nixon was a pressing creditor, much involved in this inventory, and would probably have listed it if it had been in the parlor in March, 1861. Lyman was short of funds in his later years so a sale might have taken place along with a number of other items.

If the coat of arms *was* sold at the auction or about that time, there are two strong possibilities regarding its purchaser and subsequent home. There is a record at the Inn from the year 1926, which tells us: "Mr. Hunt says the original Howe family coat of arms was purchased by J. Calvin Howe, the son of Buckley, and that he later sold it..." This Mr. Hunt would have been Mr. George Hunt, postmaster, the son of Emory Hunt who was Lyman's friend. His recollections, collected before his death, are a major source of information about the inn in Lyman's time. J. Calvin Howe's father, Buckley Howe, worked for Lyman, and his brother was the Buckley Howe who later moved with his family to Colorado.

Another equally plausible theory is that Lyman Howe sold the coat of arms to his distant cousin, Israel How Brown, with whom he had other business dealings, in the decade before his death. Or Israel How Brown may have purchased or otherwise acquired the coat of arms before the auction to make sure it remained in the family. Israel How Brown was directly descended from David How, the first innkeeper, through his mother, Alice How, who was David How's granddaughter. She married John Brown and Israel was one of their sons. Israel would have had a strong interest in keeping the coat of arms in the family.

There are three sources for this idea. First, the coat of arms now hanging in the Inn has on the back of it a stamped letter 'B,' such as an auctioneer would use, suggesting that the item was stamped 'B' for 'Brown' at the auction in 1861. Second, Longfellow refers, in his letter of thanks to Miss Eaton, to seeing the coat of arms and the clock at 'Mr. How Brown's.' Third, a descendant of Israel How Brown, Barbara Eaton Deveneau, remembers that her great-grandmother, [Alice How Jones Parmenter] recalled meeting Mr. Longfellow at the house of *her* grandfather, Israel How Brown, on the day in October, 1862, that the poet stopped there after his visit to the inn. (See Chapter XIII.)

In any case, the coat of arms left the inn, one way or another, in or near 1861. Newspaper clippings in the next three decades do not mention it. There are several articles—most notably in 1865, 1868 and 1872—which say nothing of it but speak, instead, of the Inn being "stripped of accouterments," the parlor particularly.

Lucie Welsh, the schoolmistress who boarded at the inn in 1887, did not mention it in her account. Lack of mention by journalists is, of course, not clear proof but it does suggest that the coat of arms was missing for at least part of the period from 1861 until 1892 because the writers were all hard up for anything new to say and would have almost certainly have mentioned the colorful crest if it had been visible.

It is questionable whether the people who printed the program of the Howe Family Gathering which took place at Harmony Grove in South Framingham on August 31, 1871, and which contains a colored painting of the coat of arms as a frontispiece, took this painting from something which was hanging at the inn at that date, or from a copy they obtained elsewhere. It is titled "a *facsimile* of the original coat of arms, said to have been brought from England by John Howe about 1630, which adorned the walls of the Wayside Inn or Howe Tavern in Sudbury for over 150 years."

Note the use of the past tense, "adorned," and the careful use of the words, "facsimile." There is also the phrase "a well executed coat of arms of the Howe family..." This suggests that the painting in the program was *not* obtained from anything in the inn. By the year 1871, as will be seen below, there were in existence several copies of whatever coat of arms first hung on the wall at the Red Horse Tavern, so it would not have been difficult for an enterprising artist to make a convincing copy. Coles's original was, without doubt, copied many times and his style is such as to make copying relatively easy for a trained painter.

The coat of arms reappears in print in the early 1890's when New York papers begin to call attention to it. A description of the parlor in September 4, 1892, says: "But perhaps the most interesting thing in the room and one of which Longfellow makes extensive mention...is the Howe coat of arms, the original copy of which gaudily engrossed on linen, rests carelessly on the mantel—"

Some coat of arms was certainly back in place when Mrs. Seymour conducted her ten-cent tours between 1889 and 1897. It was several times mentioned in the accounts of visitors. Also, soon after Edward Lemon's take-over in 1897, it was appraised for $15.00, as part of the antiquarian's overall valuation of the contents of the inn for mortgage purposes.

The Wayside Inn Diaries, kept as a daily log of events from the start of the Ford era, provide helpful clues about the travels of the coat of arms, or several coats of arms, at the end of the nineteenth century. They make it clear that in addition to Jerusha's known copies, there were several other copies of the coat of arms in existence in different locations.

In 1924 several letters to Mr. Ford and his agents were received from a Mr. David Howe of Taunton, Mass. He claimed to be a direct descendant of David, the first innkeeper, through David's son, David, Jr. His proofs were most convincing and he had inherited a number of family heirlooms. A letter of February 1924 is particularly interesting:

> I possess a copy of the Coat of Arms painted by Isaac Sprague, an artist who travelled with Audubon, the Naturalist. My father sent Mr. Sprague to the inn and had the copy made then over seventy years ago. It is in heraldic color and on metal now framed in a gilt frame.

This letter tells us flatly that sometime in the 1850's the father of this David Howe of Taunton commissioned Isaac Sprague, a young painter accustomed to fine detail, to make a good copy, possibly because he feared Lyman's finances might force him to sell.*

The Inn Diaries also throw light on what happened to Buckley Howe's copy. On November 26, 1932, there is this entry:

> Mr. George Hubbard Howe of Wakefield came to the inn this afternoon...when he was ten years old he knew Lyman Howe. Mr. Howe also claimed to possess the orginal How coat of arms and has had correspondence with Mr. Ford about it....

This man was the son of the Buckley Hubbard Howe who went to Colorado. He later returned to Wakefield, Mass., in retirement and lived there from 1928 onwards. If his father purchased the coat of arms from his uncle, J. Calvin Howe, as George Hunt infers by saying that J. Calvin Howe "later sold it," George Hubbard undoubtedly brought it back with him when he retuned to Massachusetts in his old age.

This probable sequence of events between 1861 and 1928 is supported by writer Alvin Jones who informed his readers in the year 1894: "The original coat of arms is owned by Buckley Howe of South Dakota." This writer seems to have been aware of what happened at the auction, since his account agrees with George Hunt's account of the purchase of the coat of arms by this same Buckley Howe. (One wonders how Jones mistook "Colorado" for "South Dakota," or if perhaps Buckley moved from one western state to another.) Gilman Howe, Judge Howe's editor, provides further corroboration in 1928, by stating that the "original" was in the hands of George Hubbard Howe of Wakefield, Mass. This all adds up if George Hubbard moved back from the west by 1928 and brought his father's copy with him.

There is yet a third possibility about the whereabouts of the "original." On June 20, 1943, the Diary records:

> The Inn was bought in 1894 by Mr. S. Herbert Howe of Marlboro. His son, Louis P. Howe, was a dinner guest today and volunteered the following information: The Howe coat of

---

*David Howe of Taunton's legitimacy was clearly established by Judge Wait Howe. (*Howe Genealogies*, #547 p. 286). He was unquestionably the sixth generation in direct descent from David the innkeeper. He was born July 17, 1848 and was alive in Taunton when Judge Howe's work was published in 1929. He was still alive there at the age of 91 when Inn hostess Priscilla Staples made a trip to see him in 1939.

arms, now in the Parlor, came from Dunstable, Mass. or 'up that way.' The original coat of arms, or the one which belonged to the inn in the old days, was later owned by a Mrs. Richardson.

This source is less precise and we cannot verify it satisfactorily. The "Mrs. Richardson" referred to may be Lauretia Howe, who in 1849 married Stephen Richardson of Nashua, New Hampshire, where she presumably lived. She was the daughter of George Howe, who was descended from Isaac How, the son of John and the Hows of Marlborough. Lauretia Howe Richardson could conceivably have purchased the coat of arms, or a reasonable copy, at the auction or at some later date. Nashua, New Hampshire, is only a few miles from Dunstable, definitely "up that way."

The most thorough and extensive inquiry to date into the legitimacy and whereabouts of the various How coats of arms was done by Judge Wait Howe as part of his genealogical work in 1900 and the years following. In the Preface to his book, published in 1929, he included a description of all the coats of arms he was able to discover at that time. Judge Howe concluded his investigation with the following statement:

> In 1901 I submitted to Mr. Henry E. Woods, Chairman of the New England Genealogical Society, and an acknowledged authority on heraldry, the various coats of arms, together with all the information about them in my possession. The conclusion of Mr. Woods was that all were spurious...John Coles was a notorious fraud who resided for a time in Boston and then disappeared, presumably returning to England.
> "The various coats or arms...are to anyone familiar with the subject and the facts, of no earthly value in determining anything..."

It will be noted that Mr. Woods's opinion in 1901 not only coincides with that of his colleague, Mr. Greenlaw, in 1927, but also with the conclusions of M.W. Farr, County Archivist in Warwick for the past decade.

We observe that Ford's purchase of the Inn in 1923, his search for important heirlooms in the years directly following, Greenlaw's letter to his "Cousin Littlefield" in 1927 and the publication of the *Howe Genealogies* by Judge Howe's editor, Gilman Howe, in 1929, all occur within a relatively short time span. We have not been able to discover an exact connection among these events as they relate to the recovery of a coat of arms for the Inn.

It is clear, however, that by Ford's time there were numerous copies of the arms in different locations. Miss Alma Littlefield, who worked for Ford as a hostess at the Inn and was William Greenlaw's cousin, may have been trying, by writing to Greenlaw, to help Ford decide among David Howe of Taunton's copy of Coles by Isaac Sprague, the copy George Hubbard Howe had in Wakefield, the copy owned by Mrs. Richardson near Dunstable, and any number of other copies in the possession of different members of the Howe family.*

As far as we know, various branches of the Howe family still possess copies of the coats of arms in widely scattered locations in this country and Canada. We have been unable, due to time constraints, to pursue this trail. However, as well as can be determined at the date of writing, these copies are all, in turn, copies of the How coat of arms created by John Coles for the Sudbury Hows or paintings that Coles previously or subsequently created for other branches of the How family.

Jerusha Howe's copy of the coat of arms, which she deeded to the American Antiquarian Society of Worcester, and which can still be seen there, was her own rendering of the Coles version which hung in the Inn during her lifetime. On the back of it is written: "To the American Antiquarian Society of Worcester the other coat of arms of my family name which I copied from the original held by my father...by Jerusha Howe of Sudbury, Massachusetts, A.D. 1830..."

The suggestion has been made that this painting was done by someone other than Jerusha, but there seems no reason to doubt the evidence left by Jerusha herself.

We have concluded—from discoveries in England as well as the opinion of experts in the United States—that there is little question that the battery of experts cited is correct: Regardless of the enticements of legend, the How coat of arms appeared for the first time on this side of the Atlantic less than two hundred years ago and was not inherited from some obscure ancestor of noble lineage in the Middle Ages in England. On this point the pale light of tradition flickers too faintly to be perceived.

*The Ford Foundation in Dearborn, Michigan, cannot shed any light on what conclusions Henry Ford came to about the various coats or arms, nor which copy he may have purchased or been given for the Wayside Inn.

Bibliography

Public Records and Documents, Private Collections, Journals, Diaries and Letters

The Black Book of Warwick 1563-1590. Ed. Thomas Kemp. Warwick: Henry Cook and Son, 1900.

The Book of John Fisher, Town Clerk and Deputy Recorder of Warwick, 1580-1588. Ed. Thomas Kemp. Warwick: Henry Cook and Son, 1898.

Boston Street Directory, 1796-1813. Boston Public Library, Boston, Mass.

Churchwardens Accounts for the Parish of St. Nicholas, Warwick, 1547-1621. Ed. Richard Savage. Stratford-upon-Avon: Shakespeare Birthplace Association, 1900.

Massachusetts Archives Collection. Columbia Point, Boston, Mass. Vols. 1, 3, 4, 7, 12, 16, 30, 38a, 40, 47, 52, 67, 113 and 244.

Middlesex County Court Record Book.

Middlesex Court of General Sessions Records, East Cambridge, Mass. 1692–1722, 1735–1748, 1748–1761.

Middlesex Registry of Deeds and Probate Court Records, East Cambridge, Mass. Deeds and estates. Books 16, 21, 47, 49, and 55. Will and Inventory numbers: 8495; 12097; 11595; 12021; 34740; 34789.

Middlesex Superior Court, County Court Folio Collection, Columbia Point, Boston, Mass. Folios: 17, 28, 31, 62x, 68.

Frank H. Noyes Collection. Research Notes on the descendants of John How of Sudbury and Marlborough. MSS 47. Boston: New England Historic Genealogical Society, 1960.

Sewall, Samuel. *Diary,* Vol. 3. New York: Arno Press, 1972.

Sudbury Town Records, Sudbury, Mass. 1639–1695; 1695–1755; 1755–1814; 1814–1855. Also *Sudbury Proprietors Records,* 1706–1805, vols. 1–2.

Stearns, Thomas. *Collection 1640-1840.* Goodnow Library, Sudbury, Mass., and New England Historical Association, 1154 Boylston Street, Boston, Mass.

Thomas, Isaiah. *Extracts from Diaries and Accounts, 1782-1804 and 1808.* Ed. Charles L. Nichols. Worcester: American Antiquarian Society, 1916.

Thoreau, Henry David. *Journal.* Ed. Bradford Torrey. Vol. 5. Boston: Houghton Mifflin, 1906.

Warwick County Records, County Record Office, Priory Place, Cape

Road, Warwick, England. Records of baptisms, marriages and deaths, 1557–1932.

Wayside Inn Archives, private collection, Wayside Inn, Sudbury, Mass.

Wayside Inn Hostess Diaries, 1929–1950. Daily log of events.

Books

Banks, Charles Edward. *Topographical Dictionary of 2885 English Emigrants to New England 1620-1650*. Philadelphia, 1937, p. 175.

Barre, William. *History of Framingham*. Boston: Arthur Forbes, 1874.

Bond, Henry. *Genealogies of Families and Descendants of Early Settlers of Watertown, Mass*. Boston: New England Historic Genealogical Society, 1860.

Brailsford H.N. *The Levellers and the English Revolution*. Ed. Christopher Hill. Stanford, Cal.: Stanford University Press, 1961, pp. 656–670.

Buchan, John. *Oliver Cromwell*. Boston: Houghton Mifflin, 1934.

Bullard, Lauriston. *Historic Summer Haunts*. Boston: Little Brown, 1912, pp. 123–132.

Crawford, Mary Caroline. *Among New England Inns*. Boston: L.C. Page and Co., 1907, p. 92.

Drake, Samuel Adams. *Historic Fields and Mansions of Middlesex*. Boston: James Osgood and Co., 1874, pp. 410–26.

Eberlein, A. D. and A. E. Richardson. *The English Inn Past and Present*. Philadelphia and London: J. B. Lippincott Co., 1926.

Farmer, John. *Genealogical Register of the First Settlers of New England*. Ed. Samuel G. Drake. Baltimore: Genealogical Publishing Co., 1829, p. 151.

Fisk, John. *Beginnings of New England*. Boston: Houghton Mifflin, 1899.

Forbes, Allan and Paul F. Cadman. *France and New England, Lafayette's Visits to Boston and Other Places in New England*. Vol. 1. Boston: State Street Trust Company, 1925, pp. 22–50.

Fraser, Antonia. *The Weaker Vessel*. New York: Knopf, 1984.

Freeman, Douglas Southall. *George Washington, a Biography*. New York: Scribners, 1934, pp. 240–254.

French, Allen. *The Day of Concord and Lexington*. Concord, Mass., 1925.

Hervey, Rev. S.A.H. *The History of Ladbroke and its Owners*. Bury St. Edmonds, 1914.

Hill, Christopher. *The Century of Revolution, 1603-1714*. 2nd ed. United Kingdom: Van Nostrand Reinhold Co., 1961.

_____. *The English Revolution, 1640*. 3rd ed. London: Lawrence and Wishart Ltd., 1955.

_____. *God's Englishman*. Singapore: Penguin Books, 1970.

————. *Reformation to Industrial Revolution*. The Pelican Economic History of Britain, Vol. 2, 1980.

Hotten, John Camden. *Lists of Emigrants to America 1600-1700*. New York: J.W. Boughton, 1974.

Howe, Daniel Wait. *Howe Genealogies Vol. 1*. Ed. Gilman Howe. Boston: New England Historic Genealogical Society, 1929.

Hudson, Alfred S. *History of Sudbury, Mass*. Sudbury, 1889.

Hudson, Charles. *History of the Town of Marlborough*. Boston: T.R. Marvin and Son, 1862.

Hughes, Ann. *Politics, Society and Civil War in Warwickshire, 1620-1660*. Cambridge: Cambridge University Press, 1987.

Larwood, Jacob and John Camden Hotten. *The History of Signboards*. London: Chatto and Windus, 1900.

Longfellow, Henry Wadsworth. *Tales of a Wayside Inn*. Boston: Ticknor and Fields, 1863.

Longfellow, Samuel. *Life of Henry Wadsworth Longfellow*. Ed. Samuel Longfellow. Vols. 1 & 2. Boston: Ticknor and Co., 1886.

Manning, Roger B. *Village Revolts, Social Protest and Popular Disturbances 1509-1640*. Oxford: Clarendon Press, 1988.

Markham, Sarah. *John Loveday of Caversham, 1711-1789, the Life and Tours of an Eighteenth Century Onlooker*. Salisbury: Michael Russell, 1984.

Nolan, J. Bennett. *Lafayette in America Day by Day*. Baltimore: Johns Hopkins Press, 1934.

Notestein, Wallace. *The English People on the Eve of Colonization, 1603-1630*. New York: Harper and Brothers, 1954.

Parsons, Thomas W. *Poems*. Boston: Houghton Mifflin, 1893, pp. 143-145.

Powell, Sumner Chilton. *Puritan Village. The Formation of a New England Town*. Middletown, Connecticut: Wesleyan University Press, 1963.

Savage, James. *General Dictionary of the First Settlers of New England*. Based on Farmer's Register. Baltimore, 1860, Vol. 2, p. 475.

Smith, L.C.H. *Edmund Rice and His Family*. Sudbury: Edmund Rice Association, 1938.

Tawney, R.H. *Agrarian Problem in the Sixteenth Century*. New York: Longmans, Green and Co., 1912, pp. 338-39.

Temple, Josiah. *History of Framingham*. Framingham, 1887, p. 599.

Tepper, Michael. *Passengers to America—A Consolidation of Ship Passenger Lists from the New England Historical and Genealogical Register*. Baltimore: Genealogical Publishing Company.

Van Schaick, John, Jr. *The Characters in the Tales of a Wayside Inn*. Boston: Universalist Publishing House, 1939.

Victoria County History of Warwickshire, Vol. 2 "Social and Economic History," pp. 161-162.

Von Bergen, Werner. *American Wool Handbook.* New York, 1938, pp. 38–52.

Ward, Andrew H. *History of the Town of Shrewsbury.* Boston: Samuel G. Drake, 1847.

Williamson, James A. *The Evolution of England.* Oxford: Clarendon Press, 1931, pp. 157–258.

Newspapers, Magazines and Pamphlets

Arts and Decoration Magazine. October 1916.

Bent, Samuel Arthur. *The Wayside Inn—Its History and Literature,* an address to the Society of Colonial Wars at the Wayside Inn, Sudbury, Mass., June 17, 1897.

Boston Globe. February 12, 1924; August 20, 1924; March 7, 1947.

Boston Herald. January 29, 1897; July 3, 1897; July 11, 1923; August 19, 1924; January 18, 1927; January 5, 1958.

Boston Post. July 12, 1923; February 10, 1924; August 14, 1924; August 21, 1924.

Boston Transcript. January 14, 1922; February 4, 1924.

Boston Traveler. February 12, 1921; February 10, 1924; August 20, 1924; January 7, 1926.

Chenoweth, Mrs. Van D. "The Landlord of the Wayside Inn," *New England Magazine* Vol. 10, No. 3, 1894.

Child, Lydia Maria. "The Red Horse Tavern as it Looked in 1828—A memory." New York: *National Standard* c. 1870.

Christian Science Monitor. August 13, 1924; August 16, 1924; February 24, 1958.

Cooke, Rev. G.E. *Historical Survey of Village and Church.* Brinklow, 1974.

Country Life in America. June 1902.

Forum Magazine. September 1938.

Garden and Home Builder. Doubleday, Page & Co. Garden City, New York, July 1926. Special Issue No. 5, Vol. 53.

Gates, P.J.E. *Warwick in Times Past.* Lancashire: Countryside Publishing Ltd., 1986.

Gloucester Republican. June 6, 1958.

Herald, The. "The Story of the Wayside Inn Schools." Dearborn, Michigan: Edison Institute, May 10, 1940.

House Beautiful. July 1904.

"Howe Family Gathering." Harmony Grove, Framingham, 1871.

Lunt, Adeline. "The Old Red Horse Tavern at Sudbury." *Harpers New Monthly Magazine.* New York, September 1880, pp. 607-12.

Lynn Item. May 6, 1958.

Marlborough Enterprise. August 14, 1924; October 1952.

Massachusetts Ploughman. November 16, 1861.

Mead, Edwin. *New England Magazine and Bay State Monthly.* September 1889–February 1890.

New York Times Magazine. April 13, 1930; March 28, 1956.
Somerville Journal. August 28, 1925.
Sudbury Town Crier. November 21, 1979.
Worcester Evening Gazette. July 12, 1923.
Worcester Telegram. July 10, 1923; November 25, 1926.